"The dividing line of the true Church will be its position on the Jew and Israel. You *must* be on God's side. Read this book!"

Sid Roth, host, *It's Supernatural!*

"This book is an amazing display of worthy passion, solid scholarship, historical grasp and sound biblical exposition. Its message could not be more needed than in this present hour of global conflict, both political and spiritual. Sandra balances conviction with compassion, and prophetic passion with objectivity and patience that will dissolve much confusion and focus on timely action and intercession. This is a handbook of immeasurable worth for every thoughtful believer—especially leaders who honor God's Word."

Pastor Jack Hayford, author, *Secrets of Intercessory Prayer*; president, The King's University

"Sandra Teplinsky takes a much-needed and fresh approach to the Arab-Israeli conflict from a Messianic Jewish Israeli point of view. With pastoral warmth and solid, balanced theology, she exposes facts and truths that every justice-minded believer should know. Readers will be left well informed and caring deeply about the Jewish people (and others) because they encountered in this book the heart and voice of God."

Jonathan Bernis, president, Jewish Voice Ministries International; author, *A Rabbi Looks at the Last Days* and *A Rabbi Looks at Jesus of Nazareth*

"Inspirationally written, biblically accurate, extensively researched and user friendly to the common believer, Bible student or seasoned minister—all these describe *Why Still Care about Israel?* I applaud Sandra Teplinsky for a job well done. This book articulates with prophetic clarity and integrity God's call to the Church regarding Israel in this tumultuous hour. A desperately needed message!"

James W. Goll, director, Encounters Network, Prayer Storm and God Encounters Training eSchool; author, *The Seer*, *The Coming Israel Awakening* and many more

"Knowing theTeplinskys well, I can attest to Sandra's heart not only for her Jewish brothers and sisters but for Palestinian Arabs as well. With 'Christian Palestinianism' on the ascent, Sandra has written a courageous book. As a former attorney, Sandra brings to light the exaggerations and fabrications of Israel's accusers, yet somehow with grace and sensitivity. *Why Still Care about Israel?* has moved into my top three reference works on this crucial subject."

Wayne Hilsden, senior pastor, King of Kings Community, Jerusalem

"Israel: What other small nation can stir such strong passions and release such heated arguments? Sandra Teplinsky's wonderful book brings together the careful thought and research of an attorney with the heart and spiritual insights of a prophetic intercessor. Even after fourteen years of living in Israel, I was challenged deeply by Sandra's writings."

Rev. Rick Ridings, founder/director, Succat Hallel (24/7 worship and prayer overlooking Mount Zion in Jerusalem), www.jerusalempraise.com

"With precision and passion, Sandra Teplinsky weaves a wealth of material and presents a compelling case for why we still need to care about Israel. It's a powerful treatise and treasure 'for such a time as this.'"

Chris Mitchell, Jerusalem bureau chief, CBN News; author, *Dateline Jerusalem*

WHY STILL CARE ABOUT ISRAEL?

WHY **STILL** CARE ABOUT **ISRAEL?**

The Sanctity of Covenant, Moral Justice and Prophetic Blessing

SANDRA TEPLINSKY

Chosen

a division of Baker Publishing Group
Minneapolis, Minnesota

Revised and updated edition of *Why Care about Israel?*

Published by Chosen Books
11400 Hampshire Avenue South
Bloomington, Minnesota 55438
www.chosenbooks.com

Chosen Books is a division of
Baker Publishing Group, Grand Rapids, Michigan

Printed in the United States of America

Library of Congress Cataloging-in-Publication Data
Teplinsky, Sandra.
 [Why care about Israel]
 Why still care about Israel? : the sanctity of covenant, moral justice, and prophetic blessing / Sandra Teplinsky ; foreword by Michael L. Brown. — Revised and updated edition.
    pages cm
 Includes bibliographical references.
 Summary: "Completely revised and updated with the clarity and urgency of today's headlines, this biblically based guide reveals why Israel matters more than ever and why it affects you"— Provided by publisher.
 ISBN 978-0-8007-9529-0 (pbk. : alk. paper)
 1. Israel (Christian theology) 2. Palestine in Christianity. I. Title.
BT93.T435 2013
231.7´6—dc23   23013017679

Cover design by Dan Pitts

13 14 15 16 17 18 19   7 6 5 4 3 2

This book is offered to the Lord and His people,
with gratitude beyond words for His mercy and grace,
the loving support and invaluable help
of my husband, Kerry, and daughter, Tasha,
the scholarly input of Dr. William J. Bjoraker
and editing expertise of Natasha Sperling.

Contents

Foreword

Sandy Teplinsky has navigated her way through a biblical and theological and political field of land mines, and she has done it with grace, with sensitivity, with compassion, with courage and with exegetical acumen, thereby helping to navigate the way for all of us. And it was not an easy task.

How can you call the Church to care for Israel without being accused of neglecting the Palestinians? How can you claim a special calling on the Jewish people without being accused of favoritism and even advocating ethnic/racial superiority? How can you have a deeply spiritual approach to the Scriptures while still maintaining the importance of a physical plot of land? How can you develop a Jesus-centered theology while claiming that the Church cannot be whole without a restored Israel?

I believe that Sandy is uniquely qualified for the task at hand. First, more than anything, she is a lover of God, desiring to please Him more than side with a people or a cause. Second, she is a woman of prayer and compassion, and she is just as moved by the plight of a suffering Muslim child in Gaza as she is by the plight of a suffering Jewish child in Jerusalem. Third, as a trained attorney, she is meticulous in her research and understands proper legal (and logical) argumentation. Fourth, as a careful student of the Scriptures and history, she knows how to avoid common interpretive errors by using reliable scholarly sources. Fifth, as a Messianic Jewish woman who lives part time in Israel with her Jewish husband, Kerry, she loves and supports the Jewish state without idealizing it (or demonizing Palestinians), as some sincere Christian Zionists have sometimes done.

I have watched Sandy work on this book for many years—burdened to be fair to all, burdened to keep pointing readers to Yeshua (Jesus), burdened to be meticulously accurate in all she writes, burdened to convey God's heart for Israel—and I wholeheartedly commend this book to you.

If you will read it with a prayerful, open mind—and a healthy dose of courage!—it might just change your life.

Michael L. Brown, Ph.D., president,
FIRE School of Ministry, Concord, North Carolina;
author, *Answering Jewish Objections to Jesus*

Why Still Care about Israel?

A vast army descends upon a desert wilderness in the ancient Middle East, signaling that life is about to change forever. Outside the camp a stalwart, lone warrior paces in resolute silence. Normally the man is seen presiding over a feisty multitude. But today his eyes lock on to the horizon ahead.

Suddenly, an imposing figure with sword in hand materializes before him. Startled, the seasoned leader demands to know: "Are you for us or against us?"

None other than the voice of God replies. "No! But as Commander of the Lord's army I come!" The figure in human form is a manifestation of Yahweh Himself.

Despite Joshua's personal history with the Almighty, his heart skips a beat. The man falls to the ground on his face, humbled. The right question is not whether God is for the Israelites or their adversaries. The right question—the one he did not ask—is, "*Who are You?*"

It is much the same for us today. Discussion about Israel in the 21st century often starts by asking, not unlike Joshua, if God is for or against the Jewish state—or the Palestinians, Arabs or Muslims. But He is not for or against nations or people groups as we tend to think. His heart, His character and His ways are different from ours. The first question must be, "Who is our God, this sovereign and supreme Creator of the universe?" From there we discover that Israel—and often the ongoing contention against her—is ultimately about *Him*.

And so, bowed low, Joshua inquires, "What does my Lord say to His servant?"

May I ask, do you want to know what the Lord is saying to you, His servant, in today's fast-changing world? Do you pray that His will be done, and His Kingdom come? Do you want to know Him better in the process? If so, then a Bible-based and factually honest understanding of Israel is essential.

Through Israel the Creator is revealing the passions of His heart for all humankind—including you—personally and intimately. In the process, He is testing Jews and Gentiles alike. He is refining the Church, shaking civilizations and establishing His Kingdom on earth. He is doing it with extravagant love—and He invites you to come, see and take part.

Who Will Benefit from This Book?

This book was written mainly for three types of readers:

- Bible believers who are interested in Israel and want to learn more, from a Messianic Jewish (Jewish Christian) Israeli perspective;
- Christians who already care much for Israel but want to stay current on issues or gain deeper insight; and

• Christians who question or doubt that God still has prophetic plans for Israel.

If you consider yourself in this last group, may I encourage you in a spirit of Messiah-like love to open your heart and mind to a new perspective? If you have never seriously studied the presuppositions of your beliefs, if you have not carefully listened to an Israeli point of view or if you've formed an opinion mostly from hearsay, could it be time to ask God if He has something fresh to say to you?

In addition to the three groups of readers described above, I have written to a fourth: *non-Christians* who are puzzled or troubled by the controversy and quandary of Israel—and are willing to view the matter through the lens of Scripture.

The book in your hands is a significantly revised update of *Why Care about Israel?* written in 2003. At that time, Israel found herself in the throes of a deadly Palestinian *intifada* ("uprising"). Practically weekly, mass suicide bombings besieged the country. Jewish blood splattered in streets, schools, shops, buses—even religious gatherings—while the world paid little heed. *Why Care about Israel?* aimed to raise consciousness about the Jewish state, opening up the Scriptures and God's heart for Israel and the Arab Middle East.

Revised for New Realities

As the book itself predicted, much has changed since then. New questions and issues have risen to the fore. Israel is no longer an obscurity to most believers. Many churches, institutions and governments have intentionally postured themselves for or against the Jewish state.

On a personal level, much has changed in my life as an author. A Messianic Jewish believer in Jesus (Yeshua), I now reside part-time in Israel. There I have been blessed with friendships not only with Messianic Jews but with Muslim-background believers, Christian Zionists, a wide spectrum of believers from the nations and Israelis who do not believe in Jesus. I have ministered, among other places, in Islamic regions of the Middle East. By God's grace, these new relationships and experiences have enabled me to gain a fuller perspective on the Arab-Israeli conflict. Therefore, *Why Still Care about Israel?* offers more of an inside, nuanced view than did its predecessor.

This book is intended to inspire Christlike love for the Jewish people—but not at the expense of any other people group. I certainly do not believe Israel does everything right. But neither do I point a finger at all her wrongdoings; too many others vociferously do so. My goal is to give you, as best as God has enabled me, revelation of His heart through biblical and factual truth, from a Messianic Israeli perspective.

In addition to summarizing topics addressed in the original *Why Care about Israel?*, this updated version unpacks—and suggests a response to—realities such as these:

- *New spiritual breakthroughs:* As the world is shaken, the Kingdom of God is taken (see Matthew 11:12). Judgment and mercy are released in tandem. Jesus wants to empower His Church at new levels of love and righteousness for the sake of the Gospel, even as darkness seems to increase on the earth.

- *New Christian anti-Israel theologies:* Growing numbers of believers wonder if Israel's existence as a state is biblically or morally justified. Some are aligning with new theologies that teach God no longer has a unique or covenant-based purpose for the Jews.

• *New levels of warfare:* Israel may be forced into major military warfare in the near future. Geopolitical and spiritual shifts related to such a war will impact every nation on earth.

• *Social justice:* Social justice compels us to assess Israel's situation, as well as that of Palestinians and others in the Middle East, with biblical integrity and moral truth.

• *Palestinian statehood:* The goal to create a sovereign Palestinian state is gaining momentum worldwide and will have worldwide repercussions.

• *Israel's delegitimization and the new anti-Semitism:* A global movement to delegitimize Israel's existence overlaps with anti-Semitism and must be addressed.

• *Islamist awakening:* The Middle East is undergoing an Islamist awakening that must be reckoned with.

• *Western ideological revolution:* Increasing globalization, secularism and socioeconomic shakings are fueling a worldwide revolution in ideology. New challenges requiring new strategies face traditional Judeo-Christianity.

• *Bible prophecy:* Many Christians want to know what lies ahead and how to navigate changing realities during this epic season.

Despite the gravity of these issues, the ultimate focus of this book is on Jesus. When everything is changing around us, we must cling to the One who is the same today as He was yesterday, and will be tomorrow. No amount of information, no plethora of prophetic insight, can substitute for a heart humbly fixed on Him, a life surrendered to the Savior. *I believe we should be quite optimistic about the future, so long as we wholeheartedly follow Him into it.* The biblical truths and factual issues unpacked in this book are intended to help you do precisely that. They are meant to serve as guiding principles for many years to come, however matters unfold in Israel, the Middle East and the rest of the world.

Pressing the Reset Button

Before we start, I would ask that you please set aside certain preconceptions, if you have them. Suspend the echo of endless indictments against an allegedly belligerent or oppressive Jewish state. Subdue the extreme opposite cries of others who might deify the Jewish people or their ancestral homeland. In fact, why not ask the Holy Spirit to gently press your "reset button" on the subject? Then, look with me at the inspired and authoritative[a] Word of God. In it we see the Creator King picked an otherwise sorry little strain of humanity called Israel for the sake of His own glory. To them He lovingly assigned irrevocable responsibility for service, *not superiority*. We will see that His concept of a chosen people differs radically from what may be portrayed by some church sermons, mainstream media, Internet posts and Facebook friends.

Do not be surprised that Israel stirs controversy no matter what she does. Not only in the Old Covenant, but also in the New, Israel has always been about something and Someone much bigger than herself. As we head into what the Bible calls the last days of this present age, the controversy of Zion will intensify. God is using the tiny Jewish state, roughly 1/500th the size of the US or China, as a microcosm of what He is doing with us all. Indeed, what He is saying through Israel He is not quite saying—or doing—any other way. He is using her to reveal and refine the hearts of humanity. About that, I would like to tell you a story.

Gazing into God's Heart

Jesus shares a striking parable in Matthew 25 about sheep and goats. The tale, as you probably know, is about more than farm animals and good deeds. What you may not know is that it concerns Israel.

When we gather before Him in judgment, the Lord says He will separate the righteous—those who feed, clothe, nurse and care for His needs—from those who do not. The righteous (sheep) receive their inheritance in the Kingdom of God; the unrighteous (goats) are cast from His presence. At that time, you and I will ask when it was that we saw and cared for Him—or did not. He will reply, "I tell you the truth, whatever you did for one of the least of these brothers and sisters of mine, you did for me" (Matthew 25:40).

I was taught, probably like you, that this passage refers to the poor and needy, the oppressed and maligned. Indeed, that is a good and proper interpretation of the parable. But it has a more fundamental meaning we often overlook.

One day, in a devotional study, I sensed the Spirit speak, *Look carefully, Sandy. These "brothers and sisters of Mine" are the Jewish people.*

Startled, I pored over Scriptures and plowed through commentaries. There I discovered the Lord was speaking to His disciples explicitly about the end times. They had asked what would be the sign of His return and end of the age. In response, Jesus described several events, indicating that Israel would endure much hardship (see Matthew 24:3–25:30). He explained how to prepare for that trying time and stand firm in faith until the end of it. He cautioned that our actions toward His "brothers and sisters" in that day would affect our eternal destiny. In this context, it is clear that Jesus' brothers and sisters refer *fundamentally* to the Jews.[1] Commenting on the parable, a team of Bible scholars writes, "Ultimately, how a person treats the Jews will reveal whether or not he is saved."[2]

Please do not misunderstand: Salvation is solely by grace through faith. But true salvation is evidenced by love and fruits of righteousness—which are reflected in our attitude and actions toward Israel. Why? As we will see in this book, how we treat Israel reflects to a real extent how we would treat the Lord Jesus Himself.

I realize that is a bold statement. As I have said, Israel is not perfect. I am not suggesting we approve of everything she does or disregard her sin. Nor do I say we should not care about, bless and lovingly reach out to Palestinians, Arabs or Muslims. In fact, if our love for Israel means we have no love for these others, then I daresay something is not right about our love for Israel.

The Creator does not play favorites with Israel. He chose her so that people like you and me in every nation and period of history would know—through her Scriptures, her Savior and her soul—His loving mercy and grace. Perhaps to the surprise of some, He is not finished with the Jewish nation—or with how He wants to bless us through her. Will we honor His choice to do so?

Do you desire to lay hold of all God has for you and stand firm to the end? (see Matthew 24:13). Then, my friend, He beckons you into His heart for His ancient covenant people. There you will discover a jealous and zealous love for the Jews, pulsating with passion. As a result, you will learn more of His love for *you* and lay hold of blessing for you personally that cannot be accessed, I am convinced, any other way.

Be forewarned: Others may not go with you. God is allowing Israel to serve as a strategic point of division. Some in the Body of Christ will stand with the sons and daughters of Jacob;

some will turn away. As conflict escalates between Israel and her enemies, your stand in the end will be less about the Jewish state and more about *Him*.

Testing and Threshing in Justice

God uniquely connects Himself to the people and land of Israel. Long ago, He picked a spot on earth to put His Name forever (see 2 Chronicles 33:7; 1 Kings 9:3). The area served for centuries as a threshing floor, where wheat was sifted from chaff. God also chose a people—the Jews—to inherit and inhabit the land of that place. At His instruction, King David purchased the site and built an altar on it (see 2 Samuel 24:15–25). On this precise plot of real estate, David's son Solomon constructed God's Holy Temple. There His glory came down, dwelling in unequaled grandeur on earth. Located in Jerusalem, the place is now known as the Temple Mount.

Today the Temple Mount serves as a threshing floor no less than it did when David bought it three thousand years ago. This dry and dusty hilltop sifts nations' souls through their contest for its control. And little wonder, for there Yeshua will rule and reign in Kingdom splendor—something His enemies are scrambling to prevent (see Isaiah 2:2–3; Psalm 132:13–14; Acts 3:21). The Temple Mount will prove the consummate testing ground, the place where Messiah and anti-Messiah, and the followers of both, will someday be exposed. It is a test God wants you to pass—because it is a test of love. And by design, it will involve the Jews.

The test would prove less genuine if issues involving Israel were simple, or the Jewish people never sinned. But sometimes Israel acts unjustly. Sometimes her government or military or citizens make mistakes. Yet, as we will see, *true* justice is often perverted by the world's collective understanding and response to Israel as nowhere else.

What does God say about the nations' unjust response to the error of Israel's ways?

> "I am very jealous for Jerusalem and Zion, and I am very angry with the nations that feel secure. I was only a little angry [at Israel], but they [the nations] went too far with the punishment. . . . Whoever touches [Israel] touches the apple of [my] eye—I will surely raise my hand against them."
>
> Zechariah 1:14–15; 2:8–9

Those who treat Israel unjustly raise their hand, so to speak, as if to brazenly poke the Almighty in His eye. In response, God raises His hand against *them*; they suffer loss of spiritual vision. In this word picture, I see an expression of God's fiery love for both Israel and the nations. Certainly He is not telling us to give Israel "blind support." To the contrary, He wants us to make choices that enable our vision to be preserved. In a fast-changing world, He wants us to see where we are going, our steps aligned with His. If that is your desire too, this book will help you walk in His ways, discerning truth in love.

In New Words of Old

The Bible's most concise yet comprehensive teaching on the relationship between Israel and the Church—which includes you if you are a Christian—is found in Romans 9–11. This book follows the general flow of those pivotal chapters. In so doing, much time and space is devoted to the Islamist/Arab/Palestinian–Israeli conflict. In that context, any denunciation of terror, fundamentalist Islam or enmity against Israel is not intended to reflect anything less than Messiah-like love toward those set against her. Recall the opening story of Joshua and his encounter with the Most High. God's perspective is Kingdom-oriented; ours must be, too.

Though not a scholarly treatise, *Why Still Care about Israel?* digs deep in the pursuit of truth. As a former attorney with a political science degree and seminary background, I have researched the theological, historical and journalistic works of others, distilling them into a format lay readers can understand. The information I share has been not only intensively investigated but drenched in years of intercessory prayer. In this book you will not encounter dry facts or superficial arguments, but reality replete with heaven's heartbeat.

A companion website, www.whystillcareaboutisrael.com, supplements this book. Helpful study aids, including notes documenting or expounding on topics mentioned in the book, may be found there. Notes available online are designated by letters (a, b, c, etc.), while notes in the back of this book are designated by numbers (1, 2, 3, etc.). Some notes contain a dual designation. In that case, a portion of the note appears in the book, but expository matter is accessible online. This book can be easily read, however, without referring to any of the notes at all. They exist solely for more serious readers as a complementary tool.

Why Still Care about Israel? employs terms that may be unfamiliar to some readers. Where Hebrew or Arabic words are used, translations are provided. Jesus' name is substituted many times with the Hebrew *Yeshua.* In some instances I refer to God as *Yahweh,* using the standard English Tetragrammaton. The words *Old Covenant* and *Hebrew Scriptures* are employed synonymously with *Old Testament.* Bear in mind, however, that the Old Covenant contains within it several different covenants.

I use *Israel* interchangeably with *Jewish state, Jewish nation, national Israel, ethnic Israel* and occasionally *Zion*, referring either to the geographic territory or the Jewish people or both. This parallels the biblical usage, which reflects a dynamic unity between the people and the land.[b] The intended referent (land, people or both) should be clear from the context. Solely for the sake of convenience, the Jews are sometimes described as God's Old Covenant people, and the Church, His New Covenant people.

During the writing of this book, the United Nations upgraded its status of the Palestinian Authority to that of nonmember observer state. Presently there is no universal agreement on the name of the resulting geopolitical entity. Therefore, at different times I use *Palestinian Authority (PA), Gaza, West Bank, Judea and Samaria* or *Palestine*. I trust that any offense taken at any of these terms will be minimal. For linguistic integrity, I have tried to use the most accurate name in each instance, given the particular context.

Where it is necessary to talk of anti-Semitism, the word refers to prejudicial hostility toward Jews, not other Semitic peoples. In discussions on Islam, the term *Islamism* or *Islamist* is used interchangeably with *fundamentalist, militant* or *extremist Islam*. The phrase *the West* or *Western world, civilization, culture* or *society* refer to all nations, wherever located, that identify with and embrace traditional Western values and freedoms.

Enmity against Israel in the Middle East can be difficult to succinctly describe. It is probably best characterized as the Islamist/Arab/Palestinian–Israeli conflict. For the sake of brevity, however, I usually use a condensed term, depending on context: *Islamist-Israeli, Arab-Israeli, Palestinian-Israeli* or a variation thereof.

As you read this book, you may feel angry or pained at times. I do not apologize for disclosing information that may provoke your emotions. Truth must be told so that we can align with righteousness and respond accordingly. I do grieve along with you, however, for the fallen nature of humankind giving rise to those disturbing facts God wants us to face. My hope is that as *Why Still Care about Israel?* brings to light compelling realities and scriptural truths, you will experience His heart of love and grace—for all parties involved—as never before. I pray that when you turn the final page of this book, you will also know *God* as never before. Because in the end, Israel is all about *Him*.

2

God's Inseparable Love

For I am convinced that neither death nor life, neither angels nor demons, neither the present nor the future, nor any powers, neither height nor depth, nor anything else in all creation, will be able to separate us from the love of God that is in Christ Jesus our Lord.

Romans 8:38–39

Like me, you have probably been personally encouraged more than once by the cherished verses above. This power-packed passage has strengthened the Church for over two thousand years. Despite life's difficulties, we can cling to the truth of God's unwavering love. Nothing, *but nothing,* can separate us from it. Why? Mercy and grace. Divine mercy and grace, described in Romans 1–8, crescendo in God's unfaltering love.[1] It is in this context of His love that we begin reading, in the very next sentence, about Israel:

> I speak the truth in Christ—I am not lying, my conscience confirms it through the Holy Spirit—I have great sorrow and unceasing anguish in my heart. For I could wish that I myself were cursed and cut off from Christ for the sake of my people, those of my own race, the people of Israel.
>
> Romans 9:1–4

The flow of Scriptures is strategic by the Spirit. Just as we are assured of Yahweh's love for the Church in Romans 8:38–39, we are reminded of the unquenchable flame in His heart for the Jews in Romans 9:1. As you may know, the original letter to the Roman church contained no chapter breaks; they were added later for our convenience. *The New Covenant's keynote message on Israel is rooted in the revelation of God's merciful, gracious love.* Believers who do not comprehend the magnificent height, depth and breadth of that love will not fully comprehend why God wants them caring about Israel.

Why God Loves Israel

The first time Yahweh speaks of His love is not at Creation, but many years later—to the children of Israel. Try to picture the scene: A throng gathers expectantly before Moses, honored leader of more than forty years. The great lawgiver, prophet and friend of God is saying good-bye to the Israelites as they stand at the precipice of the Promised Land. Moses is about to die, and so (I imagine) the hushed crowd clings to his every word. Nobody pays heed to the punishing desert sun, crying babies or unending demands of life-on-the-go. Here and now, for the first time, Moses tells the Israelites that God loves them:

> The LORD your God has chosen you to be a people for His own possession out of all the peoples who are on the face of the earth. The LORD did not set His love on you nor choose you because you were more in number than any of the peoples, for you were the fewest of all peoples, but because the LORD loved you and kept the oath which He swore to your forefathers.
>
> Deuteronomy 7:6–8 NASB

Why does God love Israel? He says that He loves Israel simply because He loved Israel. He does not say Israel is lovable; He does not even say her forefathers with whom He covenanted were lovable. Yahweh offers no explanation conforming to human logic for His love for the Jewish people. This does not mean His love for them is irrational or misplaced. It is according to divine reasoning, sovereign purpose—and most of all, mercy and grace.

The Creator's love for His people exists ultimately for His own sake. Peer into the chambers of His heart; He loves because He *is* love (see 1 John 4:8, 16). He loves *you* because love is His nature and character.[a] He cannot *not* love you. "Thou art Thyself the reason for the love wherewith we are loved," said the twentieth-century theologian A. W. Tozer.[2]

God ties His love for the Jewish people to the oath He swore to them. He unconditionally binds Himself by His word to Abraham, Isaac and Jacob. It has been said that love is spelled c-o-m-m-i-t-m-e-n-t. Sovereign God loves Israel because of His covenant commitment to her. At the same time, His commitment flows from His love. In other words, God loves Israel because He loved Israel, because He committed to love Israel. Therefore, if you are a New Covenant son or daughter, He also loves *you*, unshakeably.

To be sure, love is not the same as approval. God does not advocate "sloppy agape." He does not approve of sin on the part of His covenant children, Jewish or Christian, and neither should we. But at the same time, sin does not extinguish unconditional love.

A renowned Bible scholar shares how he came to this realization. He once firmly believed God had ceased loving Israel and replaced her with the Church. But in studying Romans 9–11, he was given a revelation of mercy and grace that radically changed his view. He writes:

> It is only where the Church . . . secretly—perhaps quite unconsciously!—believes that its own existence is based on human achievement, and so fails to understand God's mercy to itself, that it is unable to believe in God's mercy for still unbelieving Israel, and so entertains the ugly and unscriptural notion that God has cast off His people Israel and simply replaced it by the Christian Church.[3]

Loving in Hebrew: *Ahav*

If you go to church, you have probably heard more than one sermon about the different Greek words used in the New Covenant for *love*. But have you ever studied the fascinating Hebrew concept? It is in Hebrew that God gives us the foundational knowledge of His love, and solid foundations are key to good constructs of any kind. So let us revisit Deuteronomy 7:7–8 (NASB), where we first hear, straight-out and plain, about God's love for His people: "The LORD . . . set His love [in Hebrew, *khashaq*] on you . . . because the LORD loved [*ahav*] you and kept the oath which He swore to your forefathers."

30

The Hebrew Scriptures use three different words to convey love. *Ahav*, a primary root, appears most frequently. *Ahav* means "to love, have affection, be attached to, delight in." *Ahav* also connotes "to lust" and "to breathe" or "pant after."[4] *Ahav* is used where Moses explains that the Lord set His love on Israel "because the Lord loved" them. The second word for love, *khashaq*, appears where Moses says the Lord "set His love on you." *Khashaq* means "to love, long for, desire and delight in." It also implies "clinging."[5] (A third word for love, *keenah*, is not found in this passage but is used elsewhere to denote Yahweh's ardor, zeal or jealousy.[6] [b])

Based on the Hebrew, Deuteronomy 7:7–8 can be accurately paraphrased: "The Lord set His longing, clinging desire, delight and love on you because of His affectionate attachment, desirous delight and love for you."

Why take so much time with definitions? The point is the passion! God is absolutely amorous toward Israel. She is the object of a divine love affair, the longest romance on record. Do I suggest His heart for her excludes Gentiles from the totality of His blessing? Absolutely not. Much to the contrary, His heart for Israel is related to His ineffable desire to bless *all* peoples on earth.

Hear God's heartbeat for His people, not only in the words of Scripture but in the very letters that comprise them. According to some Jewish schools of allegorical thought, each letter of the Hebrew alphabet carries with it a deposit of the divine. Since God is the Author of language and Hebrew is the original tongue in which He communicates to His people, it is said that not only every word, but every letter of every word bespeaks something of His nature.[7]

In the word *ahav*, the first letter is *aleph*, said to designate sacrifice, strength and servant leadership. *Hey*, the second letter, connotes an opening or open window. It is also used as a substitute for writing God's name. The third letter is a modification of *bet*, meaning "house" or "family." *Bet* implies covenantal, affectionate relationship.[8]

By its three component letters, *ahav* communicates sacrifice, strength, communion with God and familial relationship. In *ahav* we catch nuances of the all-powerful One sacrificing so His people can relate freely to Him as family. J. I. Packer, in his classic *Knowing God,* describes the intimacy implicit in the word *ahav*: God's "love reaches its highest form in personal fellowship in which each lives in the life of the other, imparting to the other, and receiving back the outflow of that other's affection."[9] What exquisite communion!

Love Synergized: The Church and Israel

As Paul trumpets the triumph of God's love, it is not surprising the Spirit turns his thoughts to Israel. Birthed from Yahweh's love for all humanity, Israel was created for His personal affections and ardor. She was to love Him back and mediate His love to others. But Israel is lost in her sin apart from her Savior. So the anointed apostle spills before us his unshakeable grief. The same Paul who exhorts us to rejoice always (see Philippians 4:4) says that he carries "great sorrow and unceasing anguish" over Israel. Why does his pain never end? Paul is gripped by the Spirit's unending burden of love for the Jews. Not once, but three times, he affirms the veracity of his passion:

> I speak the truth in Christ—I am not lying, my conscience confirms it in the Holy Spirit—I have great sorrow and unceasing anguish in my heart . . . for the sake of . . . those of my own race, the people of Israel.
>
> Romans 9:1–4

Paul's petitioning heart echoes that of Moses, who pleaded with God on Israel's behalf: "Please forgive their sin—but if not, then blot me out of the book you have written" (Exodus 32:32). Paul, like Moses, carries the unchanging heart cry of God. Do you want to know the burden of the Lord—His Kingdom purposes—for today? Think *Israel.* Does this mean others are excluded from a special place in our Father's heart? To the contrary, God's burden for Israel is central to His redemptive plans for all peoples. Not for her sake but His, the destiny He designed for Israel will someday be fulfilled.

To be sure, some believers with little grasp of God's heart for the Jews undeniably love Him deeply. For over two thousand years, countless numbers of such saints have even laid down their lives for Jesus. In no way do I impugn their integrity or spirituality. But in these last days, the world is different. In it Israel has been placed center stage before a global audience. God's love story is on divine display as the nations lock in on the tiny Jewish state. And He is noting our response. Will it be one of love, "the most excellent way" (1 Corinthians 12:31)?

According to 1 Corinthians 13, without love we are nothing. Without love, even the priceless gifts of the Spirit and His mantles for ministry add zero to our worth. If we speak in tongues or prophesy without love, we make only noise. Lacking love, our faith may move mountains but fail to bless. If we give all we possess to the poor or become martyrs for Messiah, we gain nothing without love. Love is the greatest gift and most excellent way. It never fails; it lasts forever. Love is the most valued substance of the universe.

Jesus cautioned that in the last days, Kingdom conflict between good and evil would greatly increase. Natural human sensibilities would be offended, embittered or hardened by the onslaught of iniquity. As a result, the love of most would grow cold (see Matthew 24:12–13). Messiah's true followers, however, will stand firm to the end. They will not just endure the times but engage with His sacrificial strength in the intimate communion of His *ahav*.

Refining Love

Pure, Messiah-like love is given without condition, solely to bless the beloved. Free of ulterior motive, such love is the ultimate substance and test of our faith. It is that which the Lord has always radically required of those who dare follow Him fully. And today, He is using Israel to help us attain to it. Take, for example, the story of one Arab believer I know, a former Muslim whom we will call "S."

"S" used to train young children to kill Israelis and took pride in personally snuffing out more than one Jewish life. But then he had a dramatic encounter with God. Now he loves and serves Jesus, the Arabs—and Jews. How was "S's" heart transformed from one of hate to love? Someone told him that to know God he would have to love a Jew (namely, Jesus). When that person set a Bible before him, "S" began to shake violently. He did not know if he was shaking from rage, fear, the presence of God or all three. But he did know the book was about Israel, his sworn enemy. "S" says that when he eventually read the Bible, and through it came to know God's love for Israel, he felt love for the first time in his life. "I grew up hating—and especially hating Jews. When I was willing to love them, God filled me with His love for *me*." Today when "S" ministers the Gospel to Jews, supernatural love softens their hearts toward the Savior.

Not unlike He did with "S," God used Israel to demonstrate His love in the life of my young friend Emily. For years Emily was fascinated with end times prophecy. Ever since she learned that Israel serves as God's prophetic "timepiece," she told me, she claimed to love the Jewish state. But whenever I saw Emily, she was intrigued with just one thing. The woman had question upon question about how the latest news events from the Holy Land could signal the Second Coming of Christ. Finally, I shared with Emily that God had another way for her to relate to the Jewish people she said she loved. As you will see momentarily, her life was subsequently transformed.

Since Israel's modern-day restoration, many believers have, like Emily, viewed the Jewish state as an exciting prophetic timepiece. Indeed, that is an aspect—albeit a secondary one—of her existence. As a prophetic people through whom God speaks, Israel uniquely reflects the hour of world history. But Jesus did not die for prophetic timepieces. Neither is the Father's heart ravished over some cosmic hourglass. Israel is His nation of treasured souls, most of whom desperately need salvation.

Certainly, God wants us cooperating with His prophetic Word and plans. But genuine love does not depend on a prophetic agenda. If our primary concern with Israel is prophecy, God wants to take our love to higher levels by taking us deeper into His heart. This He tenderly did with Emily, who began visiting Israel to minister in compassion to Holocaust survivors and terror victims. Instead of living for the news, she *is* good news to Israel.

Will you, like "S" or Emily, choose the most excellent way in loving God's ancient covenant people—not because her land is holy, not because prophecy gets fulfilled there, not because you seek to convert Jews and not because you want to get blessed? He is asking you to love Israel because He loves Israel, unconditionally, uncompromisingly. The prophet Ezekiel shows us how.

Mercy and Grace[c]

Ezekiel tells a rapturous tale of love, inviting us to explore the recesses of God's heart. The story starts in chapter 16 with Yahweh recounting His adoring, doting care for Israel. On the day she was born, He says, she was despised. She was thrown into a field, unbathed, unwanted, naked and alone. Not a soul had pity or compassion on her. But He passed by and saw her kicking in her blood. As she lay there helpless, He said, "Live!" God grew her like "a plant of the field." Years later, He saw that she was "old enough for love." So He spread the corner of His garment over her, covering her nakedness. He gave her His "solemn oath" and she became His. He dressed her in fine linen and costly embroidery, fitting leather sandals onto her feet. He adorned her with jewels, silver and gold. He placed a crown on her head. He nourished her with fine flour, honey and olive oil. "You became very beautiful and rose to be a queen," God said. "And your fame spread among the nations on account of your beauty, because the splendor I had given you made your beauty perfect" (Ezekiel 16:13–14).

In return, Israel took her beauty and fame and ran off to become a whore:

> You lavished your favors on anyone who passed by and your beauty became his. You took some of your garments to make gaudy high places, where you carried on your prostitution. . . . You also took the fine jewelry I gave you . . . and you made for yourself male idols and engaged in prostitution with them. And you took your embroidered clothes to put on them, and you offered my oil and incense before them. Also the food I provided for you—the flour, olive oil and honey I gave you to eat—you offered as fragrant incense before them. That is what happened, declares the Sovereign LORD.
>
> Ezekiel 16:15–19

How does God respond to Israel now that she has spurned His attention and affection only to disgrace herself? He declares: "Yet I will remember the covenant I made with you in the days of your youth, and I will establish an everlasting covenant with you" (Ezekiel 16:60).

Do you hear the long-suffering ache despite the anger in His voice? The Father's heart is ravaged yet forever faithful. In spite of her sin—for which severe chastening follows—He loves Israel unconditionally. He will not quit or give up on her. God will save Israel by mercy and grace, and she will love Him back. The same message is repeated over and again by the prophets, apostles and Yeshua Himself.

One biblical portrayal—Yahweh as Israel's husband—seems downright scandalous: the story of Hosea and Gomer.

Tough Love

In extraordinary fashion, the prophet Hosea dramatically plays out God's covenant love for all to see. Here it is more than mere story; it is flesh-and-blood reality. God startles us, and no doubt Hosea, by telling him to marry a harlot, a sex addict who will repeatedly prove unfaithful. Despite his wife's rebellion, Hosea must love and keep covenant with her. So the prophet finds and marries a prostitute named Gomer, and their marriage depicts Israel's adulterous relationship with God (see Hosea 3:1).

From this reality show of infidelity comes the word of the Lord to His people. Israel, like Gomer, has deplorably prostituted herself to sin. Her jealous God, however, will not stand for it. He will do whatever it takes to win her back—if not the easy way, then the hard. Therefore, Yahweh "will be like a lion" to the Jewish nation. He will "tear her to pieces," then hide

Himself and make sure nobody comes to her rescue. Meanwhile, He will wait patiently for her to admit her guilt, turn back and earnestly seek Him (see Hosea 5:14–15).

The story bespeaks the tough love of an incomparably gracious God. In wrath, He remembers mercy; His own love constrains Him. Hear His heart pounding with anticipation for the hour of His beloved's return:

> "In that day," declares the LORD, "you will call me 'my husband'; you will no longer call me 'my master.' . . . I will betroth you to me forever; I will betroth you in righteousness and justice, in love and compassion. I will betroth you in faithfulness, and you will acknowledge the LORD."
>
> Hosea 2:16, 19–20

The book of Hosea closes with some of the most beautiful, romantic poetry in the Bible. On Israel our long-suffering Creator, knowing the end from the beginning, stoutly refuses to give up. Rest assured, says Hosea, the Jewish nation will be transformed by mercy and grace:

> "I will heal their waywardness and love them freely, for my anger has turned away from them. I will be like the dew to Israel; he will blossom like a lily. . . . His splendor will be like an olive tree, his fragrance like a cedar of Lebanon. People will dwell again in his shade; they will flourish like the grain, they will blossom like the vine—Israel's fame will be like the wine from Lebanon."
>
> Hosea 14:4–7

A New Covenant

Not only in Hosea, but throughout the Old Covenant, it is in the context of Israel's failure and sin—and God's judgment—that

He shockingly interjects, "I love you." Just when it seems He is about to disown His people (and rightly so), He declares instead His undying love, affirming His covenant still stands. When it appears all fair and legal grounds for dissolution of the relationship exist, He renews His vows instead. Amid deserved chastisement, God dispenses compassion. Israel spurns the Creator—again and with impunity—and receives an engraved invitation to repent. His mercy and grace are appalling; His kisses, outrageous. Discipline Israel He must, but destroy or disown her completely? Never!

Eventually there came a time when sin so screamed for justice that God exiled the Jews from their land. Captive Israelites lay broken and bleeding, defeated and displaced on foreign soil. Surely they wondered if Yahweh would ever favor them again.

In this unlikely context of misery and despair came a dizzying word from the Lord. Like a windfall, hope from heaven descended on the Jews. Never before had He spoken explicitly of it—this future "new covenant":

> "Behold, the days are coming," says the LORD, "when I will make a new covenant with the house of Israel and with the house of Judah. . . . I will put My law in their minds and write it on their hearts; and I will be their God, and they shall be My people. . . . For I will forgive their iniquity, and their sin I will remember no more."
>
> Jeremiah 31:31, 33–34 NKJV

Notice that the New Covenant was not made here with the Church; it was originally made with Israel. Holy God is wholly in love with Israel; therefore, she must and will be made holy. By mercy and grace, the New Covenant guarantees it. That same mercy and grace extends to all nations—but keeps His covenant with Israel intact.

Next, as if this all-surpassing promise were not enough, God reaffirms His commitment to sustain Israel as a nation forever:

> This is what the LORD says, he who appoints the sun to shine by day, who decrees the moon and stars to shine by night, who stirs up the sea so that its waves roar—the LORD Almighty is his name: "Only if these decrees vanish from my sight," declares the LORD, "will Israel ever cease being a nation before me." This is what the LORD says: "Only if the heavens above can be measured and the foundations of the earth below be searched out will I reject all the descendants of Israel because of all they have done," declares the LORD.
>
> Jeremiah 31:35–37

Have the sun, moon and stars stopped shining? Have the waves of the sea stopped roaring? If not, then the descendants of Jacob have not ceased being a nation before God. Have men measured the heavens or plumbed the deepest bowels of the earth? Then neither has God rejected Israel because of her sin! Assured He will never reject His Old Covenant people, we can trust He will never reject His New Covenant people, either.

If you are a Christian, God's love, mercy and grace for you are no less than they are for Israel. Her story is very much yours. In the next chapter, you'll discover how to read that story anew.

The Sanctity of Covenant

Theirs is . . . the covenants . . . and the promises.

Romans 9:4

In the ancient world of the Bible, covenant defined and sealed relationship. A solemn covenant-making ceremony resulted in an agreement that was sacred in nature. But it was a bloody affair, involving the cutting of flesh.[1] Symbolically, the parties created a recognizable entity having, in a sense, a life of its own. A covenant was, and still should be, an oath scrupulously honored and protected by all.

Romans 9:4–5 describes the riches of God's mercy and grace in His covenant with the Jewish people. In this passage the apostle Paul outlines Israel's inheritance and prophetic calling. Invested in her is blessing for all humankind—guaranteed by a blood-mediated covenant with Yahweh.

The Abrahamic Covenant

As we unpack God's covenant with Israel, please note at the outset one little word in Romans 9:4: *is*. Israel's "is" the "adoption as sons," "the covenants," "the promises" and much more. Now, as it *is* in English, so it *is* in the Greek,[2] in which *is* refers to something that currently exists. If Paul writes that Israel's "is" something, he means it still *is* in an ongoing sense. The covenants and promises *are still* Israel's.

The apostle makes the same point later in his letter: "They are loved on account of the patriarchs, for God's gifts and his call are irrevocable" (Romans 11:28–29).[3] Israel's destiny has not expired. It has not been transferred to the Church or anyone else. To be sure, the Church partakes of all the blessings of salvation and is in no way inferior to Israel. But she does not replace or supersede Israel in God's heart or plans for humankind. His blessings and irrevocable callings are by mercy and grace, and He has enough of that for everyone.

Not long after the Church in Rome was established, however, a question arose as to whether Christians had replaced Israel in the purposes of God. Many Jewish leaders had rejected Jesus as Messiah. To the Romans this posed a double dilemma. First, were they Yahweh's new, reinvented "Israel"? Second, if they were, and His Word had failed the Jews, how could they trust His promises now for *them*?[3] Paul's inspired response is based on the concept of covenant. He explains as clearly as possible that God's covenant with Israel *is* still hers; it *is* still in effect. It cannot be revoked; it is *unconditional*.

In the Bible, a covenant can be either conditional or unconditional in nature. If conditional, that covenant's fulfillment depends on certain prerequisite conditions being met. If God makes a conditional covenant, the person(s) with whom He makes it must do something first before He fulfills His end of the deal. But if the covenant is unconditional, then God binds only Himself to do anything. His fulfillment of an unconditional covenant is not conditioned on, or affected by, human response. In other words, sin cannot void or cancel God's unconditional covenant. Amazing grace, is it not?

The Covenant Is Unconditional

Yahweh's foundational covenant with Israel traces to Abraham:

> The LORD had said to Abram, "Go from your country, your people and your father's household to the land I will show you. I will make you into a great nation, and I will bless you; I will make your name great, and you will be a blessing. I will bless those who bless you, and whoever curses you I will curse; and all peoples on earth will be blessed through you."
>
> Genesis 12:1–3

The covenant explodes with the hope of redemption and blessing for all humankind. Moreover, the covenant is unconditionally guaranteed—specifically in the context of the Promised Land. In Genesis 15:7, Yahweh reminds his friend, "I am the LORD, who brought you out of Ur of the Chaldeans to give you this land to take possession of it."

Abraham asks, "How can I know that I will gain possession of it?" (verse 8). God's answer leaves no room for doubt. He instructs the patriarch-to-be to slaughter and sacrifice various animals, placing pieces of their cut-up bodies on the ground. Then, with Abraham in a Spirit-induced sleep, God passes as holy fire between the pieces. He declares, "To your descendants I give this land" (verse 18).

The ritual enacted in Genesis 15 was the same procedure used in Abraham's day to formalize a legal covenant. Animals were cut, then covenanting parties walked between the pieces in solemn oath to perform their duties. If only one party passed through the bodies, however, only that one party undertook to perform covenant duties. Fulfillment of the covenant would not depend on the actions of any other party to the covenant.[4] So the fact that Yahweh alone passed between the animals, and Abraham did not, cannot be overemphasized. It establishes that God's covenant with Abraham, which later passed to Isaac and Jacob, is radically, graciously unconditional.[b] The esteemed J. Dwight Pentecost wrote that it was "impossible for God to make any clearer that what was promised to Abraham was given him without any conditions, to be fulfilled by the integrity of God alone."[5]

Inheritors of the Covenant

Time goes by and Ishmael is born. With no son by Sarah, the patriarch asks God if Ishmael can inherit the covenant. But his request is unequivocally denied: "No, Sarah your wife shall bear you a son, and you shall call his name Isaac; I will establish my covenant with him for an everlasting covenant, and with his descendants after him" (Genesis 17:19 NKJV).

Many years later, Isaac fathers Esau and Jacob. Between them, Sovereign God chooses Jacob and decrees, "In you and in your seed all the families of the earth shall be blessed" (Genesis 28:14 NKJV). Eventually Jacob's name is changed to Israel, the name his descendants have been called ever since. His children become the flesh-and-blood inheritors of the unconditional Abrahamic covenant.

And so, Paul reminds the Church the covenant "is" still Israel's, despite her collective—and lamentable—decision not to embrace Yeshua. Hebrews 6:13–14, 17 affirms: "When God made His promise to Abraham . . . he swore by himself . . . because God wanted to make the unchanging nature of his purpose very clear."

God followed the Abrahamic covenant with three other covenants. In chronological order, these are known as the Mosaic or Sinai covenant (the Law); the Davidic covenant (pertaining to the Messianic Kingdom); and the New Covenant. Each builds upon all previous covenants—but does *not* cancel any of them out (see Matthew 5:17–20; Luke 1:68–73; Hebrews 6:17).

"Correctly Handle the Word of Truth"[6]

Why does heated controversy swirl over God's covenant with Abraham? For Christians, confusion often traces back to how we have learned to interpret the Bible. God wants us to "correctly handle the word of truth" (2 Timothy 2:15) lest our understanding of Scripture be influenced by undue emotion, flawed discernment or faulty assumption. *An incorrect handling of truth will usually result, among other things, in an incorrect understanding of God's covenant with Israel.* So the question must be asked: To know our God in Spirit and truth, walk intimately with Him and avoid error, how should we interpret His Holy Word?

A full study on Bible interpretation is beyond the scope of this book.[c] It is important, however, that we overview the basics to settle in our minds, as well as our hearts, why God still wants us caring about Israel. Rest assured, the basics are simple. But some theologians have developed complex and contorted arguments against them. Many times these arguments and novel interpretation methods seek, consciously or unconsciously, to exclude any hope for Israel's national restoration. Too often, believers who are not familiar with sound principles of Bible interpretation are ensnared by them.

I trust you want to "do your best to present yourself to God as one approved, a worker who does not need to be ashamed and who correctly handles the word of truth" (2 Timothy 2:15). So please join me for the remainder of this chapter in a ministudy on how to interpret the Scriptures. I think you'll agree the Creator King is worthy of the endeavor!

To begin, Bible scholars agree that the best interpreter of Scripture is Scripture itself. Writer and teacher of the first five books of the Bible, Moses was the premier interpreter of Holy Scripture. His inspired understandings laid the foundation for all subsequent Old and New Covenant writings. The prophets followed Moses' approach, and Yeshua's teachings reflect, amplify and authenticate what we can call a Hebraic-based method of interpretation.[d] (Messiah criticized hypocritical Pharisaic applications of the Scriptures, but not the Hebraic interpretive principles themselves.) Following Yeshua's example, all the Messianic Jewish apostles and New Covenant authors adhered to the same broad approach.[7]

Now, any method of Bible interpretation (or "hermeneutic") will inevitably reflect underlying presuppositions about the character of God. A traditional, Hebraic approach draws its presuppositions from the biblical text itself. The most foundational of these presuppositions is that God is relational, sincerely desiring to communicate with you and me, and quite able to do so. This one assumption can dramatically affect our understanding of Scripture and, therefore, of Israel.

A Hebraic Approach to Bible Interpretation: Pardes

Because God delights to reveal Himself to those He loves, He generally speaks in a plain, straightforward manner that we can understand. The Master Communicator, He means what He says and says what He means. His Word "is not too mysterious . . . nor is it far off. . . . But the word is very near you, in your mouth and in your heart, that you may do it" (Deuteronomy 30:11, 14 NKJV).

Based on the assumption God wants to be understood, a Hebraic approach to Bible interpretation can be summarized: Words of Scripture are fundamentally—but not exclusively—understood according to their plain, ordinary meaning, in consideration of the literary and historical context in which they were originally written.[8] Simply put, biblical text should be understood in context. Words should first be given their plain sense or straightforward meaning before any deeper meanings are sought out and assigned to them.

A traditional Hebraic hermeneutic used since the third century BC is known as *Pardes*.[c] The *Pardes* approach to understanding and communicating Scripture is reflected throughout the New Covenant as well as the Old. Consisting of four main principles, *Pardes* offers a solid introduction to Hebraic-based Bible interpretation sufficient for our purposes in this book. Although we will refer to the principles of *Pardes* by their traditional Hebrew names, the concepts and techniques they describe are what is most important. We will look at them in the same order they are to be applied.

According to *Pardes*, the first and fundamental meaning of a biblical text is called *p'shat* ("plain"). *P'shat* refers to the plain sense and straightforward, literal meaning of the words used. This is determined in consideration of the grammatical and historical context in which those words were originally communicated. The purpose is to understand what the text said to its original readers or hearers—without our reading anything else into it. Other layers of meaning in a text may exist, but they are ascertained only after the *p'shat* is first determined. This is because additional layers build upon, but do not replace, the fundamental or *p'shat* level.

God's Word is interspersed with beautiful allegory, powerful symbolism and deep meanings. So a Hebraic-based hermeneutic is not rigidly literal. The second *Pardes* category, known as *remez* ("hints"), refers to the symbolic or allegorical understanding of Scripture at which a passage only hints. Many times there is both a plain sense and symbolic interpretation of a passage. But occasionally, a biblical text makes no sense according to its literal meaning. In that case—and *only* in that case—are we to interpret the text *fundamentally* as symbolic or allegorical.

Next, the *derash* ("association") level of meaning is determined by comparing Scripture with Scripture. For example, passages on a certain topic are interpreted in association with other passages on the same topic. Writings from a certain biblical author or time period are studied in association with other writings from the same author or time period. Lastly, *sod* ("secret") levels of esoteric, mystical or uniquely personal meanings may also be found in God's Word. But like the *remez* level, *derash* and *sod* levels must not dismiss or exclude a fundamental *p'shat* interpretation.

Interpreting the New Covenant is not much different from interpreting the Old. The New Covenant is a Jewish book written by Jewish authors, expounding on Jewish concepts, using Jewish hermeneutics. It extends God's gracious blessings to new dimensions centered in Messiah. But like the Old Covenant, whenever possible, the fundamental interpretation and application of New Covenant text is according to the *p'shat* principle. Words should be understood according to their plain meaning, given the context in which they were originally communicated. After the *p'shat* is established, additional levels of understanding and application may then be found.

Symbolizing the Scriptures

Pardes, along with more intricate Hebrew hermeneutical techniques, fell into disuse by much of the Church shortly after the first-century apostles. By the third century, most believers were Gentile rather than Jewish, and naturally so; there have always been many more Gentiles in the world than Jews. Gentile Church leaders felt a different approach to Bible interpretation would better suit their own traditions and prove more user-friendly to pagan society. So they developed an approach that reflected the Greco-Roman, rather than biblically Jewish, worldview.

Not surprisingly, soon our Church fathers started to think of God as unrelational, distant and aloof from humanity. Contrary to the Messianic Jewish apostles, they concluded He spoke only in language intrinsically difficult, if not impossible, to understand.[9] By the fourth and fifth centuries, they adopted a new hermeneutic based on new presuppositions that are not founded in Scripture. Their fundamental approach to Bible interpretation became symbolic or allegorical, instead of plain sense or literal. In essence, they jettisoned the *p'shat* principle and went wild with *remez, derash* and *sod*.

As a result, God's words were understood as mostly referring to the ethereal rather than earthly realm. Words such as *book, house* or *land,* for instance, did not suggest a literal book, house or piece of land. Rather, they were understood as referring exclusively to realities and mysteries that were spiritual and intangible. By this reasoning, terms like *Israel* and *Jew* no longer applied to the literal descendants of Abraham, Isaac and Jacob. Instead they symbolized Christians or the Church. References to the Promised Land were seen as referring exclusively to spiritual blessings. At times, the whole Old Covenant was treated as merely a spiritual type or shadow of the New. Now, the Old Covenant does contain types and shadows of the New—but not at the expense of the fundamental meaning of the passages in which those types and shadows appear.

What fruit has the allegorical method borne? "Fantasy unlimited," according to one theologian.[10] Take, for example, an insight from Origen, third-century Church father, based on Jesus' triumphal entry into Jerusalem. Dispelling any literal reference to Jerusalem, Origen reasoned that the donkey represents the Old Covenant, while its colt depicts the New. The two apostles, he concluded, picture the moral and mystic senses of Scripture. According to Origen, a straightforward understanding of a city, donkey, colt or the apostles is irrelevant. Jesus never meant for anyone to fetch an animal for Him and did not ride one into Jerusalem. Apparently He entered the Holy City sitting on the New Covenant—even though it was not yet written, and even though Zechariah had prophesied, as a recognizable sign to Israel, that her King would come riding on a colt to her (Zechariah 9:9).[f]

In overemphasizing symbolism, an allegorical hermeneutic does not explain or account for the hundreds of past literal fulfillments in the Bible of Old and New Covenant prophecy. As you might expect, it does not allow for literal *future* fulfillments of prophecy either. Therefore, Christians who interpret God's Word according to this approach rarely regard modern Israel as a fulfillment of prophecy. Some of them strongly oppose her existence today as a restored Jewish state.

Supersessionism: Replacement Theology

Following the Great Reformation, Protestant evangelicals gradually recouped the essence of the *p'shat* principle of *Pardes*. This gave rise to the widely used "literal-grammatical-historical" approach to Bible interpretation that became the evangelical mainstay for hundreds of years. But in overemphasizing the fundamental *p'shat* level, the symbolic *remez, derash* and *sod* levels ("hints," "association" and "secret") were sometimes minimized or ignored. To correctly handle the Word of truth, we must maintain the fundamental strength of the literal-grammatical-historical hermeneutic. But God wants us accessing the full, rich treasure of His Word. This we can do by restoring the breadth and depth of *all* the categories reflected in a Hebraic-based approach such as *Pardes*.

In recent decades, different streams of Christianity have sought to recover many aspects of Hebraic-based hermeneutics.[g] But most traditional denominations and seminaries still rely heavily on the allegorical approach. As a result, we still regularly hear teachings that take prophetic Scriptures about Israel and interpret them as merely symbolic of the spiritual life of the Christian. No regard at all is given to literal, physical Israel. To illustrate, look with me at Isaiah 60:1: "Arise, shine, for your light has come, and the glory of the LORD rises upon you." In context, this prophetic verse refers fundamentally, at the level of *p'shat*, to Israel. Applying principles of *remez, derash* and *sod*, there is much personal blessing in the verse for Christians, too. But the original meaning pertaining to original Israel is still the original meaning. The prophecy has a future, tangible fulfillment for the Jewish nation. If we regularly ignore such fundamental meanings, and apply Scriptures like Isaiah 60:1

exclusively to the Church, we may fall prey to the serious error of supersessionism.

Supersessionism mistakenly teaches that God's prophetic promises and Kingdom purposes for the Jews have been superseded, transferred or replaced. Through history, supersessionist theologies have inevitably brought about tragic expressions of Christian anti-Semitism. As we will see, the apostle Paul denounces all forms of supersessionism in Romans 9–11. A respected Bible scholar notes that faulty hermeneutics, especially regarding prophecy, paved way for the problem:

> In the history of the Church . . . the prophetic portions of Scripture have suffered more from inadequate interpretation than any other major theological subject [because] the Church turned aside from a normal and grammatical/literal interpretation of prophecy to one that is . . . subject to the caprice of the interpreter.[11]

Classic supersessionism is known as replacement theology. Replacement theology erroneously teaches that Israel has been replaced by the Church in God's heart and plans. All the blessings He ever gave to the Jews now belong exclusively to the Church. Left to Israel are all God's curses and judgments.

As we will see in chapter 12, a new supersessionism has developed out of the Palestinian-Israeli conflict, called Palestinian fulfillment theology or Christian Palestinianism. This new supersessionism is being used by some as a theological justification and political tool for anti-Zionism and anti-Israelism. It is fast gaining popularity—though many respected scholars regard it as outright anti-Semitic. Sadly, like the old supersessionism, the new is marked by misguided hermeneutics and mistaken presuppositions about God, such as that described below.

Valuing the Physical Realm

The approach we take to Scripture study will be impacted by another critical, though sometimes unconscious, presupposition. Whether we realize it or not, most of us attach different values of importance to the spiritual versus physical realms. If we believe the physical realm that God created is essentially good, we have little trouble understanding the significance of that realm—including physical Israel—to His redemptive plans.[12] A Hebraic-based hermeneutic assumes that material reality is quite valuable to its Creator, who declared all that He had made to be "very good" (Genesis 1:4, 10, 12, 18, 21, 31). It is because of God's loving esteem for the earth realm that He purposed to do what is necessary to redeem it (see Romans 8:19–21).

In contrast, Greco-Roman thought held a dualistic view. It regarded the intangible spirit realm as intrinsically good but tangible matter as intrinsically bad.[h] The New Covenant writers recognized and denounced the influence of this pagan perspective. Subsequent Church fathers, however, reverted back to it. In the fifth century, a treatise by Augustine entitled *City of God*[13] sharply polarized spiritual from material reality. Rejecting Hebraic hermeneutics, Augustine viewed the earth realm as irredeemably bad. As a result, he saw no hope of restoration for physical, literal Israel. Augustine's profound impact on the development and institutionalization of supersessionism cannot be overstated.[14]

If, like Augustine, we consciously or unconsciously regard the material realm as evil, we may be quick to spiritualize away biblical references to physical persons, places or things. In the process, we will likely dismiss important passages referring to the prophetic destiny of flesh-and-blood Israel. We will also hinder the expression of God's love to and through *us* as physical human beings.

Interpreting the Old Covenant in Light of the New

Augustine and other Church fathers correctly pointed out that Jesus came to fulfill the Hebrew Scriptures (see Matthew 5:17–19). But Jesus did not *abolish* those Scriptures or the covenants they contain. Their truths and prophetic promises have not expired or vanished from the earth realm. How, then, are Christians to interpret the Old Covenant in light of realities subsequently affected by Jesus in the New?

First, we must keep in mind that to correctly handle the Word of truth, we are not to read later text into previously written passages. In order to understand the fundamental or *p'shat* meaning of Scripture, we must discern how its original authors, hearers and readers would have understood the text. Obviously, Old Covenant writers and readers did not have access to New Covenant writings; therefore, they would not have understood Old Covenant teachings from a New Covenant perspective.

Second, the Bible itself shows us how to properly interpret fresh truths. When new, prophetic revelation was given to Old Covenant authors, they never reinterpreted preexisting Scriptures in light of their subsequent insights. Rather, new revelation was accepted as divine truth based on what had been previously acknowledged to be true.[15] To qualify as part of the holy canon, no new text could ever refute or replace preexisting text.[16] An important measure for judging the inspiration of proposed, new writing was its consistency with all prior biblical writings. The Jewish authors of the New Covenant were strongly influenced by this sacred principle. So when apostolic writers give fresh meaning to an Old Covenant passage, they expand, not extinguish, the original meaning of the passage—as it would have been understood by its original hearers or readers. The new meaning never contradicts the old. Recall the principles of *Pardes* in which levels build upon levels.

Therefore, while the New Covenant may amplify the Old Covenant's narrower, more literal meaning, it does not abolish or abrogate that original meaning. Where certain spiritual realities have dramatically changed, such as atonement for sin and Jewish-Gentile relationships in Christ, the New Covenant is specific and straightforward, not ambiguous or muddled. The writers try to show as clearly as possible, in the language of the day, how new realities have resulted from prophetic fulfillments of Old Covenant promises.

This does not mean that we cannot see Jesus in the Old Covenant. Messiah is the crowning centerpiece of the Hebrew Scriptures! But He is not there at the expense of the content of those Scriptures as they were originally written and understood. As the saying goes, the Old Covenant is the New concealed; the New Covenant is the Old revealed.

How, then, should we interpret Old Covenant passages about Israel in light of the New? Where the Scriptures deal with the Jewish people and their destiny, it is most accurate and aligned with God's intent to apply these passages to Israel first and with fundamental priority. Then, having honored His original intentions, we may apply those passages to other situations in light of the New Covenant. In this manner, believers can benefit from a solid biblical foundation, keep Yeshua at the center, navigate issues on Israel with integrity and receive rich blessing by the Spirit's personal application to them of the Word.

Romans 9 and the Promised Land

God's promises can be life itself. They sustain and nourish us, they offer us hope, they strengthen our faith. All believers are invited to engage in and enjoy God's universal promises. At the same time, in Romans 9:4–5 Paul reminds us that God's promises to Israel, about Israel, are still Israel's. Among them is the promise of land, a core component of the Abrahamic covenant:

> "Go . . . to the land I will show you. . . . To your offspring I will give this land. . . . Sarah will bear you a son, and you will call him Isaac. I will establish my covenant with him as an everlasting covenant for his descendants after him."
>
> Genesis 12:1, 7; 17:19

Paul does not explicitly mention the promise of land in Romans 9:4–5. This does not mean, however, that he intentionally excludes the promise from his list. If Paul had intended to exclude the land promise, he would have clearly done so.[17] A self-described "Hebrew of Hebrews" (Philippians 3:5), the apostle would have certainly meant to include, in his broad reference to "promises," God's seminal promise of land to Israel.[18] There was simply no need for him to repeat all the specific promises to Israel already revealed in the Scriptures. The word *promises* would succinctly encompass them.

Paul's original readers in Rome, schooled in the Old Covenant, would have naturally assumed he was including the land when writing about covenants and promises. They would read, just two chapters later, his implicit reference to the land promise in connection with Israel's future national salvation (see Romans 11:26–27). To think the apostle no longer recognized this unconditional and everlasting promise is to impose on him a later, non-Jewish perspective that he probably never even considered.[19]

The Mosaic Covenant and the Land Promise

Sometimes Christians wonder if Israel's land promise has expired, not due to the New Covenant, but on account of the Mosaic covenant. Unlike the unconditional Abrahamic covenant, the Mosaic covenant is conditional. Blessings and curses depend on and follow our obedience or disobedience to the law.

The Mosaic Law places clear conditions on Israel's ability to inhabit or physically possess the land. It does not, however, nullify the land promise itself or cancel its future fulfillment. The Abrahamic covenant that contains the land promise is everlasting.[20]

The Hebrew prophets help clarify the relationship of the law to the unconditional promise of land. At times they speak of territorial exile, but they also promise a return—based on grace, not good works. They describe how, when Israel disobeyed God, she temporarily lost physical possession of the land. But she never lost its promised ownership. The New Covenant explains it like this:

> The law, introduced 430 years later, does not set aside the covenant previously established by God and thus do away with the promise. For if the inheritance depends on the law, then it no longer depends on the promise; but God in his grace gave it to Abraham through a promise.
>
> Galatians 3:17–18

To be sure, God ultimately owns the land—just as He owns all the earth. We could say that He has given Israel irrevocable title deed to the property. Whether or not she lives on the ground, she alone holds title to it. If she is exiled temporarily due to disobedience, she takes title deed along with her. Israel's promised, irrevocable ownership is no cause for arrogance or excuse for sin on her part, but remains a covenant reality that cannot be extinguished.

The New Covenant Upholds the Land Promise

The New Covenant never explicitly repeals the land promise to Israel. But to be fair, we must note that it does not explicitly repeat the promise, either. Does this suggest the New Covenant does not support the existence of a modern Jewish state? Not at all.

We have seen that a proper hermeneutic assumes ongoing relevance for every promise that is not specifically canceled in subsequent Scripture. So if the New Covenant is silent about a specific promise, that promise is still in effect. Logically and linguistically, when silence surrounds an important matter that has been previously addressed, the presumption lies in favor of continued applicability of that matter.[21] (How many of us have experienced seasons of not hearing from God, and then discovered He wanted us, in such times, simply trusting and obeying what He had previously said?)

Because the New Covenant does not directly and clearly re-state the land promise, some believers are perplexed by a few scattered, isolated verses that, *superficially and out of context*, can seem to spiritualize it away.[i] When these verses are interpreted carefully and correctly, however, they are readily seen to uphold rather than upend the promise.[j] They are consistent with other New Covenant teachings that reflect Israel would, at least in the distant future, be physically restored and living in the Promised Land.

Yeshua said, "Jerusalem will be trampled on by the Gentiles until the times of the Gentiles are fulfilled" and the Jews "taken as prisoners to all the nations" (Luke 21:24). This refers to the period in God's plan in which the Gentiles are prominent and trample the land (see Matthew 24:15–20; 2 Thessalonians 2:3–4). As the times change, however, Jerusalem—and the land—will be returned to the Jews, those to whom it was promised. Yeshua also said that Jerusalem would not see Him again until the holy city, which rejected His first coming, blessed and welcomed Him back (see Matthew 23:39). For this to occur, Israel's religious leaders would have to be in Jerusalem, with the Jews back in their land.

Like Yeshua, Paul implicitly affirms the land promise in Romans 11:25–27. In context, he is writing about Israel's future national salvation.[22] He states that Israel's deliverer will come out of Zion and turn godlessness away from Jacob. The apostle foresees the Jews living in the Promised Land when Messiah (Israel's deliverer) comes again.[23]

Lastly, bear in mind that reaffirming the Jewish homeland did not have the importance in New Covenant times that it has now. The Jews had returned from exile hundreds of years earlier.[k] Their inhabitation of the land was an accepted fact. That being the case, Messiah's focus was not on the land promise as such, but on more intangible or spiritual aspects of the Kingdom.

When Yeshua was asked about the tangible aspects of the Kingdom, His teachings reflect and implicitly affirm Israel's future presence in the land. In Acts 1:6–7, for example, the disciples ask if He would restore the Kingdom to Israel "at this time." The Kingdom to which they refer—after forty days of intense teaching by the resurrected King—is physical as well as spiritual. Therefore, they give Yeshua an ideal opportunity to correct them—and us—if in fact no such Kingdom is going to be restored physically to Israel. But Messiah does not correct them. Instead He replies, "It is not for you to know the times or dates the Father has set by his own authority." Then He redirects their focus to taking the Gospel to the Gentiles. Shortly thereafter, Peter teaches about the literal and future restoration of Israel in God's Kingdom on earth: "Heaven must receive him until the time comes for God to restore everything, as he promised long ago through his holy prophets" (Acts 3:21).

Both Old and New Covenants promise that a time will come when God's focus shifts back to national Israel, both physically and spiritually. Her restoration will reflect the same mercy and grace that extended the Kingdom to the Gentiles. Virtually every prophet was shown a glimpse of this covenant-based restoration. Collectively, they describe a gradual process of a literal return by the Jews to the land, followed by a spiritual return to the Lord. When Israel's return reaches its consummate fulfillment, heaven will break gloriously loose on earth, as we next see.

4

Israel's Prophetic Destiny

Theirs is the adoption to sonship, theirs the divine glory . . .
the receiving of the law, the temple worship . . . Theirs are the
patriarchs, and from them is traced the human ancestry of the
Messiah, who is God over all, forever praised! Amen.

Romans 9:4–5

Nobel laureate Elie Wiesel, a Holocaust survivor and prominent author, reportedly once compared the Jewish people to
a messenger who had been hit on the head and knocked out.
When he woke up, he could not remember the message, who
had sent him, to whom he had been sent or the fact he was a
messenger.

In these last days, Israel is awakening—and she is beginning
to remember the Messenger, the message and those to whom
she was sent. Gifts and callings still resident in her are being

revived for the sake of the nations. So look with me at Israel's covenant-based inheritance, outlined in Romans 9:4–5, destined to unleash blessing in heaven and earth.

Adoption as Sons

According to Romans 9:4, the Jewish people are God's adopted firstborn son (see also Exodus 4:22). In the ancient Middle East, a firstborn son was not loved more than his younger siblings, but he did hold a distinct role in the family. He was uniquely consecrated to God[a] and respected as family leader,[1] even family priest.[2] Particular authority, accountability and the right of succession rested with him.[3]

Even today, various privileges—and problems—often rest with the firstborn. They are typically the first to be blessed for good choices and the first to suffer for bad ones. They are their parents' first love—which is not the same as most loved. In healthy families, parents do not love one child more than another. They do, however, relate their love to each child differently, because each child *is* different.

As Yahweh's firstborn, the Jewish nation is typically the first to get whatever He has in store for the rest of us. For that reason, Israel serves as an example and prophetic microcosm of His larger dealings with humanity. All who do good receive a blessing, "first for the Jew, then for the Gentile." Likewise, tribulation and distress come to all who do evil, "first for the Jew, then for the Gentile" (Romans 2:9–10). When spiritual shifts occur on the earth, Israel typically reverberates first—first blessed, first distressed. Because she is the firstborn, sometimes she gets a double portion—whether of blessing or cursing (see

Isaiah 40:2; 61:7; Jeremiah 16:18). She is given a certain priority, but not superiority.

To be sure, Gentiles who give their lives to Jesus are also adopted as full sons or daughters into God's family of faith (see Romans 8:15–16). Bear in mind that many of His chosen ones, including Isaac, Jacob, Moses and David, were not born first in their families. No need for sibling rivalry here; birth order is God's gift to every child. Father loves each of us best.

Divine Glory

Israel's "is" the divine glory, Paul goes on to say. To Israel appeared the theophanies, God's visitations in human or angelic form. His personal glory led her through forty years of wandering in the wilderness. After she settled in the Promised Land, His manifest presence rested in her Temple. Throughout Israel's history, God gloriously intervened on her behalf, parting bodies of water, crumbling city walls, engraving laws on stone, impregnating a virgin and more. The Holy Scriptures themselves, God's Word with which Israel has been entrusted, reflect His incomparable glory (see 2 Corinthians 3:7–11).

A singular dimension of His divine glory still remains with Israel.[4] In the process of her miraculous restoration, in her growing Messianic remnant ablaze with faith—and much more—she offers the world a glimpse of the Creator. He is preparing Israel to humbly serve the nations in a future, greater glory that will converge heaven with earth. Someday, Yeshua will return to rule and reign in Jerusalem, from where His glory will cover the globe "as the waters cover the sea" (Habakkuk 2:14, see also Isaiah 60:1–2; Ezekiel 43:1–5).

Receiving of the Law

Because theirs is "the receiving of the law," a certain anointing "is" on Israel to love, comprehend and minister God's Word. Her people scrupulously wrote the Scriptures and guarded its integrity, at times paying for it with their lives. For that reason Paul asks and answers, "What advantage, then, is there in being a Jew . . . ? Much in every way! First of all, the Jews have been entrusted with the very words of God" (Romans 3:1–2).

God's words embodied in His laws are still relevant to all who want to follow Him. In recent years, He has been restoring to the Church a Yeshua-centered love for His entire Word, including truths reflected in His laws. He is not putting us in bondage, as some might fear; He is setting us free. Allow me to explain.

Fulfilling the Law

"Christ is the *end* of the law," Paul writes, "for righteousness to everyone who believes" (Romans 10:4 NKJV). From this little sentence, two questions arise. First, what exactly is the "law"? And second, what is the "end" of it?

The word translated "law" is the Greek word *nomos*. But—and this is critical—*nomos* is the same word used throughout the New Covenant for *Torah*. The Hebrew word *Torah* means "instruction" or "teaching." The Torah technically constitutes the first five books of the Bible, but can also refer to all the Hebrew Scriptures. When the Jewish writers of the New Covenant speak of Torah, they often refer to the whole body of Old Covenant teaching. In using the term *nomos,* they do not speak strictly of the commands and statutes, or lists of dos and don'ts that we today call "the law." They speak of the Spirit-empowered means by which believers grow in grace by appropriating God's instruction in holy love. They refer to His Word engraved on our hearts (see Jeremiah 31:33).

That is why Paul writes, "All Scripture is God-breathed and is useful for teaching, rebuking, correcting and training in righteousness, so that the servant of God may be thoroughly equipped for every good work" (2 Timothy 3:16–17). Bear in mind the New Covenant did not exist as canonized Scripture in Paul's day. The "all Scripture" to which he refers—and the importance of which he affirms—is the Old Covenant.

Now, if "the law" refers to Old Covenant teaching as a whole, what is the "end" of it? Yeshua Himself clarifies that He did not repeal the Old Covenant: "Do not think that I have come to abolish the Law or the Prophets; I have not come to abolish them, but to fulfill them" (Matthew 5:17). Messiah encourages Torah teaching for New Covenant believers: "Every teacher of the law [*nomos*] who has been instructed about the kingdom of heaven is like the owner of a house who brings out of his storeroom new treasures *as well as old*" (Matthew 13:52 NIV1984, emphasis mine).

In Romans 10:4, the Greek word *telos*, traditionally translated "end," does not mean cessation or termination. God's teachings are not over and they have not come to a halt. The more correct meaning of *telos* here refers to goal attainment or maturity. An accurate translation of the verse, reflecting Hebraic concepts underlying it, is found in the *Complete Jewish Bible*: "For the goal at which the Torah aims is the Messiah, who offers righteousness to everyone who trusts."

Lawlessness

The world today cries for a cure for lawlessness. We have rebelled against God's laws under a pretense of living free and reaped death. The rotten fruits of lawlessness—killings, corruptions, immorality and more—threaten to shred society. We have misunderstood and abused His grace, shirking at the prospect of the law and "coming under" it, as if the Word were a thing of bondage rather than beauty.

Would you allow the Lord to dispel a myth about the Torah? Somehow we have nurtured the notion that any New Covenant believer embracing the Old has lapsed into legalism. But nowhere does Yeshua, or any apostolic author, tell us to throw off the law. The New Covenant cautions that lawlessness is sin, and sin is lawlessness (see 1 John 3:4). To be sure, our relationship to the law has dramatically changed since Messiah's atonement, the resurrection and Pentecost. We are not to follow the dictates of Torah in the same way Israel did in the Old Covenant. We are to avoid unbalanced, excessive or self-righteous applications of the law—but not the law itself.[b] For New Covenant believers, the Yeshua-centered law is a means by which we express our love for Him: "If you love me, keep my commands" (John 14:15).

In contrast to shouldering a load of legalism, hear how one Hebrew psalmist exults in God's law. The fervid worshiper is not bound up in statutory restriction; I hear free and intimate, high praise:

> "I delight in your law. . . . The law from your mouth is more precious to me than . . . silver and gold. . . . Oh, how I love your law! . . . I stand in awe of your laws. . . . Blessed is the one . . . whose delight is in the law of the LORD."
>
> Psalm 119:70, 72, 97, 120; 1:1–2

How much greater praise ought we, as New Covenant believers, have for God's laws!

Legally Restoring Everything

There is coming a day in which "the law will go out from Zion" to all nations (Isaiah 2:3). It will be a time of unprecedented peace (see Isaiah 2:4), when lambs snuggle up to wolves, calves cuddle with lions and weapons of war till the soil. Christians call this glorious period the Millennium, based on Revelation 20:3–6. Jews have traditionally understood it as the Messianic Age, or Kingdom of heaven on earth.

How does this future epoch affect us now? When Yeshua came to earth, He announced the Kingdom of heaven (or God) was at hand. But He did not declare it was manifest in absolute fullness (see Matthew 4:17; Luke 12:51–53). The Kingdom has, we could say, broken into present reality, but it is not yet here in consummate totality.[5] The earth has not been completely restored to its pre-Fall condition. That is why, for example, some believers are divinely healed of disease but others are not. Some Christians are delivered from evil; others are delivered through it. In short, this present, transitional age is one of overlapping kingdoms, an "in-between" era. You and I live in between the time Yeshua first came—the Kingdom of heaven breaking dynamically into the earth realm—and the time He will come again, climactically restoring "everything" (Acts 3:21). On the one hand, His glory abounds; on the other hand, the gory can impact us, too.

What does this have to do with the law and Jesus' fulfillment of it? God ensures that in the future His law will be followed and honored in all nations. Far from irrelevant, the law will mediate supreme justice, based on truth and righteousness, under Messiah's Kingdom rule. Don't you suppose, therefore, we ought to give it some prayerful attention *now*?

The Temple Worship

Israel's "is" also "the temple worship," according to Romans 9:4–5. Yet the Temple in Jerusalem is no more; perched in its place sits the Dome of the Rock and Al Aqsa Mosque. Maybe you wonder if that matters: Isn't worship in spirit and truth the pinnacle of praise on earth? Doesn't the "tabernacle of David" movement, with round-the-clock worship and prayer, replace Israel's Temple worship?

In a real sense, Christian worship can bring heaven's kiss down to earth. But there is more to the tabernacle of David described in Amos 9:11 and partly fulfilled in Acts 15:16. The tabernacle prophecy was originally given in the context of Israel's national restoration in the Messianic Age. In that day, the flesh-and-blood descendants of the ancient Levites and priests will join us in worshiping Messiah in spirit and truth. Together, we will bow before His holy throne, in His holy Temple, in His holy city (see Ezekiel 40–47). The reality will be gloriously out of (yet in) this world.

Israel's temple worship, in both Old and New Covenants, refers to much more than making music, singing and dancing. To convey the whole concept, some Bible translations use terms such as the "service of God" (Romans 9:4 NKJV) or "temple service" (NASB). The Old Covenant Hebrew word actually combines acts of service with worship.[6] Because the two functions are inseparable, the same Greek word used for worship is also used in reference to the temple ritual of animal sacrifice. Taken together, temple worship and service reflect a priestly ministry. Indeed, God called Israel to be a nation of priests: "You will be for me a kingdom of priests and a holy nation" (Exodus 19:6).

Nation of Priests

Israel's destiny as a nation of priests can be seen as beginning with Abraham, when God tells him to sacrifice Isaac. Scholars suggest the patriarch performs a type of intercessory act by willingly offering up his son.[7] Abraham's sacrificial response is regarded as a priestly oblation—even though Yahweh prevents Isaac's actual slaying. Foreshadowing Yeshua's ultimate sacrifice, Abraham's faith releases the next phase of redemption history.

Hundreds of years later, God expands the priestly function, assigning it to a lineage in the tribe of Levi. The Levitical priesthood performs ongoing intercession, all of which points to Yeshua and serves an essential role in His first coming. Ancient Israel's ministry of combined intercession, sacrifice and worship—offered on the basis of a Messianic atonement that God would someday provide—reconciled heaven to earth not only for her sake but for the Gentiles as well. Through history, faithful Jews have always recognized that an aspect of their service to God is specifically for the blessing of others.[8]

Israel's priestly calling did not totally cease with the New Covenant. Together with the Church, she has been assigned an irrevocable intercessory role to play in Yeshua's return. This is reflected in the fact that her restoration brings "life from the dead":

> But if [Israel's] transgression means riches for the world, and their loss means riches for the Gentiles, how much greater riches will their full inclusion bring! . . . For if their rejection brought reconciliation to the world, what will their acceptance be but life from the dead?
>
> Romans 11:12, 15

At its zenith, life from the dead refers to the Second Coming. It also, however, means revival of the nations even *now*. A direct relationship exists: As God restores Israel, fullness of life is released through her to the Gentiles.

Israel, God's Servant

"You are My Servant, Israel, in Whom I will show My glory" (Isaiah 49:3 NASB). Israel serves God's purposes whether she knows it or not. She serves Him when she loves and obeys Him— and she serves Him when she does not. Though at times she may be spiritually dull, God still calls her His servant: "Who is blind but my servant, and deaf like the messenger I send?" (Isaiah 42:19).

How does Israel serve the Lord in disobedience? First, since much of the Bible is a record of her failure to serve in obedience, her history provides an example from which we can benefit and learn (see 2 Timothy 3:16). Second, on account of Israel's corporate rejection of Messiah, the Gospel has gone to the Gentiles (see Romans 11:11). Third, God uses Israel to refine the Church in love. Fourth, Israel reminds the nations of the sovereignty of their Creator—and by implication, of sin. Of their own sin, however, the nations rarely wish to be reminded. As a result Israel has suffered much.

The "Suffering Servant" of the Bible, Yeshua stands apart as *the* quintessential Servant of the Lord and High Priest of humankind. He alone atoned for our sin—not Israel. Yet the prophetic Scriptures apply the term "servant of the Lord" on another level to the Jewish people.[9] Basilea Schlink, a Nazi-era survivor and German nun, wrote about Israel's Messiah-like, sacrificial service in her book *Israel, My Chosen People*:

Israel, unintentionally and unwittingly, has become a spectacle before heaven and mankind, because she bears the features of the Servant of God. The sight of her should continually remind Christians of Jesus, despised, destitute, covered with bruises, afflicted, hated, persecuted, tormented, and hounded to death . . . We as Christians are to hold in high esteem this people who bears such a close resemblance to Jesus.[10]

Could Israel's suffering at the hands of the nations somehow be in service to those nations? As a nation of priests, might Israel absorb the world's evil to some extent—and then, not unlike Yeshua, get blamed for it? If so, the One who appointed and anointed her to serve watches and weighs our response. He looks for those who will lovingly honor the sacrifice of this "ransom nation" with which He still identifies.

The Scapegoat

I suspect that since you are reading this book, you have given at least some thought to the issue of Jewish suffering. The historical enormity of my people's pain is staggering and perplexing. Tomes have been written about it from countless perspectives.[11] The anguish of the Jews over four thousand years appears a mystery, an ongoing puzzle, and highly disproportionate to our sins. Anti-Semitism, or animosity toward Jews, is described as the world's everlasting hatred, demonstrably illogical and irrepressible. Allow me to illustrate, personally.

Many years ago I ministered in the former Soviet Union. During the course of one evangelistic outreach in Moscow, I received numerous irate scoldings from churchgoers for sharing the Gospel with Russian Jews. The rebuke was the same every time: "You Jews are the reason for all our troubles!" With intriguing logic, one person would chastise me because so many

Jews had left Russia and emigrated abroad with their "skills and money-making abilities." The next churchgoing person would reprimand me because the Jews had *stayed* and caused problems with their "skills and money-making abilities." Of one thing I became certain: We Jews, once more, were the scapegoat.

The term *scapegoat* refers to one who is blamed, with irrational hostility, for the wrongdoing of others.[12] The concept originates in the Bible, based on the Day of Atonement (see Leviticus 16). On that most solemn occasion, Israel's high priest followed prescribed steps to secure atonement for the whole nation. He confessed and vicariously laid the people's sins on two different goats. One would be killed as Israel's sin-bearer; the other—called the scapegoat—went free. The scapegoat served as a sign of God's forgiveness. But it was also a visible and uncomfortable reminder of His demand for obedience.

It is said that like an ancient scapegoat, the Jewish nation serves to remind the world (often unconsciously) of her God and His holy demands. But this is a message the world loves to hate. So true to the adage, many times it seeks to kill the messenger.

The Ancient Root of Anti-Semitism

At this writing, global hatred toward Jews is at an all-time high. In some respects (and later in this book we learn why) it exceeds in scope that which preceded the Nazi Holocaust. Much of the hatred is currently directed at Israel. But as we will also see, world animus against Israel has as much or more to do with the Jewish people as with the Jewish state. Award-winning British journalist Melanie Phillips insightfully notes:

> There is no other world conflict that is so obsessively falsified. Where Israel is involved, truth and reason are totally suspended.

Irrationality and hysteria rule instead. . . . No other conflict in the world attracts such a frenzy of falsification, distortion . . . moral inversion . . . viciousness and imputation of bad faith. And there is an adamantine refusal to acknowledge that this is the latest manifestation of the unique prejudice of antisemitism.[13]

The mystery of Israel's suffering, though comprehendible this side of eternity only in part, points ultimately to the existence of evil and Satan himself. The devil despises who God loves and opposes what God does. This is not to say Israel is entirely fault-free; she is not. But the nations' perception of her wrongdoing is so extremely exaggerated, and their reaction to her sin so inordinately harsh, as to reflect demonic inspiration behind both. How, you may ask, did it all begin?

The seedbed of anti-Semitism is found in the Garden of Eden. There Satan tempts the woman with a lie, she succumbs, the man follows and humankind tragically falls. Only the Creator Himself can redeem what has happened. Stunningly, this is precisely what He sets out to do. In mercy and grace, Deity decrees, "I will put enmity between you [Satan/the serpent] and the woman, and between your seed and her Seed; He shall bruise your head, and you shall bruise His heel" (Genesis 3:15 NKJV). From then on, Satan fumes with fury over his impending ruin.

Millennia go by and redemption history unfolds. God covenants with Abraham, then Isaac and Jacob, to bless all nations through them. As a result, satanic rage is directed at Israel—and ultimately her Messiah, the woman's Seed whose crucifixion and resurrection redeem humankind. But more is yet to come. Yeshua is returning to establish His kingly dominion on earth—and He has specifically linked His return to Israel. God is not finished with the Jews; therefore, neither is the devil (see Matthew 23:39; Acts 3:17–21; Revelation 12:1–5, 13). In chapter 6 we will see that if Satan could ever totally upend Israel, he could also upend the Second Coming—and his own dreaded demise. Though doomed to fail, he will not cease to oppose God's plans, aiming to annihilate Israel with a vengeance.

The Patriarchs

In Romans 9:5, Paul brings to a close his summary of Israel's inheritance: "Theirs are the patriarchs, and from them is traced the human ancestry of the Messiah." Could any greater honor—and responsibility—be given any nation?

The Savior of humankind was birthed from a Jewish womb with Jewish DNA, grew up in a Jewish home with a Jewish family and observed Jewish traditions. I suppose Yeshua played Jewish games, ate Jewish food and had a Jewish sense of humor. Moreover, He is coming back to earth as a Jew, with a distinctly Jewish title, "The Offspring of David" (Revelation 22:16).

According to the Scriptures Yeshua had siblings, who themselves presumably had children of their own. Some of their children's children may still be around—perhaps even your Jewish neighbor, co-worker or friend. Recall that in the parable of sheep and goats, Messiah referred to the ethnic Jews of the end times as His brothers and sisters. For them He remains jealous and zealous (see Zechariah 1:14–15). He does not want His flesh-and-blood relations maligned or mistreated.

Ethnic Distinctions and Racism

Sometimes, any mention of ethnicity stirs rancor and brings charges of racism. Many feel the nations comprise one, autologous global community. National distinctions place barriers between us, they say, causing wars and injustice. Others insist that in a world where many individuals claim combined racial bloodlines, ethnicity is irrelevant. Because such thinking is used today in efforts to invalidate Israel's existence, we must address it.

Let us remember that God created the nations for our own good. Long ago, humankind spoke one language and acted as one. Pooling our pride, we built a high tower called Babel for our eternal renown. Responding in mercy and grace, Yahweh confused our communications, devising different tongues (see Genesis 11:1–9). Presumably based on who could understand whom, we gathered in different people groups. From that gathering, followed by scattering, the nations evolved. Though the world's first globalization project did not fare well, God redeemed the results.

I believe the Creator intends different nations, like the many facets of a diamond, to reflect different dimensions of His divine character. Each has received special blessings and a diversity of gifts with which to serve Him and others (see Genesis 49:3–27; Deuteronomy 33:6–25; Isaiah 19:25). But the Sovereign of the Universe is no racist (see Ephesians 2:14–16). Absolutely no nation is inherently better or worse, no ethnic group intrinsically superior or inferior to any other.

In God's redemptive plans, however, nations do have unique callings and destinies. These distinctions are maintained in the end times and even into the Messianic Age.ᶜ For example, referring to this period the Creator declares, "Blessed be Egypt my people, Assyria my handiwork, and Israel my inheritance" (Isaiah 19:25). At His return, Yeshua deals with nations: "The survivors from all the nations that have attacked Jerusalem will go up year after year to worship the King, the LORD Almighty, and to celebrate the Festival of Tabernacles" (Zechariah 14:16).

The nations that refuse to go will not receive rain (see Zechariah 14:17). God created the nations, each is special to His heart and He loves them all.

Sadly, apart from Yeshua, men have historically formed hostilities and hatreds based on bloodlines. A consequence is racism, the devilish perversion of God's good designs. Racism is defined as the false belief that race is the chief determinant of human traits and abilities, giving inherent superiority or inferiority to individuals.[14] This, the Bible emphatically does not promote.

The Holy Scriptures teach we are all created in God's image with equal human dignity and inherent worth. They promote a framework for human freedoms and "rights." At the same time, the Scriptures do not teach that individuals or nations all have the same or equal gifts, destinies and functions (see 1 Corinthians 12:14–31). We are not universally alike in every trait and ability. We should not, therefore, always be treated exactly the same in every respect. To do so would prove unjust.

Nevertheless, around the world, many oppose the existence of a Jewish state because they believe it racist for a nation to exist uniquely for Jews. Jewish people, they argue, are no different from anyone else. Such individuals confuse, among other things, equality, uniformity and moral justice.[d] God has a different plan.

God Forever Praised

After profiling Israel's inheritance and explaining what her destiny "is" today, Paul exults: "Messiah, who is God over all, forever praised!" (Romans 9:5). The apostle revels in the Creator's plan to make Himself known to the ends of the earth. Like Paul, another Messianic believer looks forward to the day when Israel's gifts and callings are fully revived to bless humankind:

There is a people on earth for whom the Bible is their own history, and not merely spiritual allegories; there is a nation who tasted real freedom as they crossed the Red Sea, who knew the flavor of the original manna in the wilderness, and who let out a loud shout and saw Jericho's walls collapse before them in a heap of rubble. There is a people who . . . slew real giants, who claimed and possessed a tangible land, and who beheld the glory come down upon and fill the temple of their God. There is a nation on earth today which carries deep within its blood and bosom a purpose and a call which must be rediscovered, cultivated and perfected, yet one last time! What will it be like when such a people come alive unto God? What hidden treasure will then explode within the Church . . . as these ancient brethren are quickened again and revived into their true identity, "Hebrew" and "Israelite"?[15]

Pray for Israel, especially Jewish believers, to embrace their prophetic destiny. Ask God to endue the Church with fresh revelation of His mercy and grace for Jews *and* Gentiles. He wants us to honor, even celebrate, our distinctive callings "in order that [His] purpose in election might stand" (Romans 9:11). The future depends on it.

5

The Contention of Election

"It is through Isaac that your offspring will be reckoned" . . . in order that God's purpose in election might stand. . . . What then shall we say? Is God unjust? Not at all! . . . It does not, therefore, depend on human desire or effort, but on God's mercy.

Romans 9:7, 11, 14–16

Through history, Israel's election has been hotly debated and widely disputed. The notion of her "chosenness" by God can offend natural human sensibilities. Even Bible-believing Christians sometimes struggle with the concept. The contention of election begins in the Scriptures, brews in the Church and boils over in the Arab/Islamist–Israeli conflict of today. Yet God chose a people purely for the purpose of redeeming and restoring all others to Himself. Is it possible, then, that much of the fuss is actually about *Him*?

The saga starts when the Creator makes a promise to Abraham laden with hope for humanity. But it depends on the apparently impossible: an heir. Years pass, until his barren wife, Sarah, conceives a scheme, if not a son. She directs her husband to deposit his seed with a surrogate, her Egyptian servant, Hagar: "Perhaps I can build a family through her" (Genesis 16:2).

Hagar becomes pregnant—and immediately sparks fly. Soon she despises her mistress, who in turn treats her roughly. Hagar runs away from home—but not the presence of God. He sees her plight and pities her in the desert of her distress. He tells her to go back and submit to Sarah, for she is carrying a special child. Then He prophesies over this woman of high destiny:

> "I will increase your descendants so much that they will be too numerous to count. . . . You will give birth to a son. You shall name him Ishmael ["God hears"], for the LORD has heard of your misery. He will be a wild donkey of a man; his hand will be against everyone and everyone's hand against him, and he will live in hostility toward all his brothers."
>
> Genesis 16:10–12

Many years later, still no son by Sarah, Abraham has another talk with his Friend. The patriarch pleads, "If only Ishmael might live under your blessing" (Genesis 17:18). Not only he, but Sarah, Hagar and consequently Ishmael himself have assumed this boy is the child of promise. But God has another plan, and His response sets the course of history. He promises bountiful blessing to Ishmael, for he is Abraham's firstborn, beloved son. Ishmael will be fruitful, spawn a great nation and father twelve rulers. "But," God reiterates, "My covenant I will establish with Isaac" (Genesis 17:21).

Abraham's Family Feud

Finally, at one hundred years of age, Abraham cradles baby Isaac in his arms. Now Ishmael is in an understandably tough spot. Suddenly the family spotlight is off him, shining instead on his younger brother. In the culture of the day, Isaac has just usurped Ishmael's birthright. I imagine the boy's whole being wracks with pain. His plight is unprecedented.

We can infer that Ishmael knows God is the One who chose Isaac; nevertheless, the boy deeply resents it. According to the Scripture, he mocks Isaac to such an extent that Sarah detects her son's inheritance is at risk. The connotation is that Ishmael's taunting and deriding is intended to belittle or diminish—actually, curse—Isaac. Galatians 4:29 says he "persecuted" his brother. From God's perspective, Ishmael sneers not so much at human favoritism but sovereign election. In effect Ishmael demands of Deity, "What You gave me is not enough; I want it all." Some say the cry still echoes in much of the Arab world today in its stance toward Israel.

To resolve the conflict, God tells Abraham to send both Hagar and Ishmael away—for good (see Genesis 21:9–12). His seemingly harsh directive would achieve good for both Isaac and Ishmael. How good could it have been for the older son to live with the constant reminder of the younger's election? In such circumstances, could Ishmael, affronted and offended, have matured so as to father twelve princes?

Isaac and Ishmael reunite at Abraham's death to bury their father. By that time they stand shoulder to shoulder, each the head of a family and nation. But Abraham "left everything he owned to Isaac" (Genesis 25:5). Normally, the law of primogeniture would have delegated at least a double portion of the patriarch's property to Ishmael. Whether Ishmael accepted this loss graciously or felt further slighted, we do not know.

We do know that many of his descendants today brood over stacks of perceived dishonor or injustice at the hands of the Jews—particularly related to land. Interestingly, a millennia-old rabbinic insight into the distant future foresaw that Ishmael's descendants would someday assail the Jewish nation with unparalleled ferocity. Reading the Genesis account alongside prophetic Scriptures, the rabbis predicted a type of symbiotic alliance between Ishmael's descendants and the rest of the world. The result, they said, would be cataclysmic war against Israel. They believed only the Messiah would overcome this end times assault, His victory inaugurating the Messianic Age.[1]

Lacking a New Covenant perspective, the rabbis did not perceive how deeply God yearns to save Ishmael's beloved children. He wants us to uphold them in prayer, reach out to them with the Gospel and help them fulfill their Kingdom destiny. Their inheritance, like Israel's through Isaac, is a question of sovereign election. The Creator need justify His choice to no one: "Who are you, a human being, to talk back to God? 'Shall what is formed say to the one who formed it, "Why did you make me like this?"'" (Romans 9:20–21; see Job 40:2).

Ishmael in Bible Prophecy

Ishmael prospered under God's blessing and multiplied quickly into twelve rulers. Today, hundreds of millions of Arabs live in over twenty sovereign states in North Africa and the Middle East, encompassing a vast area of oil-rich land. The existence of these mighty nations, capable of generating tremendous wealth, is evidence of God's blessing.

At the same time, history recounts how Ishmael's children are noted for "hostility toward all their brothers" (Genesis 16:12).[a] Tribal grudges, based on ubiquitous legends of plunder and murder, have gone back for generations, screaming for revenge. Now, I do not believe God cursed Ishmael or caused his descendants to live at odds with each other. But He did know in advance the choices they would make. He alone knows the extent to which those choices reflect resentment over sovereign election.

In the prophecy given before Ishmael was born, God also described him as a "wild donkey of a man." In the culture of the ancient Middle East, the wild donkey was highly admired.[2] The Bible portrays it as a fierce and sturdy animal, capable of thriving in a barren wasteland (see Job 39:5–8). Independent and untamable, a wild donkey spurns the approval or restriction of men for its boundless freedom.

Someday, I believe Ishmael's hostilities and wild donkey disposition will be magnificently transformed in Messiah. Arab nations will redirect their passions to please only Him. Ishmael's descendants will reflect the humble yet honorable servant character of the donkey Jesus once rode into Jerusalem (see Matthew 21:2–29). Collectively, they will carry the presence and glory of the King in a unique, intimate way, tapping into their Abrahamic legacy as never before. They will discover the power of their ancient familial connection to Israel. Hints of conciliatory revival between the children of Ishmael and Isaac glimmer at us from the Scriptures:

> In that day there will be a highway from Egypt to Assyria [modern-day Iraq]. The Assyrians will go to Egypt and the Egyptians to Assyria. The Egyptians and Assyrians will worship together. In that day Israel will be the third, along with Egypt and Assyria, a blessing on the earth. The LORD Almighty will bless them,

saying, "Blessed be Egypt my people, Assyria my handiwork, and Israel my inheritance."

Isaiah 19:23–25

The world has yet to behold the beauty and blessing that will flow from Ishmael's fulfilled redemptive destiny (see Isaiah 60:4–7). Someday, upon a great highway, these children of Abraham will metaphorically roll out a red carpet for the nations—drenched not with the blood of man, but the blood of the Lamb. I believe they will bring to the international Body restored concepts of honor, community, hospitality and sacrificial zeal. Ultimately, the children of Ishmael will reveal to the world how "God hears," in prophetic fulfillment of their forebear's name.[3]

Abraham's Other Sons

The descendants of Ishmael represent only a portion of the Arabic peoples. Many other nations comprise this vast company the Creator desires to captivate, not with the saber but with His Spirit. They, too, are affected by ancient hostilities that will give way to the love of Yeshua through sacrificial intercession and evangelism.

After the departure of Hagar and Ishmael, the death of Sarah and the marriage of Isaac to Rebekah, Abraham takes another wife, Keturah. By Keturah, the rejuvenated patriarch fathers six more sons: Zimran, Jokshan, Medan, Midian, Ishbak and Shuah. He sends them to live in the region east of the Promised Land that Isaac inhabits, toward the area where Ishmael dwells. There in the Arabian Peninsula, the clans intermingle and intermarry (see Genesis 25:1–6).

We can assume that Abraham teaches all his sons to worship Yahweh before they leave home. Very few, however, follow in their father's faith. Instead they turn to idolatry and enmity against Israel, for which they are all eventually judged. Their descendants, together with the Ishmaelites and other nations such as Persia, Egypt and Moab, intermix and are collectively known as Arabs.

By New Covenant times, Arabs dwell from the Euphrates all the way to the Red Sea. Today they possess nearly 5.5 million square miles,[4] or 12 percent, of the earth's surface. These lands total 650 times the size of the state of Israel. For a fast visual comparison, picture two and a quarter copies of this book stacked one atop another. If you were to remove just one page of one book, that page would represent the approximate size of Israel's land space relative to that of the Arabs.

Esau and Jacob: War in the Womb

The contention of election resumes in Bible history with Isaac's pregnant wife, Rebekah. The matriarch-to-be finds herself enduring a veritable fetal feud. I imagine her mopping a sweaty brow as she puzzles before God: "Why is this happening to me?" (Genesis 25:22).

The Sovereign of the Universe replies, "Two nations are in your womb, and two peoples from within you will be separated; one people will be stronger than the other, and the older will serve the younger" (verse 23).

When the twins are born, the baby delivered first is named Esau ("Red" or "Hairy"). The second is called Jacob ("Heelgrabber"). In the course of time, the twins grow up.

One day, Jacob is home cooking stew when Esau arrives, tired and hungry, after working hard outdoors. He prevails upon his brother, "Quick, let me have some of that red stew! I'm famished!" Jacob replies, "First sell me your birthright." Esau mutters, "Look, I am about to die. What good is the birthright to me?" The story concludes:

> So he swore an oath to him, selling his birthright to Jacob. Then Jacob gave Esau some bread and some lentil stew. He ate and drank, and then got up and left. So Esau despised his birthright.
>
> Genesis 25:33–34

Might Esau have inherited the birthright if he had not despised it? Weaving human free will together with sovereign election, God is not unjust. In despising his birthright, Esau has shown a woeful disregard for the One who gave it to him. God foreknew the choice he would make; therefore He says, "Jacob I loved, but Esau I hated" (Romans 9:13).

Years go by and Isaac prepares to die. At Rebekah's behest, Jacob resorts to deceiving his father to "steal," and this time seal, the birthright blessing. Thus Isaac lays his hands on Jacob and by the Spirit pronounces a powerful word:

> May God give you heaven's dew and earth's richness. . . . May nations serve you and peoples bow down to you. Be lord over your brothers, and may the sons of your mother bow down to you. May those who curse you be cursed and those who bless you be blessed.
>
> Genesis 27:28–29

Jacob irrevocably inherits the covenant promise, and Esau is enraged. He implores Isaac to retract the blessing, but this his father cannot do: "I have made him lord over you and have made all his relatives his servants. . . . So what can I possibly do for you, my son?" (Genesis 27:37). Esau weeps at Isaac's feet—over his personal loss, not in repentance—until Isaac prophesies over him, too. But the "blessing" proves unenviable:

> Your dwelling will be away from the earth's richness, away from the dew of heaven above. You will live by the sword and you will serve your brother. But when you grow restless, you will throw his yoke from off your neck.
>
> Genesis 27:39–40

Esau is devastated, embittered and bent on revenge: "I will kill my brother Jacob" (verse 41). The Scriptures tell us to learn from his example:

> See to it that no one falls short of the grace of God and that no bitter root grows up to cause trouble and defile many. See that no one . . . is godless like Esau, who for a single meal sold his inheritance rights as the oldest son. Afterward . . . he was rejected. Even though he sought the blessing with tears, he could not change what he had done.
>
> Hebrews 12:15–17

To escape Esau's wrath, Jacob is forced to flee for his life. But while he is on the run, God graciously visits him. He sovereignly and unequivocally passes His covenant with Abraham and Isaac down to Jacob. Though seemingly obtained by trickery, the inheritance was destined for him all along:

> "I will give you and your descendants the land on which you are lying. Your descendants will be like the dust of the earth, and you will spread out to the west and to the east, to the north and to the south. All peoples on earth will be blessed through you and your offspring. I am with you and will watch over you wherever you go, and I will bring you back to this land."
>
> Genesis 28:13–15

Many years later, Jacob is involved in a dramatic struggle with the Angel of the Lord. Contending for blessing, he secures it—but only after he is forcibly weakened to the point of surrender. At that moment Jacob is so transformed that his name is changed to Israel. The meaning of *Israel* is twofold: "Striving with God" and "Prince with God" (see Genesis 32:28). Today, as with Jacob long ago, Israel's striving with God is being transformed into a humble surrender to His princely calling.

Esau's Descendants at Enmity with Israel

When Yahweh changes Jacob's name and identity, He also changes Esau's heart to one of love for his long-lost brother. The two men reconcile and seem to live peaceably side by side. But Esau spawns a nation known as Edom, which throughout its existence harbors enmity against the children of Israel. They refuse to let the Israelites pass through their land after the exodus from Egypt (see Numbers 20:21), the Edomite ruler Amalek cruelly attacking them. As a result, God swears He will war against Amalek from generation to generation (see Exodus 17:8, 14). Centuries later, a descendant of Amalek named Haman attempts to annihilate all the Jews of Persia (see Esther 3:1, 6). The royal Herods in the New Covenant are Edomites[5] who continue to oppose the ways of God.

For their historically persistent, anti-Israel, anti-God hatred, the Edomites are sternly judged (see Ezekiel 36:5; Joel 3:19; Obadiah 1–15). God is particularly displeased because He sees them as Israel's brother:

> "For three sins of Edom, even for four, I will not turn back my
> wrath. Because he pursued his brother with a sword, stifling all

compassion, because his anger raged continually and his fury flamed unchecked, I will send fire upon [Edom]."

Amos 1:11–12 NIV1984

Throughout the Scriptures, Edom typifies the nations' contention against Israel's election.

The Offense of Election

In the New Covenant, the question of election carries over into the Gentile Church. Some struggled with the idea of a chosen people, most of whom did not believe in Jesus, distinct from the Body of Christ. So Paul addresses the issue forthrightly in Romans 9:6–29. Right after he describes Israel's inheritance, the apostle explains how and why their election still stands.

Paul uses Bible history to illustrate that only a small remnant within Israel has ever stayed faithful to God. Only the elect remnant within Israel has ever engaged personally with Him in full covenant blessing and calling. This remnant serves to maintain the election of the whole nation. The apostle reminds us that Israel's collective disobedience through history never canceled God's unconditional covenant with her, and does not cancel it now. "So too, at the present time there is a remnant [faithful Messianic Jews] chosen by grace" (Romans 11:5).

Ironically, scattered verses in Romans 9 are sometimes taken out of context and used to argue *against* Israel's ongoing election. If only superficially read, for example, Paul's words in verses 6–8 can be misunderstood to mean the opposite of what the passage actually teaches:

> For not all who are descended from Israel are Israel. Nor because they are his descendants are they all Abraham's children. . . . In

other words, it is not the children by physical descent who are God's children, but it is the children of the promise who are regarded as Abraham's offspring.

In context, it is clear that Paul is not denying the Jews' ongoing election as a nation here—or anywhere else.[6][b] Rather, he is referring specifically to the Messianic Jewish remnant as the "Israel" that is spiritually *as well as* physically "descended from Israel." A spiritual separation in Yeshua exists between unbelieving ethnic Israel and believing ethnic Israel. The latter are the "children of the promise" who are *fully* "Abraham's children" and "offspring." It is abundantly clear from the context of Paul's broader teaching in Romans 9–11 that he believes the Jewish people are in fact physically descended from Abraham—and that the Jewish people are still Israel. But they are not all, so to speak, the "Israel" that is "descended from Israel" in the sense of *personally* surrendering to and walking in God's full calling on Israel, as Abraham did.

In explaining election, Paul is pointing out that Jewish DNA is not a guarantee of salvation or a place in God's family. Those are matters of mercy and grace, not race. The elect remnant within Israel exists by mercy and grace. Likewise, His covenant election is maintained with the whole nation by mercy and grace (see 2 Chronicles 6:14).

Does election still seem unfair? "Is God unjust? Not at all! For he says . . . 'I will have mercy on whom I have mercy, and I will have compassion on whom I have compassion'" (Romans 9:14–15). The reality of election should bring us all to our knees before God. Election is designed to extravagantly bless the Gentiles just as much as the Jews. Unless we deliberately choose otherwise.

"I Will Bless Those Who Bless You"

The seminal Scripture on election, Genesis 12:2–3, comes with a peculiar blessing—or curse. Speaking to Abraham (then Isaac and Jacob), God states, "I will bless those who bless you, and whoever curses you I will curse." What might this profound promise mean for us today? Probably not what you would think.

The popular 21st-century notion of a blessing differs dramatically from the biblical concept. In Genesis 12:3, the word used for "bless" is *barekh*. Some scholars say that *barekh* stems from a Hebrew root which means "to kneel."[7] The implication is that blessing involves kneeling. To bless another, therefore, suggests one has a humbled posture of heart, if not always in body. *Barekh* itself denotes spiritual and physical enrichment.[8] Putting the two concepts together, we realize that when God blesses, He kneels, so to speak, to enrich us. Quite a mind-numbing and heart-humbling construct!

Indeed, Yeshua empties Himself of glory to dwell among us, embodied in mere dust. At the near pinnacle of His career, He stoops to wash twelve disciples' dirty feet. Then He hangs to death, agonizing and bleeding on a tree. He humbly kneels to eternally enrich you and me, calling us to follow Him and do likewise.

If we desire to follow Messiah, we, too, must humbly kneel to enrich others. But kneeling can offend our pride; we must go low and decrease. Yet as we do, Yeshua in us graciously increases (see John 3:30). We discover that in exchange for the sacrifice of self, He has given us more of *Himself*. A prominent theologian wrote, "The blessing God promises is not, cannot be, any external thing apart from Himself. All that He has to give or can give is only more of Himself."[9]

What does this have to do with Israel? When God makes good on His promise, "I will bless those who bless you," He "kneels to enrich" all those who "kneel to enrich" the Jewish people. Now, metaphorically kneeling before the Jews (or anyone else) does not suggest worshiping them. It merely reflects a heart posture of honor and preference, flowing from Messiah-like humility. This same humility is required of Israel toward "all peoples on earth" (Genesis 12:3). It is this humility, the diminishing of oneself in pure love to enrich another, that moves God to bless back. In its highest expression, those who bless Israel are blessed with more of the Blesser Himself.

"Whoever Curses You I Will Curse"

In contrast to blessing, consider the concept of a curse—and whether one might still pertain to Israel. The Hebrew definition of a curse is threefold: (1) to stop or impose a barrier; (2) to treat lightly, make light of, belittle or make little; or (3) to despise, disdain or regard with contempt.[10] In Genesis 12:3, a particularly strong form of the word is used. Based on the sentence structure, the verse could be accurately phrased, "The one who stops you from fulfilling your calling or belittles you, I must severely curse."[11]

That God *must* severely curse is a sobering, almost chilling thought. If it is true He must curse those cursing Israel—or those stopping her from fulfilling her calling or belittling her—the implications are immense. Is there any evidence to suggest this principle actually plays out?

Soon after God promises blessing or cursing through Abraham, King Abimelech unwittingly mishandles the patriarch's wife. As a result, he turns infertile and almost loses his life (see

Genesis 20:1–18). Years later, Joseph is favored and blessed by an Egyptian pharaoh; consequently, Egypt prospers in difficult times. Another pharaoh enslaves the Hebrews, kills their babies and imprisons them; Egypt is then laid waste. Soon thereafter, the Moabites hire a soothsayer named Balaam to curse the Israelites on their way to Canaan. Instead, God curses the Moabites and Balaam is killed (see Nehemiah 13:1–2; Numbers 31:8). Centuries later, after their exile, Jews in Persia are threatened with annihilation by an evil ruler named Haman. His sinister plan backfires and Haman himself hangs on gallows he had built for a Jewish neck (see Esther 3; 5:14; 7:9–10).

Throughout the Old Covenant, when Israel strays from God, He uses other nations to call her back to Him. But invariably those nations go too far and viciously abuse her. God then turns to judge *those* nations—without the mercy He reextends to the Jews. Those cursing the children of Israel—Amalekites, Amorites, Assyrians, Hittites, Moabites, Perrizites, Gibeonites, Midianites, Edomites, Babylonians, Philistines and others—only force God's hand against themselves.

With its focus shifted to the Gospel of the Kingdom, the New Covenant does not record specific instances of Gentiles cursing Israel. There are indirect references to Roman cruelty—including the crucifixion—and Paul's admonitions not to mistreat the Jews. But post-biblical history shows that the curse pattern of the Old Covenant did not change after the New.

The Pattern Persists

When the New Covenant was written, the Roman Empire loomed over a large portion of the world and continued to flourish for hundreds of years. Then Constantine came to power and made Christianity the official religion of his expansive state. He adopted and enforced virulently anti-Jewish laws, embedding replacement theology in the institutional Church. Very soon thereafter, the great Roman Empire fell. The Church sank into a spiritual abyss known as the Dark Ages, during which time Islam rose to the fore. From its inception, Islam intended to replace the Church in much the same way the Church had tried to replace Israel.

The eleventh and twelfth centuries ushered in the so-called Holy Crusades. Dispatched by popes and kings, Christian soldiers marched from England and France down through the Middle East, seeking to liberate Jerusalem. But liberation meant, in effect, liquidation. Along their way, Crusaders needlessly slaughtered tens of thousands of unarmed Jews (and Muslims) in the name of Jesus Christ. What happened next? The bubonic plague decimated much of Europe; England and France re-aimed their weapons against each other in the Hundred Years' War.

A few centuries later, large numbers of Jews migrated to Spain. There they rose to prominent positions and helped transform the nation into a world power. The Golden Age of Spain ended, however, with its nefarious Inquisitions forcing Jews either to convert to Christianity or to leave the country. After that, the Spanish empire plunged into a period of political, military, economic and social decline, never to reclaim its global position or prestige.[12]

Approximately five hundred years ago, many Jewish people migrated to Great Britain. There they enjoyed favor and eventually support from a small but vocal Christian minority. With revived insight, these early Christian Zionists understood that prophetic promises and covenant blessings to Israel still applied to the literal sons and daughters of Jacob.[13] (Christian Zionism, a faith-based expression of God's love for Israel, is at least four hundred years old.[14]) By the late 1800s, British believers were offering strategic vision and practical help to European Jews in the return and rebuilding of their ancestral home.[15] Indeed, as long as Great Britain treated the Jewish people kindly, things went well for her. Her global empire thrived. But a turning point came in the aftermath of World War I, when the international community delegated to her a sizeable honor and responsibility. She was to supervise the reestablishment of a sovereign Jewish state in the Middle East.

Britain, however, took 78 percent of the land given her to hold in trust for the Jews and handed it to the Arabs instead. Then, during and after the Holocaust, she blockaded the remaining 22 percent to reduce Jewish immigration to a trickle. With vast oil reserves in the Middle East at stake, she felt it best to appease Palestinian Arabs objecting to the Jews' return.[16] As a result, millions of Nazi-hunted Jews found no place of escape. As you know, the once-great British Empire is no more.

World War II, with its Nazi-generated, draconian Jewish genocide, left Germany in shambles, divided and humiliated. But in the years following the Holocaust, at least part of the nation turned; a remnant of Christian believers repented. Germany sincerely blessed Israel with war reparations and strategic aid. In large measure, Germany has been restored.

A grand-scale drama of the late twentieth century played out in the once-formidable Soviet Union. Throughout Soviet history, reports of widespread, murderous anti-Semitism made their way to Jewish communities abroad. Demand was made for decades, inside the Soviet Empire and out: "Let my people go!" But Communists refused—until suddenly and surprisingly the fearsome USSR imploded. An exodus of more than a million Jews followed, most of them immigrating to Israel.

Concerning the United States, sobering parallels seem to exist between America's treatment of Israel and her present-day problems. Now, to a very important degree, she has been Israel's best friend. But a best friend is not always a good or lifelong friend. Recently, some American Christians have recounted widespread devastations, treacherous weather aberrations and economic upheavals in the US—and showed how they do not seem to randomly transpire. The traumatic events have often occurred on the heels of specific actions taken by America to stop or impose a barrier or ban on Israel, treat her lightly or belittle her (as in trying to make her little land even littler).[17] Coincidence—or curse?

Meanwhile, for over a century, every Arab nation in North Africa and the Middle East has opposed the Jewish state. Still cursing the day of Israel's rebirth, they languish in repressive spiritual darkness, poverty and social injustice at the hands of their own leaders.

History presents a recurring pattern. Those who bless Israel get blessed; those who curse her get cursed. As the international community increasingly aligns against the Jewish state, what might that mean for us all?

In the next chapter, we look at an alternative to cursing. We discover the greatest blessing any believer can release over Israel, from any nation.

6

The Salvation of Israel

Brothers and sisters, my heart's desire and prayer to God for the Israelites is that they may be saved.

Romans 10:1

Thirty years ago, I was happily serving the Lord in a fast-growing nondenominational church in California birthed from the Jesus movement. I was not involved in Jewish ministry and had no plans to be. But one day when I was quietly worshiping the Lord at home, He dramatically encountered me. A life-altering experience followed. Suddenly and sovereignly, He opened up to me His heart—His immense love and longing—for Israel. Undone by His undying burden, I have not been able to cease praying and caring for the Jews ever since. Decades later, I remain convinced that He wants our hearts' "desire and prayer to God for Israel [to be] for their salvation" (Romans 10:1 TLV).

Certainly it is important to pray for Israel's peace and protection, security and safety, comfort in her crises, wisdom for her leaders and righteousness in her policies. These are issues for which I encourage you to petition heaven wholeheartedly. But God's priority "for the Israelites is that they may be saved."

At this writing in 2013, as many as 20,000 Israeli Jews believe in Yeshua.[1] Worldwide, it is conservatively estimated that 500,000 Jewish people have given their lives to the Lord.[2] [a] Not since the days of the book of Acts have the sons and daughters of Jacob responded so positively to the Gospel.[b]

How Are Jews Saved?

Sometimes Christians are surprised to learn that Jews are saved the same as everyone else—by grace through faith in God's Son. The day before His crucifixion, Yeshua said to a roomful of Jews, "I am the way and the truth and the life. No one comes to the Father except through me" (John 14:6). Peter declared to a gathering of Jewish leaders, "Salvation is found in no one else, for there is no other name under heaven given to mankind by which we must be saved" (Acts 4:12). Only the Jewish Messiah fulfills the Jewish hope for Jewish redemption. All of Romans 10 is dedicated to making the point. In it Paul writes there is no distinction in the way Jews and Gentiles are saved:

> There is no difference between Jew and Gentile—the same Lord is Lord of all and richly blesses all who call on him, for, "Everyone who calls on the name of the Lord will be saved."
>
> Romans 10:12–13

Please do not misunderstand. The apostle is not teaching here that there is no distinction at all between Jews and Gentiles. If that were his intent, he would not distinguish over and again between Jews and Gentiles throughout the same chapter and entire letter to the Romans. In context, what he is saying is that there is no difference between Jew and Gentile *concerning the manner of salvation.*[3]

Whether you are Jewish or Gentile, God loves you so much that He gave His Son, so that *whoever* you are, if you believe in Him, you may receive eternal life. Yeshua is the only One through whom your sins are forgiven and your relationship with the Creator made right (see John 3:16).

To many of you I am stating the obvious. But some Christians take exception with me on this point. They say something like this: "The Jews are God's chosen people. They have a special covenant with Him and do not need Jesus." To this, and other common hindrances to sharing the Gospel with the Jewish people, we now turn.

Dual Covenants

A doctrine known as dual covenant teaches there are two ways to get saved: one for the Jews, and another for everybody else. To simplify, the Jews get saved via the Old Covenant, while the Gentiles get saved through the New. Dual covenant teaching grew in popularity over the twentieth century partly to compensate for past theological error. For nearly two thousand years, much of the institutional Church had taught that God's heart toward Israel was one of so-called divine contempt or disdain. Christians were convinced the Father now scorned the "despicable" Jewish nation guilty of killing His Son. Believers were encouraged to relate to Jews with the same allegedly deserving disdain. Not surprisingly, centuries of institutionalized contempt gave way to outright hate, crusades, inquisitions, murderous pogroms and, eventually, a theological grid to justify the Holocaust. Such treatment by Christians embedded into the collective Jewish mind-set that Jews absolutely cannot—or at least must not—believe in Jesus.

In search of a more sensitive and compassionate way to relate to the Jews, some believers traded divine contempt for dual covenant. As a result, many mainline churches issued formal manifestos, still in effect, exempting the Jews from evangelism. One such statement was signed not long ago by representatives of over twenty different Christian—including evangelical—denominations. It concludes, "In view of our conviction that Jews are in an eternal covenant with God, we renounce missionary efforts directed at [them]. . . . Christians need new ways of understanding the universal significance of Christ."[4]

Now, I am very grateful for Christian sensitivity and compassion toward the Jews. I sincerely appreciate the acceptance and respect, affection and friendship that many believers demonstrate toward my people who do not—and may never—believe in Yeshua. But in the process of trying to rectify the past, is it possible we have moved from one extreme to the other? Has the Church gone from condemning Israel for her rejection of Messiah to condoning it?

Certainly, respect and friendship are essential components of the Great Commission—but they do not substitute for it. Far better to share the truth in love and humility with Jewish people, if we are sincerely their friends, than to deliberately withhold it from them. Would a real friend do anything less?

Related to the idea of dual covenant is the misconception that all Jews who ever lived will get saved, whether or not they hear the Gospel. Usually this belief comes from a well-intended but mistaken interpretation of Romans 11:26: "In this way all Israel will be saved. As it is written: 'The deliverer will come from

Zion; he will turn godlessness away from Jacob.'" A promising phrase indeed! But it cannot be given a meaning that is inconsistent with the overall teaching of the Scriptures. As we saw in chapter 5, Paul, Yeshua and other New Covenant authors teach that Jewish DNA does *not* guarantee salvation. In view of the apparent contradiction in Romans 11:26, recall that context is critical. When we read *all* of verse 26, and not just part of it, we discover it relates specifically to the Second Coming. So the "all Israel" that gets saved refers, in context, specifically to the people of Israel who are living when Yeshua returns.ᶜ Meanwhile, those Jewish people alive today need to hear the Gospel from believers like you and me.

Times of the Gentiles

Some Christians say they have another reason for not sharing Yeshua with the Jews: It's not time.

According to 2 Corinthians 6:2, "now is the day of salvation." But Yeshua uses a phrase, "times of the Gentiles" (Luke 21:24), that, taken out of context and read alongside Romans 11:25, has sometimes led to confusion. This is because most modern Bibles translate Romans 11:25 similar to the NIV: "I do not want you to be ignorant of this mystery, brothers and sisters, so that you may not be conceited: Israel has experienced a hardening in part until the *full number* of the Gentiles has come in" (emphasis mine). Reading Luke 21:24 with this translation of Romans 11:25, some have assumed that not until the full number of Gentiles comes into the Kingdom will the "times of the Gentiles" come to an end. Then—and only then—will Israel stop being spiritually hardened to the Gospel.

Older Bible versions, however, offer a different view: "Blindness in part has happened to Israel, until the *fullness* of the

Gentiles has come in" (NKJV, emphasis mine; see also KJV, NASB). The *Complete Jewish Bible* puts it like this: "Stoniness, to a degree, has come upon Israel, until the Gentile world enters its *fullness*" (emphasis mine). According to a recent translation by a team of Messianic scholars, "A partial hardening has come upon Israel until the *fullness* of the Gentiles has come in" (TLV, emphasis mine). The difference between "full number" and "fullness," as we will momentarily see, can be monumental.

"Fullness" or "full number" is translated from the Greek word *pleroma*.[5] *Pleroma* appears seventeen times in the New Covenant, and most contemporary Bibles translate it "fullness" all seventeen times—except in Romans 11:25. There alone does *pleroma* become "full number." Especially odd about this sole exception is that just a few verses earlier, in the same letter on the same topic, *pleroma* is translated "fullness" or a close variant thereof. With all due respect to the "full number" of Bible translators, I join the ranks of those who suspect this singular interpretation of *pleroma* reflects an unfounded theological bias. As one scholar comments, "There is certainly no linguistic reason why 'fullness' [*pleroma*] should take on a numeric quality, as it has to do with 'that which is brought to fullness or completion.'"[6]

The practical distinction between "full number" and "fullness" of the Gentiles is critical. For some, it may mean the difference between eternal life and death. Here is why: If Israel is Gospel resistant until the *full number* of Gentiles comes to faith, there is little point sharing the Lord with her today, or tomorrow, or probably the day after that. Not until the last Gentile numbered for the Kingdom, in the remotest region on earth, finally gets saved will it be time to turn to the Jews. But if Israel's hardness is removed when the *fullness* of the Gentiles comes in, then our approach to Jewish evangelism should be quite different.

Fullness of the Gentiles

To what does "fullness" of the Gentiles refer? Romans 11:11 reveals that "salvation has come to the Gentiles to make Israel envious." We can think of fullness, quite simply, as Spirit-fullness. From a practical perspective, fullness is that quality of mature Christlikeness that provokes Jewish people to godly envy for their Messiah. It is another way to describe the regenerate and Spirit-filled life to which you and I are called as His followers. God's will for every believer has always been the attaining of this fullness. Indeed, right after Romans 11:25 tells us the Jewish people will be hardened "until the fullness of the Gentiles," verse 26 states, "and in this way all Israel will be saved." The way Israel turns to Yeshua, between now and the Second Coming, is by the fullness or spiritual maturity of the Gentiles reaching out to them. The implication is that "in this way" the fullness of the Gentiles also impacts the timing of the Second Coming.[d]

Meanwhile, it is the *quality* of Gentile Christianity encountered by Jewish people that leads to their salvation, not the *quantity* of Gentile Christians they encounter. I myself came to the Lord partly out of envy for the relationship a Gentile Christian friend had with Yeshua. She was obviously full of God's Spirit, bubbling with joy and exuding peace and righteousness. I puzzled, *What is* she *doing with* my *God—and having such a good time with Him?* I was not only envious, I was outright indignant. I absolutely had to have a relationship with Him like that, too!

Sharing the Gospel with Jewish people should not be intimidating. Most are not highly religious and have less familiarity with the Scriptures than you do. Many harbor an interest in spiritual matters and unresolved questions about Yeshua. If you know and love the Lord, you have no reason not to prayerfully follow His leading in forthrightly but respectfully telling others, including Jews, the truth about Him. If you feel you need guidance with Jewish sensitivities, most Messianic ministries are glad to help.[e]

Jewish "Hardness" or "Blindness"

Maybe you want to see Jewish people come to Yeshua but feel they are too spiritually hardened or blind to believe. At times I was tempted to think that way about my own father. Dad was raised Orthodox, and when he learned that I proclaimed faith in Messiah, he hung his head low, went to his father's grave and apologized. For sixteen years I prayed for Dad, during which time he would not even speak the name *Yeshua* or *Jesus*. But then my father got sick. As he lay on his deathbed, he remembered the conversations we had had over the years. Weeks went by, until one day he told me good news: Dad had given himself to Yeshua. The next day he lost consciousness, and the day after that he awoke in heaven. From then on, I purposed never to resign anyone as too hard or blind to surrender to God in response to persevering prayer.

Bear in mind that nowhere does the New Covenant attribute Gospel resistance to all of Israel. A degree of spiritual hardening—or according to some translations, blindness—is on part, but not all, of the Jewish nation. Romans 11:7 says that while Israel's elect sought salvation by grace through faith, "the others were hardened." Part of Israel responds to the Gospel, while part of Israel does not. The reality is similar to how some Gentiles respond to the Gospel while others do not. If we forget this and assume that all Israel—or all but a miniscule fraction—is hopelessly hardened to Yeshua, will we make any effort at all to reach them with the Gospel?

Even those Jews who are hardened usually are not *totally* hardened: "A *partial* hardening has come upon Israel until the fullness of the Gentiles has come in" (Romans 11:25 TLV, emphasis mine). There are varying degrees of openness and resistance, not unlike the varying degrees of openness and resistance among Gentiles.

Place Is Not a Problem

The Bible promises that in the last days, the Jewish people will be restored physically to their land and then spiritually to their Lord (see Romans 11:25–27; Matthew 23:39; Ezekiel 36:24–37:14; Zechariah 12:2–12). Does this mean, therefore, that Jews must first immigrate to Israel before they can come to Yeshua? The answer is yes—and no. Consider the facts: Thousands of Israeli Jews pass into eternity each year without knowing Messiah. Meanwhile, significant numbers of Jewish people living outside their ancestral home are turning to Him.

The Scriptures indicate that Jews can and will be saved in more than one place at a time. In this transitional season, some will turn to the Lord outside of Israel, and then return to the land (see Deuteronomy 30:1–5; Nehemiah 1:8–9; Jeremiah 29:13–14). But many others will come to the land first, and only then to the Lord. Steadily growing numbers of Israelis are coming to faith, and the Scriptures indicate those numbers will increase as we move toward the end of the age. *Aliyah* (immigration) to Israel is most certainly to be encouraged. But regardless of time or place or anything else, God's mercy and grace are unlimited; the Gospel can be shared with the Jews wherever they happen to be.

Opposing the Salvation of the Jewish People

The devil fights hard against Jewish people coming to faith. When a Jew turns to Yeshua, it can seem that spiritual havoc is wreaked all around him or her. Family, friends and colleagues may feel betrayed, even outraged. But our enemy is *the* enemy, not our loved ones or religious community.

We have seen that Satan is uniquely threatened by Israel's restoration because it precipitates his personal ruin. Yeshua explicitly connects His return—and earthly removal of the devil—to the time when Jewish Jerusalem welcomes Him back:

> "Jerusalem, Jerusalem, you who kill the prophets and stone those sent to you, how often I have longed to gather your children together, as a hen gathers her chicks under her wings, and you were not willing. Look, your house is left to you desolate. For I tell you, you will not see me again until you say, 'Blessed is he who comes in the name of the Lord.'"
>
> Matthew 23:37–39

Over two thousand years ago, religious leaders in Jerusalem rejected Jesus as Israel's Messiah. But someday in the future they will wholeheartedly bless His return. This pinnacle event will inaugurate the Second Coming—and the devil's eviction from earth (see Acts 3:17–21; Revelation 20:2). Meanwhile, like a trapped and frenzied beast, Satan is scrambling to prevent the scenario from materializing (see Revelation 12:13, 17). I imagine him terror-stricken at the growing remnant of Jewish believers in Yeshua—especially Israelis—prophetically crying, *"Barukh haba b'shem Adonai!"* ("Blessed is He who comes in the name of the Lord!") Therefore, when Messianic believers face opposition from other Jews, we pray in love for those who persecute us. We know our battle is not against flesh and blood; our enemy is *the* enemy.

Organized opposition against sharing the Gospel with Jews comes mainly through the Jewish counter-missionary (or anti-missionary) movement. Counter-missionaries are usually religious or ultra-Orthodox Jews whose *raison d'être* is to prevent other Jews from believing in Yeshua. In their opinion, faith in Messiah is tantamount to excommunication from biblical Judaism. Very much "anti" missions, they resemble the Pharisees who opposed Yeshua and His followers.[f] They tail Jewish evangelists around the globe, steadfastly working to undermine their efforts and invoking ritual curses against them. Paul describes the anti-missionaries of his day as "loved enemies":

> They are zealous for God, but their zeal is not based on knowledge. . . . As far as the gospel is concerned, they are enemies for your sake; but as far as election is concerned, they are loved on account of the patriarchs.
>
> Romans 10:2; 11:28

Discrimination against Israeli Messianic Jews

Israel is presently the only country in the Middle East where Christianity is freely and openly growing, not diminishing. Nowhere else in the region may Christians worship as they do in the Jewish state. Israel tries very hard to protect the personal and religious rights of believers in Jesus—so long as those believers are Arabs or other Gentiles. For Messianic Jews, however, the situation is different.[g] Counter-missionaries have for decades firebombed Messianic congregations and homes, assaulted or beat up believers, vandalized their personal property, shut down their businesses, hurled death threats—and attempts—at them and more. Israeli police are notoriously slow to respond to counter-missionary crime. If there is an arrest, a judicial prosecution rarely follows.[7] If it does, a verdict rarely brings justice.[h]

In spite of anti-missionary harassment, Israel is a freedom-loving and robustly democratic society, not a repressive regime. Israeli believers do not suffer systematic, violent persecution, but we do endure governmental discrimination at various levels.[i] This is because ultra-Orthodox Jews have historically held disproportionately great political power in the country,[j] and are easily influenced by counter-missionaries. The effect trickles down into much of Israeli society.

Friend, please do not begrudge Israel for her treatment of Messianic Jews. God's heart is big enough to love her unconditionally despite her flaws, and ours must be, too. I make you aware of the matter so you can seek strategies from heaven to stand with your brothers and sisters in Christ. Already, signs of positive change are on the horizon. Pray for anti-missionaries who are "enemies for [our] sake, but . . . loved on account of the patriarchs" (Romans 11:28). At the same time, please pray for God's beloved friends, Israel's remnant.

Blessing Israel's Remnant

Speaking as one member of the Israeli body of believers, I would like to be blunt: We are more needy than you may think! Mostly, like believers everywhere, we need more of Yeshua. We need to be conformed more and more to His likeness. We need more of His Kingdom reality manifest in our lives. We need Holy Spirit empowering to be and to share the Good News, embracing our full biblical destiny. For all these things, we need your friendship and ongoing prayer.

But there is more I must share. Due to counter-missionary pressure, Israeli believers sometimes lose their jobs—or find it difficult to obtain one—if their faith is made known. Consequently, some live in chronic financial distress. Those who have emigrated from other countries are typically hardest hit. The situation is made worse by the fact that Christian and Jewish relief funds rarely get into Messianic hands. The government, which regulates and disperses most charitable aid from abroad, precludes Messianic organizations or individuals from receiving monies they themselves have not raised.[k] These huge sums often end up in the hands of groups that actively support counter-missionaries, who in turn intentionally and seriously harm Israeli believers in Yeshua.[l]

One renowned, international philanthropic organization says it has raised 100 million US dollars for Israel, for each of the past several years. Many Christians have generously given to this organization on the basis of Romans 15:27: "For if the Gentiles have shared in the Jews' spiritual blessings, they owe it to the Jews to share with them their material blessings" (see also Galatians 2:10). But the founder-director of the group has steadfastly refused to aid or deal with Messianic Jews:

> I have always had one red line: that I would never work with any group involved in missionary activity targeting the Jewish community. [Practically speaking, this means any group that does not *exclude* Jews from Gospel outreach.] . . . I will never work with groups like Jews for Jesus or the Messianic community.[8]

To "never work with" Messianic groups is a politically correct way to say he never agrees to dispense funds to us, either.

Despite the obstacles, the Body of Messiah thrives. No Israeli city is without at least one Messianic congregation in which Yeshua is exalted. More and more, indigenous believers are penetrating society around them. Some are quite financially blessed, and certainly, the majority is not poor. God provides for His people. (Several Messianic ministries, including ours, collect and distribute funds to needy believers.)

One New Humanity

The Messianic Jewish remnant of Israel is an integral part of the universal Body of Christ. We are your brothers and sisters in the "household of faith" (Galatians 6:10 NKJV). Ephesians 2 describes us as "one new humanity":

> You who are Gentiles by birth . . . now in Christ Jesus . . . have been brought near. . . . His purpose was to create in himself one new humanity out of the two. . . . Consequently, you are no longer foreigners and strangers, but fellow citizens with God's people and also members of his household. . . . This mystery is that through the gospel the Gentiles are heirs together with Israel, members together of one body.
>
> Ephesians 2:11, 13, 15, 19; 3:6

Christian friend, you and I need each other. The Body of Christ is incomplete without Jews and Gentiles reciprocally loving and blessing the other. The story of Ruth vividly illustrates how, together as one in Yeshua, we are destined to change history.

"Your People Will Be My People"

The book of Ruth is fundamentally a Spirit-breathed account of literal, historical events. But it can also be seen as a prophetic allegory applicable to Israel and the Church, each humbly blessing the other. (Recall the *p'shat* and *remez* levels of Scripture interpretation.) Allegorically, Naomi (meaning in Hebrew "Pleasant"), represents Israel, and Ruth ("Friend" or "Clinging One") represents faithful Gentile followers of Jesus.

When the story begins, Naomi is married with two sons. Due to a severe famine, she and her family leave Israel, seeking refuge and sustenance in neighboring Moab. There both young men marry, but not for long; they die within a few years. Sadly, Naomi's husband dies, too. She is left penniless and alone, except for her Gentile daughters-in-law, Orpah and Ruth.

Eventually the famine in Israel ends and Naomi decides to go home. She urges Orpah and Ruth to stay behind, find new husbands and start new lives. Though at first reluctant, Orpah departs, "going back to her people and her gods" (Ruth 1:15). But Ruth refuses. Instead she vows:

> Where you go I will go, and wherever you stay I will stay. Your people will be my people and your God my God. Where you die I will die, and there I will be buried. May the LORD deal with me, be it ever so severely, if even death separates you and me.

> Ruth 1:16–17

Now, life has been so hard for Naomi that she is about to change her name from "Pleasant" to Mara ("Bitter"). Nonetheless—and this is where the story carries unction for today—Ruth continues clinging to her. This Gentile believer in the God of Israel will not let go of her mother-in-law, no matter how embittered she seems. She knows that she can go forward in God only by going forward with Naomi.

Arm in arm, the two impoverished women return to the place of God's promise. When they arrive it is harvest time, so they are able to eat by gleaning leftover grain from some of the local crops. Ruth dutifully goes out to the fields, literally kneeling to enrich Naomi as she gleans. This sacrificial act blesses Naomi deeply. From then on, Ruth is no longer a daughter-in-law; Naomi calls her "my daughter."

While she is gleaning, Ruth catches the admiring eye of a gentleman named Boaz. He has heard of her love and commitment to Naomi, and his heart is smitten when he meets her. Unbeknown to Ruth, Boaz (a prophetic depiction of Messiah) is Naomi's near kinsman and potential redeemer. With Boaz on the scene, the hope of redemption comes into view.

Up until now in the story, Ruth has been the one kneeling to enrich, and thereby blessing, Naomi. But at this juncture matters dramatically turn. For the right of redemption through Boaz legally belongs to Naomi alone (see Deuteronomy 25:5). Accordingly, Naomi has every reason to regard this upstanding, wealthy man—closer to her age than Ruth's—as quite a good catch for *herself*. But she has been profoundly blessed by Ruth; now it is her turn to humbly kneel to enrich her daughter. Stunningly and selflessly, Naomi gives up her right of redemption to Ruth and, with it, any real hope of gaining a better life. She is willing to sacrifice all.

Naomi details step-by-step the protocol of redemption required of Ruth. Glamoured and perfumed, she must go in the night to Boaz, then lie down at his feet while he sleeps (see Ruth 3:4). Now, I suspect a virtuous young woman like Ruth could have naturally thought, *Hey, I've gone along far enough with the whole "Israel thing," but this is just too much! I'm an Arab—and this isn't how we do things!* But no; instead, she forthrightly complies.

Boaz responds to Ruth's humble gesture, eagerly claiming her as his bride. The Jews joyfully bless their marriage: "May the LORD make the woman who is coming into your home like Rachel and Leah, who together built up the family of Israel" (Ruth 4:11). Their blessing comes to pass; before long Boaz and Ruth have a baby named Obed. Meanwhile, Ruth remains true to her vow to Naomi, clinging to her as mother. As a result, little Obed so thrills Naomi's heart that she sheds her bitterness, together with the name "Mara." Through Ruth (representing the Gentile Bride of Messiah) and the fruit of Ruth's relationship with her redeemer, Naomi (representing Israel) is revived.

Over time, Obed fathers Jesse, who fathers David, the progenitor of Jesus. Ruth is astoundingly blessed for her blessing of Naomi; she gains standing forever as a mother in Israel, in the direct lineage of Messiah.

Together Ruth and Naomi—Gentile and Jew blessing the other—helped prepare the way of the Lord's first coming. So it will be, I am convinced, with His Second Coming. Yeshua's return will be preceded by a remnant of Gentile believers who, in the spirit of Ruth, cling to the Jews to the very end. They will so captivate the Lord's heart that, like Boaz, He will joyfully come to claim His Bride (see Revelation 22:17), fully redeeming Israel as well.

In the next chapter, we see how and why nothing so magnificent has yet to take place.

Rejected Roots
and Broken Branches

Do not be arrogant, but tremble. For if God did not spare the
natural [Jewish] branches, he will not spare you either. . . . I do
not want you to be ignorant of this mystery, brothers and sisters,
so that you may not be conceited [about] Israel.

Romans 11:20, 25

Flash back with me, if you would, to an early childhood experience that seared my soul about "Christianity": I stare in puzzled
horror at a parade of living skeletons, sunken cheeks and bulging
eyes, the victims of macabre Nazi "medical" experiments. Seconds later, corpses—countless piles of them—are bulldozed and
dumped into a gargantuan pit, like refuse heaped in a junkyard.

Then the film stops. The rabbi fumbles with the movie projec-
tor, an old reel-to-reel, and switches on the lights. He shuffles

slowly to the front of the room. Everyone is very quiet, and I can tell he has something important to say. "This is what Christians will do to you, if you let them," he warns. "You must never let them; no, never again!"

No . . . never again! I vow silently. I am five.

From then on, I land in more than a few schoolyard scruffs after being jeered a Christ-killer. I must fight back to survive; for whoever this Christ is, I am certain He wants me dead. His people keep telling me so.

I am ignorant, and so are they.

Ignorance of the Word Is No Excuse

At certain times the Word of God explicitly cautions us not to be "ignorant" or "arrogant." These warnings flash and bleep like red alerts—meant to be read, alert. When I come to these passages, I hear the Lord saying, in that tender but firm voice of His, *This is really important, Sandy. You need to hear what follows—and for your own good, remember.*

In Romans 9–11, we have been told about God's love for Israel, her election and prophetic destiny, and her need for salvation. Now the Spirit through Paul turns to the linchpin issue of the Church's heart toward the Jews. The apostle reminds us (once again) that God has not rejected them, replaced them or rescinded His gifts from them. Instead He is using their national spurning of Messiah to release blessing to the Gentiles. Then he instructs, cautions and pleads, "Do not be arrogant [toward Israel], but tremble"—or God "will not spare *you*" (11:20–21, emphasis mine).

Paul continues, "I do not want you to be ignorant of this mystery [about Israel], brothers and sisters, so that you may not be conceited" (verse 25). Here's how serious the stakes are: Consider His kindness toward the Jews, even if some were cut off from faith. "Continue in his kindness" toward them; "*otherwise, you will also be cut off*" (verse 22, emphasis mine). Paul teaches that our rightstanding with God, maybe even our salvation, is linked to our treatment of Israel.

Sadly, much of the Church has remained "ignorant," "arrogant" or "conceited" of exactly that which we are enjoined against. Now, ignorance in itself is not sin. But concerning Israel, history demonstrates that ignorance easily breeds arrogance, and arrogance of heart feeds further ignorance of mind. In other words, if I know nothing about Jewish people, I am simply ignorant about them. But if I am reading the Bible with a humble spirit, or am even vaguely aware of current international events, I must know *something* about them. If not, I dare say I am arrogant. And if I am arrogant, I will likely stay ignorant. ("Why bother? I know everything about 'troublesome' Israel that I need to know.") If I love the Lord and His Word, however, that is not the attitude I want.

Severing Jewish Roots

As we saw earlier, much ignorance and arrogance about Israel stem from Christianity's historical severance of its Old Covenant Jewish roots. God intended for the Church to "share in the nourishing sap from the . . . root" (Romans 11:17). Instead, it turned away, tapping headlong into the pernicious poison of anti-Semitism. Soon a false notion of "spiritual Israel" evolved,[1] along with supersessionist theology. The result is Christian anti-Semitism—something that should be an oxymoron, but sadly is not.

One Gentile Christian scholar summarizes what went awry:

Paul's warning to Gentile believers about pride went unheeded. The Church had become overwhelmingly Gentile, so it reasoned that there was no more need for the support of the root (Israel). What presumption! . . . Gentiles claimed to have replaced Israel. . . . Church fathers taught that the unfaithfulness of the Jewish people resulted in a collective guilt which made them subject to the permanent curse of God [divine contempt].[2]

A respected Church historian describes what happened next:

The so-called "parting of the ways" between Christians and Jews would take place gradually over two or three centuries. . . . Church fathers, well into the fourth century, warn against Christian participation in Jewish observances . . . [and] carried the idea of supersessionist "fulfillment" to its logical conclusion, arguing that the Jewish Scriptures no longer had validity as the revealed Word of God. . . . It would be impossible for a believing Jew to accept a Jesus whose meaning, by definition, involved a *de*meaning of the Jewish Scriptures. . . . A Jew could accept Jesus only by rejecting—betraying—everything Jesus himself believed.[3]

Shortly after the Messianic Jewish apostles, Gentile Church fathers formulated their theology of divine contempt for the Jews. Sermons inciting murderous cruelty toward them were routinely preached. The venerated John Chrysostom left no margin for misinterpretation: "The synagogue is . . . the cavern of devils. . . . As for me, I hate the synagogue. . . . I hate the Jews."[4] Before long, Christians began stripping Jews of their civil and religious rights. Paul's admonition to the Church against ignorance and arrogance was upended in less than four hundred years. Over time, matters grew even worse.

In 1543 the beloved herald of the Protestant Reformation, Martin Luther, instructed his followers with these words:

> Wherever they [Jews] have their synagogues, nothing is found but a den of devils. . . . What shall we Christians do with this rejected and condemned people, the Jews? . . . First set fire to their synagogues or schools. . . . I advise that their houses also be razed and destroyed. . . . I advise that their rabbis be forbidden to teach henceforth on pain of loss of life. . . . I advise that safe conduct on the highways be abolished completely for the Jews. If this does not help we must drive them out like mad dogs.[5]

Tragically, Luther's words were proudly cited by Adolf Hitler four hundred years later.[a] That such a man of faith as the Great Reformer could be seduced by Satan to write such monstrous fodder for the Nazi Holocaust should cause us all to "tremble" in the spirit of Romans 11:20. Like Luther and some of his predecessors, we, too, can be ignorant of his schemes. For as we see later in this chapter, the devil has not abated his insidious campaign—in the Church—against Israel.

Outlawing Messianic Judaism

In rejecting its Old Covenant roots, Christianity took aim at one small sector in particular—Messiah-following Jews. The following is an abbreviated sample of official Church canon and decrees that renounced Messianic Jewish faith or any Christian expression of Jewishness.[6] Because they have not been revoked, these directives still carry varying degrees of spiritual weight. I do not include this list to instill resentment but to inspire restoration. God wants the Body revived with "nourishing sap" and lovingly reconciled as one new humanity in Messiah.

- First- and second-century Church fathers issue various anti-Jewish statements that are binding in regions where they hold authority.

- Pope Victor condemns use of the Bible's Jewish calendar for dating Christian holy days; AD 175.

- Council of Elvira, Spain, forbids Christians to marry Jews on threat of excommunication (Canon 16), forbids Christians from receiving Jewish prayers or blessing (Canon 49) and prohibits Christians from eating with Jews (Canon 50); AD 306.

- Council of Nicea I rejects the biblical date for celebrating Resurrection Day, for the specified purpose of severing Jewish connections to Passover; AD 325.

- Council of Antioch excommunicates any Christian celebrating Passover with a Jew and defrocks any cleric who communicates with such a Christian (Canon 1); AD 345.

- Council of Laodicia forbids Christians from attending Jewish festivals (Canon 37) or receiving unleavened bread from them (Canon 38); AD 360.

- Council of Agde, France, prescribes strict rules for the baptism of Messianic Jews, "as it is well known that they return easily to their vomit" (Canon 34), and again prohibits clerics from taking part in Jewish festivals (Canon 40); AD 506.

- Council of Toledo IV prevents Jews, and specifically Messianic Jews, from holding public office, and authorizes excommunication of noncomplying Gentile officials, an edict that is reissued over the centuries; AD 633.

- Council of Nicea II requires Jews who fellowship with or join the Church first to reveal names of other Jews who openly or secretly follow the Old Covenant, observe the Sabbath or honor other biblical festivals. Baptized Messianic Jews must formally renounce and condemn all their traditional expressions of worship, and then be watched to ensure "that they depart from Hebrew practices" (Canon 8); AD 787. (From this point on, Jesus and the apostles would have been banned from the Church.)

- Pope Gregory IX authorizes investigations against Messianic Jews allegedly embracing their Jewish roots; AD 1231.

- Spain expels all Jews, including Messianic Jews, who do not renounce Judaism and all Old Covenant practices. Those who do not comply, including many Messianic Jews, are burned at the stake. Jewish believers are forced to sign pledges that state curses against unbelieving Jews and vow not to interact with them; AD 1492.

- Congregation of the Holy Office tortures and burns at the stake Messianic Jews who follow Old Covenant practices; AD 1542.

- Germany's National Reich Church requires pastors to take oaths of allegiance to Hitler and expel from churches all Messianic Jews or Christians of Jewish descent; AD 1935.[7]

A historical review of the tender mercies and affections of Jesus Christ? No Messiah-loving Jew of integrity could have identified with this fellowship of scorn. Indeed, most Jews who joined the Church were in reality choosing forced conversion over death. Nevertheless, God miraculously reserved for Himself among them a true remnant, saved and sustained by grace.

In an act of historic and laudable reform, in 1965 the Roman Catholic Church officially repudiated its ancient accusation against the Jews of "deicide" (killing God), the teaching of divine contempt and all forms of supersessionism. Catholics reaffirmed Israel's election, based specifically on Romans 9:1–4.[8] [b] Shortly thereafter, and in connection with the Jesus movement, Jews started coming to faith in Yeshua in remarkable waves. Evangelicals took note, and some began supporting the

Messianic Jewish movement a decade later. As one prophetic leader writes, the days ahead can be different from the past:

> We can learn from the mistakes of the past and prevent history from repeating itself. . . . Our faithful prayers and righteous deeds must provide proof that we have recovered from our spiritual bankruptcy and now have more than enough of God's love to extend . . . to the Jews. . . . We can no longer afford to look the other way. Our Master just will not have it.[9]

Grafted into the Olive Tree

In recent years, more and more Christians around the world have begun embracing the Jewish roots of their faith. Many feel they are recouping lost spiritual treasure. Admittedly, sometimes there are imbalances or mistakes made in the process. These growing pains, however, do not diminish the underlying reality the Spirit seeks to restore.

The phrase *Jewish roots* derives from a vivid metaphor in Romans 11:17–21:

> If some of the branches have been broken off, and you, though a wild olive shoot, have been grafted in among the others and now share in the nourishing sap from the olive root, do not consider yourself to be superior to those other branches. If you do, consider this: You do not support the root, but the root supports you. You will say then, "Branches were broken off so that I could be grafted in." Granted. But they were broken off because of unbelief, and you stand by faith. Do not be arrogant, but tremble. For if God did not spare the natural branches, he will not spare you either.

When Paul penned his letter to the Romans, a horticultural practice in the ancient Middle East was to reinvigorate a cultivated olive tree that had stopped bearing fruit by grafting wild olive branches into it.[10] The fresh sap, or lifeblood, of the wild olive branches would revive the cultivated tree. The original branches could then begin to bear fruit again. The wild branches, formerly untended and unwieldy, would beautifully flourish because of the nourishing sap received from the roots. What's more, with both wild and cultivated branches intermingled, the whole tree yielded prized and plentiful fruit that was impossible to grow any other way. When Gentile branches grafted into a Jewish-rooted tree function as God intends, the fruit is spectacular.

I have seen some gargantuan olive trees in Israel, hundreds or perhaps thousands of years old. Their gnarly roots span maybe half a city block, sturdily protruding above ground and firmly entrenched (so it seems) until Messiah comes again. Breathtaking in appearance, they grow knotty, wild and alone, bearing poor fruit compared with the carefully planted and tended olive groves that dot the land.

I can imagine the Divine Husbandman gently lopping off a few branches from one of these untamed specimens and hand carrying them to a failing tree. Next He cuts off some of the natural, cultivated branches, protectively setting them aside for future use. I picture Him lovingly linking the foreign branches to the host, oozing a good dab of humility—His grafting agent— between them. Then He blesses the tree and waits. Will this transplant "take"?

Jewish roots support new Gentile branches—but the engrafted branches are needed with their fresh vigor and vitality to save the whole tree. If it is ever to bear fruit again, the original tree must accommodate the transplant, freely sharing all the life it has left. *The two must become one for their mutual survival.* God's grafting agent, humility, makes the miracle possible.

What if, however, things go wrong and grafted (Gentile) branches poison rather than preserve the life of the tree? I suppose the Master could stand idly by, watching wistfully as the branches perish along with the tree they have choked. But that is not His nature. Rather than let the whole tree die, I imagine He will slice off and discard the foreign branches. Then He will try again—using others.

Theologians have different interpretations as to the "root" of the olive tree. Some say it refers to God Himself, some say the patriarchs and some say the Jewish remnant of the Jewish nation. Still others say the root of the tree is God's Word. I say, why not receive it all? If you are grafted into the olive tree, God Himself is your portion. He wants the words of the Jewish Scriptures spoken by the Jewish Messiah, patriarchs, prophets and apostles to flow in you like nourishing sap. If you can, why not enjoy Jewish fellowship along the way?

The New Christian Anti-Semitism

For multitudes of believers bereft of their Jewish roots, the story is different. Smoldering embers of hate for the Jews have assumed a new form of acceptable expression in the 21st century. "The new anti-Semitism," as it is called, is directly tied to anti-Zionism, hate for Israel or both. Accordingly, by 2013, violent anti-Semitic acts committed around the world were increasing by an alarming 30 percent per year[11]—with perpetrators typically faulting Israel.

Israel is being blamed in our day for everything from airliners crashing into skyscrapers and nose dives on stock exchanges to global wars and global warming. Some point fingers at Israel for being the villain, rather than victim, in the spread of Islamist terror. Relentless world castigation is reserved for Israel alone, daily distorting facts beyond any fair sense of reasonableness.

Just who is this "Israel"? We might ask the hundreds of European and South American Jews who, in recent years, have been brutally beaten (some, to death); the North American college students subject to raging, anti-Israel harassment on campus; or the thousands of Jews across the earth whose synagogues, shops and loved ones' graves have been vandalized. Perhaps the bereaved families of those murdered in Jew-targeting bombings in New Delhi, Bangkok, Bulgaria and the Republic of Georgia[c]— all of which took place during the writing of this book—could help answer the question. I suspect they would agree the people of Israel are the sons and daughters of Jacob—the Jews—wherever they happen to be.

How has mainstream, institutionalized Christianity responded to re-stoked flames of anti-Semitism? The World Council of Churches (WCC) is the world's largest operating interchurch organization, consisting in 2013 of 345 denominations. Included are Baptist, Catholic, Lutheran, Orthodox, Pentecostal, Reformed, evangelical and other churches, representing 560 million Christians in over 110 nations.[12] Stating that Israel is "a sin," it declares that resistance against her is a Christian right and duty.[13] Sadly, the WCC has repeatedly distorted facts to denounce and demonize the Jewish state.[14] It has established two bodies, the Ecumenical Accompaniment Programme in Palestine and Israel, and the Palestine Israel Ecumenical Forum, for the singular purpose of ending Israeli "occupation and injustice" in Palestine.[15] It has nothing similar, however, for ending the cold-blooded terror by Palestinians against Israeli civilians or the well-documented persecution and slaughter of Christians by Islamist nations in the Middle East—including putative Palestine.[16]

In the US, the National Council of Churches (NCC) is composed of over 45 million believers in more than 100,000 Protestant, Anglican, African American, Orthodox, evangelical and other denominational congregations. It calls itself the "leading ecumenical force for cooperation among Christians in America."[17] The NCC harshly condemns the Jewish state for her alleged treatment of Palestinians, but not Palestinians for terror against Jews.[18] It has pushed strenuously for a resolution of the Palestinian-Israeli conflict based on land borders that would shrink Israel down to a size she could not possibly defend from military attack.[19]

The largest Canadian Protestant denomination, the United Church of Canada, sanctioned Israel in 2012 by boycotting and divesting from the Jewish state (see chapter 11).[20] Numerous other denominations representing millions of Christians threaten to do the same. Meanwhile, they have joined with Arab and Palestinian churches—notably excluding Messianic Jewish congregations—to form Churches for Middle East Peace. Their peace initiatives aim to create a sovereign Palestinian state. Problem is, they do not address the extensively documented Palestinian plan to annihilate Israel once that sovereign state is established.[21] Like some of the other groups above, Churches for Middle East Peace seeks to divide Jerusalem into a capital city for Israel to share cooperatively with a militant Islamist state.[22]

At the core of Christian anti-Israel[d] sentiment is usually a refusal to believe the Jewish state is an expression of God's everlasting, unconditional covenant. Therefore, Israel is not regarded as a fulfillment of prophecy. Typically, no biblical promise for her future, national restoration is acknowledged. As we have seen, these beliefs almost always stem from either an anti-Hebraic hermeneutic of the Scriptures; misunderstanding of God's love, mercy and grace; personal offense at election; or ignorance fostering arrogance. Sadly, new supersessionist theologies offer revived expression to all the above (see chapter 12).

An Alternative Christian Approach

Thankfully, some Christian leaders and organizations offer a well-reasoned response to the anti-Israel strategies of their peers. One example is the Protestant Consultation on Israel and the Middle East, which encourages an honest approach to both sides of the Arab/Palestinian–Israeli conflict. The Consultation takes into account the enormity of injustice sustained by Israelis as well as Palestinians. Though not Christian Zionist, the organization firmly disavows supersessionism. It expresses love and support for Israelis, Palestinians and Arabs throughout the Middle East. Regarding the "peace strategies" of traditional church organizations, it astutely states:

> Whether this effect is intended or not, such strategies lend encouragement to the forces that have vowed to destroy Israel— [Islamist] forces that launch rockets at Israeli civilians on a daily basis. We fear that this approach is not motivated by Christian love for anyone, but quite the opposite. We ask the zealous promoters of those strategies to examine their consciences in this matter.[23]

As most traditional churches wrestle with the Jewish state, Christian Zionists have shown themselves to be Israel's closest friends. Some are politically active; others extend love and support in a variety of other creative and helpful ways. Personally, I deeply appreciate how some Gentile believers, particularly leaders, have sacrificed much for the sake of their friendship with Israel. May their commitment to God's heart and purposes for the Jewish people unleash abundant blessing to them through eternity. May He be the "exceedingly great reward" (Genesis 15:1 NKJV) of these brothers and sisters who serve as examples of the "fullness of the Gentiles." Of such believers who carry and convey God's passion for Israel, a former Israeli Foreign Minister has said:

> With Christians now reaching out to the Jewish people in genuine contrition and love, we are witnessing a remarkable phenomenon . . . that will, please God, usher in the final redemption of the Jewish people and of all humankind.[24]

Indeed, final redemption is coming. But first we must consider the incursion of Islam—which God may use to precipitate it.

8

The Islamic Middle East
and Anti-Semitism

God has bound everyone over to disobedience so that he may have
mercy on them all. Oh, the depth of the riches of the wisdom
and knowledge of God! How unsearchable his judgments, and
his paths beyond tracing out!

Romans 11:32–33

Fourteen hundred years ago, secluded in a cave in the Arabian
Desert, a Meccan named Muhammad said he encountered the
angel Gabriel. According to Islamic writings, Gabriel violently
overpowered him, then commanded him to recite and record new
holy verses, known as the Quran. Arab history documents that
initially Muhammad, as well as some of his contemporaries,
believed he had been demon possessed. Distraught, he attempted

suicide but was stopped by a voice affirming his prophetic mission. Thus Islam was born.[1] [a]

The Quran claimed to replace the Bible,[b] and so Muhammad's revelations were rebuffed by most Jews and Christians of his day. He did gain a wide following, however, among pagan Arabs.[2] Under Muhammad's leadership, Islam spread sometimes peaceably, but at other times quite violently through terror.

Currently the fastest-growing faith in the Western world, Islam claims over 90 percent of the Arab population.[3] In 2013, nearly one fourth of people alive identified as Muslim.[4] Demographers expect the global Muslim population to increase by approximately 35 percent by the year 2030.[5]

As with any religion, Islam has branched into divergent expressions, with varying interpretations of the Quran and other sacred texts.[c] Certainly at this writing, most Muslims are not militant fundamentalists. But across the Middle East political realities are fueled by fundamentalist Islam (Islamism). In this chapter we will see how certain Islamist doctrines have inflamed the Arab world and set it on a collision course with Israel. As we do, please bear in mind that God loves even the most militant of Muslims. Many harbor deep personal pain, their lives commandeered by oppressive regimes. My purpose is not to demean or incite resentment toward human beings created in God's image but to lay informational groundwork for strategic prayer and response to realities He wants to change—starting, perhaps, with ourselves.

A Christian Root of Islam?

Islam originated and rose to the fore during the so-called Dark Ages of history (late fifth through tenth centuries). This was a period shrouded in spiritual—with resultant political and cultural—darkness. The Church weakened, evangelism ebbed and the Gospel gained little ground. Christianity's bright light seemed to have grown dim.

Earlier we saw that not long before this sordid era, Christian leaders renounced their Old Covenant heritage, cutting off the Jewish roots of their faith. The doctrine of divine contempt led many to persecute and kill—in Jesus' name—Jews who would not convert. Some Jewish historians are convinced Christians would have attempted to completely annihilate the Jewish people if their attention had not been diverted by the rising tide of Islam.[6]

Similar to how Christianity had lapsed into replacement theology, Islam adopted "replacement-of-replacement theology" with a vengeance. First, the Church claimed to supersede Israel; next, Muslims asserted they superseded both Jews and Christians. And so the logical question becomes: Could the Body of Christ have opened the door to the devil, so to speak, by ignoring the exhortation of Scripture not to be arrogant or ignorant toward Israel? Is it possible the Church has reaped for itself the same treatment it meted out to the Jews?

In the sixteenth-century classic *Foxe's Annals of Martyrs,* historian John Foxe paralleled persecution by the Church with persecution *of* the Church: "We fight against a persecutor, being no less persecutors ourselves. We wrestle against a bloody tyrant, and our hands be as full of blood as his."[7] Foxe attributed the rise of Islam to the infirm condition of the Church:[8]

Early in the seventh century a new enemy of Christianity arose. . . . The rapid success of this adventurer [Muhammad] must be classed among the mournful proofs furnished by that age of the decay into which practical Christianity had fallen. . . . It was, unquestionably, the abuses and infirmities of the Christian church that gave Muhammadanism room and leisure to mature its strength.[9]

As believers in Jesus today face revived fundamentalist Islam, it is critical that we purge ourselves of any vestige of theological anti-Semitism. By God's grace we must learn from history—so that we need not repeat it.

Islamic Jesus and the End Times

Fundamentalist Islam in the 21st century is to a large extent apocalypse-driven, with militantly messianic aspirations. But Islam's messiah is unequivocally not the Jesus of the Holy Bible. According to the Quran, Jesus was a strictly human prophet who never died on a cross—and is definitely not God's Son.[10] This is publicly declared in plain view from the Temple Mount in Jerusalem. A Quranic engraving on the ceiling of the Dome of the Rock reads, "Far be it from God to have a son. . . . It is not for God to beget a son."[11]

Fundamental Islam teaches that Jesus was supernaturally spared death, having been taken directly to heaven like Moses or Elijah. In the end times, he is expected to return—as a Muslim serving the Islamic messiah (*mahdi*). The *mahdi* appears during a period of violent global unrest. He demonstrates supernatural signs and wonders, promising peace, justice and righteousness. But to prepare for the *mahdi*'s coming, Muslims must first put into place an Islamic caliphate, or political empire adhering to totalitarian, Islamic religious law (*shari'a*). The caliphate is to be established through holy wars (*jihad*). These bloody campaigns are aimed especially, but not exclusively, at Jews and Christians. In the process, Israel must be overrun and Jerusalem must be captured.

Fundamentalist Islam is obsessed with Jerusalem because the city is to serve as Islamic holy headquarters. Now, the only time Muhammad ever entered Jerusalem was in his sleep, in a dream en route to heaven. But sacred texts assert the *mahdi* will rule from the Temple Mount, with Jesus helping him establish the kingdom of Allah. Jesus will accomplish this by abolishing Christianity, teaching *shari'a* and slaughtering Jews who refuse to convert. Then Jesus will marry, father several children and die.[12] But that's not all.

Muslims expect two Jesuses to return. The personality described above (an imposter by biblical standards) will appear first. The second Jesus (the Bible's Messiah) claims to be both a Jewish man and divine. He defends Israel in a major military operation against the *mahdi* and his hordes. Islamic texts describe this second Jesus as the Antichrist (*dajjal*) who gets defeated by Allah's forces.[13]

As you can see, on all these points, Islamic eschatology presents an inverse parallel or mirror image of the end times outlined in Scripture.[14] The *mahdi* (Islamic messiah) would fit the role of the Antichrist in the Bible. The Islamic Jesus would represent the Antichrist's false prophet (see Revelation 16:13; 19:20; 20:10). Islam's *dajjal* appears to describe the true Messiah (except for His alleged defeat by Allah). Because fundamentalist Islam presents such a strikingly opposite view of the end times described in the Bible, explicitly denying that Jesus is God's Son, some Christians suspect it may be part of the religious system of the Antichrist (see 1 John 4:3).

Who Is Allah and What Does He Want?

Since Muslims are monotheists and there is only one true God, is it necessarily Him whom they worship? To be sure, *Allah* is the only word in Arabic meaning "God," and Arab Christians use the name with reverence specifically for Yahweh. But by all accounts, the Islamist Allah does not resemble the divine personality of the Creator portrayed in Scripture.[15] The nature and attributes of the two differ dramatically. Moved by the power of love, Father God offers the sacrifice of His Son on our behalf. In contrast, moved by the love of power, Allah orders the sacrifice of his followers' sons on his own behalf.

Islam means "submission," and Allah requires submission to him willingly, forcibly or by the torturous killing of those who refuse. Submission is universally applicable to everyone on earth. As "people of the Book," Christians and Jews who do not convert are sometimes allowed to live as persecuted second-class citizens if they submit to *shari'a* law and pay an exorbitant tax.

The Islamist's highest duty is *jihad* and his ultimate reward, martyrdom. Jihad is not an option; it is a compelling sacrament. It is not, as some say, fundamentally limited to inner striving toward personal growth. Islamists must strive for outward, global domination at all times, not wait idly for the *mahdi* and Islamic (false) Jesus to achieve it for them.[16] Recall that the establishment of an Islamic caliphate is a prerequisite for the arrival of both.

Despite claims to the contrary, fundamentalist Islam is not a recently invented reality to oppose the Jewish state. Muhammad himself instigated *jihad* against pagans, Christians and Jews from Africa to India and China, and up into Spain.[d] Under his orders, Muslim warriors savagely slaughtered masses of believers, overrunning churches and converting them into mosques.[17]

Muhammad's mandate to conquer the whole world and compel submission to *shari'a* law has never been relinquished. According to Mark Gabriel, an author on Islam, the Quran contains 114 verses about love, forgiveness and peace. All are abrogated, however, by "The Verse of the Sword," penned later in Muhammad's life: "Find and slay the pagans wherever you find them, beleaguer them, and lie in wait for them, in every stratagem of war; but if they repent [convert to Islam] . . . open up a way for them."[18]

Moderate Muslims interpret the Quran more liberally, just as less fundamentalist Christians interpret the Bible more liberally. Most moderate Muslims are peaceful, upright citizens of goodwill. I know some personally, enjoy their friendship and admire their dedication to principled ethics and family values. They have little predilection for their radical co-religionists. But the moderates hold small sway in the overall Islamic world. *The agenda of fundamentalist Islam includes overtaking and eventually forcing them to conform to extremism, too.* Some moderates know this and are openly concerned; many cope by denying it; others are simply unaware. Most recognize, however, that they can rarely trust what the fundamentalists say or do.

Islam and "Truth"

Sadly, Islamic sacred texts are replete with perversions of biblical truth, many of which target the Jews. The Quran teaches, for instance, that the Jewish authors of Scripture intentionally distorted both Old and New Testaments for their own selfish interests. Abraham—like Adam and Eve—is said to have really been a Muslim, and Ishmael, his rightful covenant heir. From Genesis through the New Covenant, the Jews are accused of falsifying the whole canon of Scripture—in a demonic attempt to supersede Islam![e]

With major distortions of biblical truth embedded in the Quran and related sacred texts, an element of dishonesty inevitably permeates the Islamist world. Truth does not—and cannot—carry the same value as it does in Judeo-Christian culture. *The worldwide impact of the fundamentalist disposition toward dishonesty cannot be overstated.* It dramatically affects what is represented, and what you and I hear and see, about the Arab/Palestinian conflict with the Jewish state.

The fundamentalist doctrine of *taqiya* mandates lying in order to preserve Islamist goals.[19] [f] According to *taqiya*, facts may be distorted, outlandishly embellished, dismissed altogether or completely concocted. *Taqiya* explains why some Islamist leaders openly insist (in Arabic) that no matter what happens regarding a sovereign Palestinian state, Israel must be destroyed—and within days, when speaking to Western officials, say that peace with Israel will result just as soon as a sovereign Palestinian state exists. Generally, what is communicated in Arabic within Islam about Israel differs greatly from what is communicated in English or other languages for Western consumption.[g]

Truthful and insightful perspectives of Islam can often be gleaned from former Muslims, some of whom now love and follow Jesus. Living in the West where they can speak freely, they consistently describe fundamentalist Islam as highly non-peaceful, with deceptive and terrorizing aspirations for global, political-religious domination. These courageous spokespeople repeatedly warn about Islam's insidious infiltration into Western democracies, including the US, to cause their collapse.[20] Most are also vocal defenders of the Jewish state. While portrayed by liberal institutions as lunatics or Islamophobes, they are usually faced with death warrants from Islamist leaders abroad. I believe they deserve and need our blessing and support—as do our Christian brothers and sisters still living in the highly tumultuous Middle East.

Arab Spring / Islamist Awakening

In 2010, Muslims across North Africa and the Middle East began rebelling against dictatorial regimes. Much of the world reacted with optimism, hoping democratic freedoms would finally transform this oppressed region. In reality, however, the revolutions have been hijacked by well-organized Islamist parties with radical agendas and ideologies. Arab Spring has morphed into what can more accurately be termed, at this writing, an Islamist awakening.

What the West did not understand is that Islamist groups boast automatic advantages in any free election in the Arab Middle East. They have long held sway over the majority through the mosque and the media. Savvy and well networked, some have waited for decades to step into political power vacuums. Barring the miraculous—which we should never bar—the governments they control will, over time, likely replace superficial democratic reform with *shari'a* law. This is because Western-style elections are part of a distinctly Western political system and culture, originally rooted in Judeo-Christian values, which has little relevance to the Arab Muslim world.[21][h]

Dr. Zuhdi Jasser is a well-known authority on Islam and human rights. He is a former US naval officer and founder-president of the respectable American Islamic Forum for Democracy. Jasser, himself a moderate Muslim, cautions that "those who say democracy and political Islam can peacefully coexist are ill-informed."[22]

As Islamic states move from one form of dictatorship to another, the more powerful regimes will compete for hegemony across the entire Middle East. They make no secret of their goal to resurrect the Islamic caliphate—but this time they anticipate forcibly inaugurating, through brutal *jihad*, a cataclysmic end times scenario along with it. Expect to see Iran and Turkey, and to an extent Egypt, contending at the forefront. As we look briefly at Middle East nations below, pray that God's light will shine through even the darkest Islamic veil.

Iran

Iran, known in the Bible as Elam or Persia, has a rich and varied history. In the book of Daniel we read about the archangel Michael wrestling tenaciously more than once against the "prince of Persia" (Daniel 10:13, 20). This dark prince is a spirit of high-ranking authority. He tries hard to keep Michael from delivering prophetic revelation about the end times—in which Iran may play a key, warring role.

Persia became the birthplace of revived fundamentalist Islam in 1979 when the Ayatollah Khomeini announced the formal resumption of Allah's rule. His declaration carried spiritual authority to stoke centuries-old smoldering flames. Iran quickly converted into a police state run on ghoulish cruelty. Terror metastasized from that country throughout the Middle East and around the world. Since 1979, Iranian oil revenues have spawned, funded, amply armed and networked militant proxy groups like Hezbollah, Hamas, Islamic Jihad and more.

Demonizing not just the Jewish state but Jewish people everywhere,[i] Iran broadcasts vociferously that Israel must be wiped off the map. Fearing a second Holocaust,[j] Israel takes this threat seriously in view of Iran's rogue nuclear program. The Jewish state has no choice but to prepare for a preemptive, defensive military strike against an Iranian attack.[k] On the one side, Israel knows such a strike could spark a long-dreaded regional war. On the other side, if Iran delivers but one nuclear bomb to her first, there will be no Israel.

Along with its nuclear program, Iran openly seeks to establish a totalitarian caliphate throughout the Middle East, then inaugurate, as it declared in 2012, a "new world order."[23] In the new order, America is neutralized and the *mahdi* comes to power. To garner support for its scheme, Iran sponsored an international summit in 2012 in Tehran. A surprising two-thirds of the world's nations attended the conference.[1]

Prophetic Scriptures indicate Yahweh will "set [His] throne in Elam," bring disaster against it, break its military might and disperse its people. But in the end—consummately, after the Second Coming—He graciously restores the nation (see Jeremiah 49:34–39). Meanwhile, missionary organizations report that a groundswell of Iranians are coming to faith in Jesus. Pray for the underground revival to increase and even shift the spiritual climate of that nation.

Syria and Lebanon

Aligned closely with Iran, Syria is a highly strategic nation in the Middle East. At this writing, a horrific civil war wages in Syria in which multitudes of civilians have been brutally killed or forced to flee the country. With its government in disarray, Syria harbors huge stockpiles of weapons of mass destruction, compliments of Iran. Some of these have already been unleashed against her own people. Many are in the hands of Iranian-backed forces and other militant groups competing for power and threatening to fire their lethal caches into Israel. Most likely, Israel will attempt to neutralize at least some of these WMDs. Biblical references to Syria pertain mostly to its capital city, Damascus, for which devastating judgment is prophesied—and our intercession needed.

Lebanon, for which we must also pray, has long served as a proxy state for both Syria and Iran. This once beautiful Christian country fell several years ago to the democratically elected leadership of the terrorist group Hezbollah. In 2012, Lebanon contained most of the 200,000 missiles in the Middle East that were positioned and ready for fire against Israel.[24] Every tenth house in the country was serving as a weapons depot,[25] with the nation poised for war. Yet a remnant of faithful followers of Jesus remains in Lebanon, praying earnestly for her.

Egypt

In 1979, Egypt and Israel entered into a historic peace treaty. Egypt recognized Israel's right to exist, and in return, Israel gave Egypt over half its land mass, the Sinai Peninsula.[m] But soon after Egypt's Arab Spring revolt, its new leadership came under the control of the fundamentalist Muslim Brotherhood, signaling that peace with Israel would probably end.[26]

From its inception the Brotherhood has been obsessed with anti-Semitism, and often monstrously so.[27] Until recently, the organization could not act directly on its ideology, so it created Hamas, a terror group whose very existence is dedicated to Israel's demise. At this writing, Hamas is the elected government of the Palestinian people living in Gaza. It is actively warring against Israel (with occasional cease-fires) and aggressively seeking to gain control of the West Bank.

Immediately after a Muslim Brotherhood candidate was elected president of Egypt in 2012, its leaders—not fringe mavericks—held massive public rallies declaring *jihad* on Israel and the conquest of Jerusalem.[n] A high-ranking Egyptian cleric bellowed in one such gathering: "We can see how the dream of the Islamic caliphate is being realized, God willing, by [President] Morsi." Morsi nodded in agreement, stating Jerusalem is "our goal" and martyrdom operations will attain it.[28] Shortly thereafter, he prayed publicly for the annihilation of the Jewish state.[29] Whether through Morsi or a successor, the Muslim Brotherhood will likely seek to undermine Egypt's peace treaty with Israel to bring about its cancellation,° and place full blame for doing so on the Jewish state.ᵖ

If the Brotherhood or the likes of it stays in power, Egypt will gradually morph into a resolutely Islamist state. Nevertheless, the prophet Isaiah portrays a final, beautiful future for Egypt, consummately fulfilled in the Messianic Age, with God declaring, "Blessed be Egypt My people" (see Isaiah 19:18–25).

Iraq

The same Scripture that prophesies blessing for Egypt also describes God's gracious touch on the land of Assyria, "My handiwork." Today, much of Assyria is known as Iraq. Ur of the Chaldees, where God first spoke to Abraham, was located in what is now Iraq. Also situated in Iraq is the ancient city of Babylon (meaning "gateway of the gods"). Babylon was grisly ground to a host of polytheistic rites and rituals in the ancient world. Former Iraqi dictator Saddam Hussein rose to power as a self-declared reincarnate of Babylon's King Nebuchadnezzar, openly drawing on its spiritual past. At his direction, the city's ruins were excavated and restored—along with demonic hosts associated with them.

An Islamist government was brought to power years ago through democratic elections in Iraq. Though some personal freedoms exist, Iraqi law must not be inconsistent with *shari'a* and the country remains highly unstable. The Scriptures are replete with prophecies of judgment against Babylon, which some believe will transpire literally in the resurrected Iraqi city.

Turkey and Other Middle East Nations

Turkey is not technically part of the Middle East and its people are not technically Arabs; they are Turks. But the Turkish nation served for hundreds of years as premier power of the Ottoman Empire (see chapter 10) and still remains a regional linchpin. Turkey has never relinquished the ideal of resuming its position as head of a future, pan-Islamic empire, thereby eliminating the Jewish state it deeply disdains. Some believe that end time prophecies indicate Turkey will regain formidable power, then spearhead calamitous war against Israel.[30]

Other nations in the Middle East are rumbling with threatened revolution. Among them is Jordan. Jordan shares a border with Israel and many years ago, the two entered into a peace treaty. But feverishly anti-Semitic, Islamist groups now seek to overtake Jordan and terminate that peace. Nearby, Saudi Arabia and other Peninsula states could also succumb to incipient uprisings. As the whole region roils, please join me in petitioning heaven for the salvation of multitudes and protection of the Church.

Over time, Arab Spring revolutions could result in disintegration or reorganization of less powerful Middle East states. As the three imperialist nations—Turkey, Iran and Egypt—contend for regional hegemony, the map may change. But one thing is certain: So long as fundamentalist Islam rages in the region, Israel will remain a target, no matter what she does or how many concessions she offers for peace. Hate for the Jews is embedded into fundamental Islam, beginning with the Quran. It forms an essential tenet of the ideology espoused by every Islamist state.

Islam and the Jews

The Quran alleges, as we have seen, that the Bible's Jewish authors intentionally falsified the Scriptures. It also teaches that

Allah despises and cursed the Jews, turning some into apes and pigs.[31] Accordingly, Muhammad ordered the wholesale slaughter of unarmed Jewish villages that existed in his day.[32] An integral supplement to the Quran, the *Hadith*, instructs the apocalyptic Day of Judgment cannot come until Muslims fight and vanquish the Jews.[33] At that time Jews will attempt to hide, but even trees and rocks will cry out, "O Muslim, there is a Jew behind me; come and kill him."[34]

Through the centuries, fundamental Islam has depicted the Jewish people as its greatest enemy. It has generated furiously anti-Semitic rhetoric predating modern Israel by over 1,300 years. A popular author on Islam writes:

> Sacred Islamic traditions of a final slaughter of all Jews cannot be attributed to the present-day conflict with the State of Israel. Although many today try to blame Muslim enmity toward Jews solely on Zionism and its alleged . . . abuse of the victimized and oppressed Palestinians, it simply cannot be done in an honest and informed manner. The enmity of Islam toward the Jews has existed since Islam's inception.[35]

Much of the world outside the Arab Middle East has been led to think that Islamic hate for Israel is the result of Israel's reluctance to create a Palestinian state. It is not. Islamic hate for Israel has been, however, the principal *cause* of that reluctance. Among themselves, Islamists admit (in Arabic) that their rage against Israel has little to do with anything she does, but rather with the fact she exists:

> They [the Jews] are enemies not because they occupied Palestine; they would have been enemies even if they did not occupy a thing. . . . We must believe that our fighting with the Jews is eternal, and it will not end until the final battle. . . . O Allah, bring your wrath, punishment, and torment down upon them.[36]

Islamic Holy Land?

Besides the intrinsic theological hate, fundamentalist Islam cannot end its conflict with Israel because, according to its holy texts, any land that was ever conquered for Allah must be recouped. If it is not, his name is besmirched and his conquest of the world delayed.

For 1,300 years, Israeli lands were under foreign Muslim rule. To be sure, a sizeable Jewish population has lived in Israel continuously since biblical times. The Jews never voluntarily relinquished claim to their land, and Palestine never existed as a sovereign Arab domain. Nevertheless, Israel—every inch of it—absolutely must, in Islamist thought, be re-subjugated to Allah's rule. Reclaiming Jerusalem is a central goal. Although Jerusalem is the least referenced of all holy cities in the Quran, it is the presumed locale for the *mahdi*'s coming rule and reign on the Temple Mount. To prepare for his arrival, Jerusalem must be recaptured from the Jews and "restored" to Islamist control.

Radical religion is the primary but not sole reason for Islamic hostility toward the Jewish state. Because of her historic alliance with the West, Israel is perceived as an insulting, imperial outpost of decadent Western civilization. Few Westerners realize that Israel's friendship with them exacerbates Islamist fury against her. Even fewer realize that, positioned on the frontlines, Israel is fighting pivotal battles against fundamentalist Islam for all of Western civilization.

Inciting Hate for Israel

Throughout the Arab world, Islamist ideology pervades secular thought; there is virtually no separation.[q] Hate-inciting sermons about Israel and the Jews are preached daily in mosques and muezzins, aired by radio and television stations and blasted through cyberspace.[r] Multiple generations of Muslims have been raised on state-sponsored, barbarously anti-Semitic literature and propaganda. Nazi materials have long been mainstays in schools, stores, the media and political institutions across the Middle East.[s] Practically everywhere in the region, Jews are portrayed as subhuman and evil, deserving of death.

Sometimes the hate is so absurd that one does not know whether to laugh or cry. Hapless Saudis are warned in the daily news of Zionists on the prowl for Gentile blood with which to bake kosher delicacies.[37] Egyptian jurists plan to sue Israel to recover the value, including over three thousand years' interest, of everything "stolen" the night of the exodus.[t] Turkey accuses Israel of spying on her through seasonally migrating birds.[u] The list goes on and on.

How do you suppose the incitement has impacted the Palestinian-Israeli conflict? The Palestinian Authority has squandered exorbitant sums of international aid to systematically indoctrinate its entire population, since early childhood, with egregious lies about Israel. School textbooks in subjects from history and science to grammar and math (using word problems) instruct students about the "cursed and oppressive Zionist regime."[v] Kindergartners are trained to conduct terror operations and to welcome death in doing so.[w] Children's camps, art and poetry contests, scouting programs and more all focus on inciting hate for Israel and encouraging martyrdom for the sake of killing Jews.[x] State-run television programs for toddlers use Disney and Sesame Street characters to promote *jihad*.[y]

As Palestinians move to establish a sovereign state, the anti-Israel frenzy saturates their society at seemingly every level.[z] Secular public events are peppered with reminders such as this: "Our war with the descendants of the apes and pigs is a war of religion and faith."[38] Suicide bombers are honored as new stadiums, tournaments, town squares, schools and other building projects, funded by the West, are named after them.[aa] A salary is paid to any Palestinian imprisoned for acts of terror committed against Israel.[bb] Publicly blasted—and internationally funded—sermons such as these inspire the murder of Jews:

> Allah willing, this unjust state will be erased—Israel will be erased. . . . Blessings to whoever put a belt of explosives on his body or on his sons' and plunged into the midst of the Jews crying, "Allah akbar [Allah is great.] There is no God but Allah and Muhammed is His messenger."[39]

> The [resurrection] hour will not come until you fight the Jews. The Jews will hide behind stones or trees. Then the stones will call: "O Muslim, servant of Allah, there is a Jew behind me; come and kill him."[40]

Subject to a relentless onslaught of lies, multiplied millions of people have become consumed with a demonic loathing of Israel. But because the propaganda campaign takes place in Arabic, it is ignored by much of the non-Islamic world.[cc] Instead, the hate is spread to the West in a more culturally palatable package. *To appeal to Western ideals of freedom and justice, a conflict based fundamentally on murderously anti-Semitic ideology is reinvented as rooted in social injustice.*

But the reinvention turns the truth upside down. Social injustice did not *cause* the conflict; it has resulted *from* the conflict. Islamist/Arab/Palestinian hate and theology have brought about facts and realities that are genuinely unjust—for both Palestinians and Israelis. Our challenge is to forthrightly ascertain those facts and realities, then assess what believers can do to change them. The remainder of this book aims to guide us, by God's grace, in that task.

To God Be the Glory

As nations rage against Israel, let us remember that Yahweh has the whole matter in hand. The apostle Paul concludes his grand sermon on Israel with a resplendent doxology—one that can help steer us in faith through difficult, perplexing times. He explains that Israel's calling, her election and even her troubles culminate in God's incomparable glory. The Spirit catapults the apostle—and us—into sweeping adoration of the Almighty. None but He could mastermind this dazzling display of redemption, this triumph of mercy and grace:

> God has bound everyone over to disobedience so that he may have mercy on them all. Oh, the depth of the riches of the wisdom and knowledge of God! How unsearchable his judgments, and his paths beyond tracing out! . . . To him be the glory forever! Amen.
>
> Romans 11:32–33, 36

Our spirits soar as we peer into the telescopic lens of God's ways. The picture is bigger than Israel or her conflict with Islamism; it is bigger than the Church. The picture displays God's sovereign splendor, forever.

The Jewish people and their story or, more accurately, their role in His story, are all about *Him*. How important then, as we see next, to get the story straight—and understand what is at stake if we don't.

9

Discerning Truth
about Israel Today

Do not conform to the pattern of this world.

Romans 12:2

In Romans 9–11, the apostle Paul has just told us of God's love for the Jewish people, their prophetic inheritance and His plans for their salvation. We have seen how reciprocal blessing flows between Gentiles and Jews as one in Messiah, to God's infinite glory. Next, in Romans 12:1–3, Paul tells us what to do with the information he has just unpacked. We must not conform to the pattern of this world; we must be transformed by the renewing of our minds in order to discern God's will. For that we must know truth.

To know the truth about a given situation, we must usually be equipped with the facts. Concerning Israel, however, this can prove a daunting task. Every form of media imaginable communicates something, every day, about the Jewish state and its contention with Islamism, Arabs and Palestinians. Often the narratives conflict and complexities are confusing. Many find it difficult to discern how reliable the seemingly boundless barrage of data can be. As a result, they may be misguided—or flatly manipulated—by raw emotion having little to do with facts or truth. They may believe whatever narrative of the conflict stirs the most sympathy—even if it happens to be fake. Allow me to share from personal experience.

World Pattern: The Media

My first visit to a Palestinian refugee camp was in 1982, but remains relevant today. From all the dreadful news reports even back then, I braced myself for the worst: row upon row of flimsily strung tents surrounded by piles of filth, men and women clothed in rags and crying children with runny noses and distended bellies. But that was not what I saw.

The camps I visited were neighborhoods quite decently built by Middle East standards of the day. The streets were calm. Women strolled casually about, groceries and other goods balanced on top of their heads. Men sat and sipped coffee together in the doorways of their shops. Palestinian children were off the streets and in school. Young Israeli soldiers leaned lazily at their posts, puffing cigarettes. Now and then a dog barked or a goat bleated.

I was more than a bit befuddled. The scene, while far from idyllic, hardly reflected the abject squalor and oppression widely reported by the media. Admittedly, I viewed only two camps, and neither would qualify for anyone's list of residential best picks. Nevertheless, the refugees' condition looked nothing like the deplorable imprisonment I had been led to expect.[a] Later, I learned that Palestinians had experienced rapid and broad-based improvements in their standard of living shortly after the Israelis began "oppressively occupying" them.[b]

Media distortions about the Arab/Palestinian–Israeli conflict have exponentially worsened since that visit decades ago. My last trip to the Palestinian West Bank left me dazzled and practically stunned. In 2012 I saw palatial homes, one after another, several times larger than my own. Businesses were thriving. Large-scale ministry organizations operated in beautifully designed buildings, equipped with sleek appliances and updated technology. Certainly I do not deny that poverty exists among Palestinians. I do, however, suggest there is another side to the West Bank story—and that it is rarely told.[c]

To gain a sense of the distortion of truth about Israel in today's public discourse, please look with me at three particular internationally publicized incidents. *These examples reflect and typify countless others still regularly occurring.* I was in Israel during each of the events described, accessing reliable sources of information in order to corroborate them. As you read, I think you will discover the highly nuanced nature of today's war on truth.

Justice in Jenin

During Passover 2002, in a city near Tel Aviv, a Palestinian terrorist walked into a hotel filled with guests celebrating the feast. Without warning, he detonated a suitcase full of explosives. Instantly, thirty Israelis were blown to bits; 143 more were seriously injured in the grisly horror.[1] Similar attacks had been carried out, murdering and maiming civilians, on an almost weekly basis across the country for over a year.[d] Restaurants, shops, buses, schools, public squares—no place was safe. Israel pleaded for help, but the world paid little heed until she was forced to take action on her own.

Days after the Passover massacre, to curtail the relentless slaughter, the Israeli army advanced into the West Bank refugee camp of Jenin. The sole purpose of the incursion was to weed out and dismantle Jenin's *known* terror nests. Each day I watched the newscasts on TV, read the papers and talked with the locals, including army reservists. Clearly this operation, called Defensive Shield, was defensive in nature. It was a necessary response to the deadliest terror wave the country had experienced. Just as clearly, the war had been started not by the Israelis but by the Palestinians in their so-called Second Intifada.

Defensive Shield was a military operation of very limited proportions. Soldiers I knew serving in Jenin told me the army undertook extreme, even heroic, measures to curtail casualties in the very difficult setting of house-to-house combat. So I was perplexed at charges of wide-scale, Holocaust-like genocidal atrocities that quickly beamed via satellite across the globe and landed in UN chambers. How had such a distortion, indeed serpentine tale, hatched?

The Palestinian Authority (PA) Minister of Local Government, I learned, had given this summation to news reporters: "The Jenin refugee camp is no longer in existence; [it is] totally destroyed."[2] Other PA officials decried a brutal massacre of five hundred innocents, their bodies buried under the rubble by Israeli bulldozers.[3] Fuming at Israel, the international media did not bother to investigate facts before releasing the story. The London news reported, "We are talking here of a massacre and cover-up of genocide" that was "every bit as repellent" as Osama bin Laden's in New York in September 2001.[4] The world was outraged; the UN launched an investigation.

What was the truth? In sharp contrast to Palestinian allegations, UN investigators—who were decidedly not pro-Israel—could find no evidence of any massacre in Jenin.[5] The only affected area was the terror nest itself—which amounted to just 10 percent of the camp. Ninety percent of Jenin had been left practically intact. Not 500, but 52 Palestinians were killed, most of whom were terrorists.[6] Palestinian News Agency reports about "mass graves" heaped under rubble and bulldozed to conceal the "Zionist massacre"[7] could never be substantiated. Months later, Israel unearthed and publicly released Palestinian documents confirming the trumped-up nature of the charges.[8]

The truth is the PA had deliberately lied. Recall the Islamist justification for dishonesty called *taqiya*. *Taqiya* affects much of what you—and the international community—hear and see about Israel today.

Eventually it was discovered that much of the property damage and death toll in Jenin had been intentionally caused by the Palestinians themselves. They had planted bombs and booby traps inside civilian homes, buildings[c] and even ambulances to maximize bloodshed, which could then be blamed on Israel. (Such tactics occur even more often today.) In reality, the Israelis had taken extraordinary precautions at great risk to themselves, tediously searching whole neighborhoods house by house to avoid unnecessary civilian deaths.

Captured Jenin-based terrorist Thabet Mardawi told CNN news reporters the Palestinians had expected Israel to attack with planes and tanks. They were elated when instead the Jews exposed themselves to harm on the ground. Said Mardawi:

I couldn't believe it when I saw the soldiers. The Israelis knew that any soldier who went into the camp like that was going to get killed. Shooting at these men as they walked cautiously down

the street was like hunting . . . like being given a prize. . . . I'd
been waiting for a moment like that for years.[9]

While the UN exonerated Israel of the massacre charge, by
the time it released its report, few folks were listening. Instead,
they were busy watching the movie. An Arab filmmaker put
together a purported documentary called *Jenin, Jenin*, based
on scenarios proven false, which went on to win prestigious
international awards.[10] Besides, other accusations against the
Zionists were competing for global attention. Devilish damage
to Israel's reputation having been done, more and more people
grew angrier and angrier at the suspect Jewish state. Some may
think 2002 was a long time ago and things have changed. *They
have not.* Precisely for that reason, we have detailed the jugger-
naut of Jenin—and turn now to lies growing in Gaza.

Gaza-Grown Lies

In 2005, Israel unilaterally withdrew its presence from Gaza,
painfully uprooting all Jewish communities and ending any
occupation of the area. This unprecedented gesture toward
peace was met with a nightmarish barrage of rockets and missiles that, at this writing, has not ended. By 2013, Palestinians
in Gaza had launched approximately 12,000 projectiles into
the Jewish state.[11] [f] The attacks reached a peak in late 2008,
when they escalated to dozens each day for over a week. Israel
pleaded to the UN for help, but (again) to no avail. When more
than sixty rockets and mortars hit civilian population centers
on a single day,[12] Israel was compelled to commence Operation
Cast Lead. The sole purpose of the operation, as in Jenin, was
to defensively dismantle terror nests and neutralize munitions
supplies.[g]

Immediately, Palestinians charged Israel with all manner of macabre crimes against humanity in the course of the operation, including the deliberate killing of babies. The UN quickly investigated, but interviewed only Palestinians—not Israelis. Consequently, its final report condemned Israel harshly.[13] But that was just the beginning.

Months later, the UN's lead investigator publicly recanted key findings in the report. He admitted that his conclusions were wrongly based on insufficient evidence and biased testimony. Only after the formal inquiry closed, he said, did he acquire evidence that Israel had never targeted civilians, particularly not babies.[14] He confessed the number of Gazans killed had been far lower than claimed, and mostly limited to militants. He noted that Israel had dedicated significant resources to investigate, on its own initiative, allegations of misconduct in Gaza. He praised the Jewish state for quickly implementing policy changes to limit future collateral casualties.[15]

As is typical, however, practically nobody listened—though there would be another opportunity in another war with Gaza in 2012 (see chapter 11). The UN report had worsened the damage to Israel's reputation to the extent that most folks did not want to be bothered with the facts. Too many new, false claims against the Jewish state were filling the air waves and flying through cyberspace. As a result, in 2010, anti-Israel activists joined together with militants to launch a naval flotilla into Israeli waters. Sadly, few suspected what was really afloat.

Facts on Flotillas

By 2010, Palestinians were complaining of a humanitarian crisis in Gaza due to the "oppressive occupation"—even though Israel had had no physical or occupational presence in Gaza for five years. Israel was, however, delivering over 100 truckloads of aid to Gaza each day—even though it was governed by Hamas, which declares in its charter its intent to destroy the Jewish state.[16]

Notably, by mid-2012, Israel facilitated the shipment into Gaza of 250 truckloads of humanitarian aid per day, or 40,000 tons weekly.[17 h] Concurrently, upscale neighborhoods and hotels, shopping malls, theme parks, beach resorts and entertainment centers sprang up in the area. In 2011, the Red Cross had determined the humanitarian crisis in Gaza was over.[18 i] This happened after impoverished Palestinians, along with some Western leaders, exposed how Hamas had been artificially maintaining the crisis as a propaganda tool against Israel.[j] But that (again) is just the beginning.

Humanitarian crisis or not, a fleet of nautical vessels launched by Turkish and other anti-Israel activists set sail for Gaza in 2010. The flotilla's stated purpose was to peacefully deliver humanitarian aid to civilians suffering from occupation. Israel countered that any humanitarian crisis was due to extreme mismanagement by Gaza's own government. The real reason for the flotilla, Israel said, was to defy its lawful and necessary maritime blockade. (The blockade was in place to prevent the extensively documented, ongoing smuggling into Gaza of materials used to build terror weapons for murdering Israeli civilians.) If the peace activists wanted to deliver aid, Israel invited them to do so via truck.

As matters turned out, most of the flotilla participants respected the blockade and turned their vessels around. The aid they brought was inspected and trucked into Gaza, under the watchful eyes of international observers. But on one vessel, the *Mavi Marmara*, the situation turned deadly.

When the *Mavi Marmara* did not respond to repeated warnings to retreat, a single Israeli soldier tried to peacefully board and commandeer it. Expecting to encounter nonviolent social activists, he was armed with only a small hand pistol. But as live video footage showed, the so-called peace activists responded by overpowering him with knives, metal bars and guns. Just as they tried to throw his pummeled body overboard, Israeli backup troops arrived. The fighting escalated, and nine militants—eight of whom had ties to recognized terror organizations—were killed.

Within minutes the world learned of the event, and by day's end, nations seethed with fury against the Jewish state. Predictably, more international investigations took place. The UN's formal report[k] concluded that flotilla activists and militants had illegally breached Israel's maritime border and blockade. Naval officers who boarded the *Mavi Marmara* had rightfully defended themselves. But no Israeli had died in the skirmish. So the UN determined the Jewish state must have used excessive force.

Now, to ascertain excessive or disproportionate force, UN standards focused almost exclusively on the relative number of combatants killed. But by this measure, the UN would have also condemned Israel for using excessive force in the Exodus, where Pharaoh's army drowned in the Red Sea while not one Jew perished (or fought). A more updated, accurate and fair determinant of excessive force considers the extent of force needed to prevent or defend against imminent assault by the other side.

With the widely publicized accusation of excessive force, frenzied lies about the Jewish state—and Jewish people—exploded at new levels.[l] Frightening Nazi cartoons and propaganda pieces slamming Israel went viral around the world. International activists and militants were emboldened to instigate all new manner of illegal land, air and sea breaches of Israel's borders—based on lies, breeding more lies.

God's Word tells us not to conform to the pattern of this world but to be transformed by the renewing of our minds in order to know and do His will. But this requires knowledge of truth, and when it comes to Israel, "the father of lies" is usually hard at work to distort it (John 8:44).

Timeless Weapons of Deceit

"What has been done will be done again; there is nothing new under the sun" (Ecclesiastes 1:9). The biblical truism has applied to Israel and her enemies since ancient times. A snapshot survey of Scripture shows how Satan has used world weapons of deceit against the Jews like no other nation on earth.

In the book of Esther, a Persian official named Haman demands that all bow down and worship him. Mordecai, a God-fearing Jew, refuses. At this Haman is outraged; to retaliate, he plots the annihilation of Jews throughout the empire. Like Israel's enemies today, Haman concocts a scheme based on lies that he reports to the government: "There is a certain people . . . who . . . do not obey the king's laws; it is not in the king's best interest to tolerate them. If it pleases the king, let a decree be issued to destroy them" (Esther 3:8–9).

The duped king concedes to Haman's request. But the sinister ploy is fabricated and undeserving. There is no mention of sin on the Jews' part; to the contrary, it is Mordecai's worship of Yahweh that stirs the enemy's wrath. While the plan providentially backfires and Haman is killed, the spirit of Haman lives on.

Consider next the book of Ezra. After exile in Babylon, many Jewish people have returned to the Promised Land. They plan to rebuild their country and at first things go well. But after the foundation of the Temple is laid, the opposition stirs. When local efforts to stop the Jews from rebuilding fail, a formal appeal is filed with the authorities. The deceitfully crafted complaint distorts reality almost beyond recognition:

> The king should know that [the Jews] . . . are rebuilding that rebellious and wicked city [Jerusalem]. . . . Furthermore, the king should know that if this city is built and its walls are restored, no more taxes, tribute or duty will be paid, and eventually the royal revenues will suffer. Now since we are under obligation to the palace and it is not proper for us to see the king dishonored, we are sending this message. . . . We inform the king that if this city is built and its walls are restored, you will be left with nothing in Trans-Euphrates.
>
> Ezra 4:12–14, 16

The threat is thoroughly fabricated. But the propaganda campaign succeeds, at least temporarily, and the king orders the construction to stop.

Five hundred years go by and Yeshua is born. Obsessed with a lie that the child will lead a revolution and usurp his royal crown, a Roman king executes every Jewish boy in the region of Messiah's birth (see Matthew 2:13–18). Decades later, another Roman ruler sentences Yeshua to death, based again on more lies (see Matthew 26:59–61; Luke 23:2).

What does the devil do to oppose God's purposes? Throughout the Bible a pattern emerges. Satan's timeless weapon of choice is deceit. The father of lies, *lies*. And his goal is murder.

Modern Myths

Fast-forward with me to the Nazi Holocaust, where lie upon lie formed the foundation for the most brutal genocide campaign the world has known. At the beginning of his rise to power, Hitler publicly noted that people fall victim more easily to a big lie, repeated often, than to a little one.[19] Accordingly, he instituted a widespread propaganda campaign—built on lies most of us would regard as outrageous—to set the stage for his future, Jew-free regime. I have listed some of these notorious "Big Lies" below, along with contemporary, Islamist variations on the theme. You may wonder how any thinking person could have believed them. I assure you that even today, many millions still do.

Each of these preposterous myths—and countless more—circulates widely through the Internet, government institutions, social and mainstream media, stores, schools and everyday society in the Palestinian, Arab and Islamist world:[m]

- Jews regularly murder non-Jews to use their blood in religious ceremonies and for baking unleavened Passover bread.[n]

- Jews are a biologically inferior people—part pig and ape—with evil genes that will destroy the human race if they are not destroyed first.

- Jews harbor a pernicious plot to subvert and take over the world, as revealed in their book *The Protocols of the Elders of Zion.* (This egregiously anti-Semitic book, purportedly written by world Zionist leaders, was proved in court to have been forged by the Russian army in the 1800s.[o] Yet the sordid tale remains a bestseller in the Arab world. It was formally presented to the UN in 2003 by an Egyptian diplomat as "historic truth."[p])

- Jews caused the Black Plague of the 1300s and, more recently, AIDS.[q] Today, Israel infects (or steals or withholds) Palestinian water[r] and will infect the whole world with dreadful disease if she is not eradicated first.

- Jews are Satan's agents on earth. That is why they killed Christ, and that is why God (or Allah) wants them killed now.

- Jews control the global economy and are at fault for every nation's money problems or economic collapse.

- Israel causes earthquakes, tsunamis, volcanoes and meteorological storms to destroy other nations.

- Jews control the media, feeding the world false information to try to dispute all of the above "facts."

Hitler's minister of propaganda, Josef Goebbels, summarized: "All Jews, by virtue of their birth and race, are part of an international conspiracy against us. . . . They started this war. . . . The treatment they receive from us is hardly unjust. They have deserved it all."[20] Goebbels' inverted logic echoes in much of the Islamist world today, in which Israel is held responsible for every assault she is forced to endure, simply because she exists. As King Solomon said, there is nothing new under the sun. What has been done to curse God's people through lies and false reports is being done again.

As a result, Israel finds herself having to fight a war on at least three different fronts.[5] In addition to the traditional military front, a public relations war of words wages against her in the media. Israel's third precarious front, known as lawfare (described later in this chapter), now exists in the sphere of international law and multinational governing bodies.

Concluding that anti-Israel "irrationality and hysteria" rules over "truth and reason" in the realms of media and lawfare, Melanie Phillips cautions us all of the consequences:

What is unique about the treatment of Israel is that a conflict subjected to an unprecedented level of scrutiny should be presented in such a way as to drive out truth and rationality. History

is turned on its head; facts and falsehoods, victims and victim-
izers are reversed; logic is suspended and a fictional narrative is
now widely accepted as incontrovertible truth. . . . Israel sits at
the epicenter of the West's repudiation of reason.[21]

Phillips discerns that today's war against Israel is a war against
truth.

Inventing and Reinventing News

A sad reality is that in reporting on the Arab/Palestinian–Israeli
conflict, facts and events may be egregiously misrepresented and
truth disregarded altogether. Investigations reveal that some
reporters and photographers regularly stage "news" events to
shoot. Scripted scenes are acted out, depicting fictitious Israeli
oppression, then released internationally as formal or informal
reporting of facts.[1] These highly distorted images, beamed elec-
tronically worldwide, aim to plant one picture in the global con-
science: a viciously oppressive, Goliath-like Israeli pitted against
brave, little Palestinian David. If, as the adage goes, one picture
is worth a thousand words, it can also spread a thousand lies.

During Israel's military operation in Jenin, for example, the
world winced at photos of hapless and heartbroken Palestinian women wailing amid rubble that used to be called home.
The untold back story was that "home" had been serving as a
terrorist hideout or munitions plant for the murder of Jews—
despite Israel's repeated warnings to quit. In 2008, Palestinians
in Gaza released presumed photographic evidence that Israel
was inhumanely withholding electricity from them. Pictures
of suffering innocents huddled in the dark were sent and seen
around the world. One photo of a roomful of "innocents,"
however, betrayed a narrow streak of sunlight beaming through

curtains that were not completely closed. The particular photo pictured Hamas leaders meeting in what was actually broad daylight, attempting to stage a nighttime scene. It turned out they had engineered the blackout themselves to gain sympathy and international support in their fight against Israel.[u]

Dishonest depictions of Israel became so widespread that in 2011, an Italian photojournalist produced an exposé of it. He showed how some photographers cooperate with Palestinians to create news events by taking images of nonexistent conflict. He personally shot pictures of his colleagues photographing Palestinians who were posing in fighting positions for the other photographers who needed scenes they could sell.[v] Once on the market, the pictures could be published with captions condemning Israel for any array of alleged abuses. The exposé cautions that today's media spins and sells to the world a narrative of the Palestinian-Israeli conflict that is biased and often unsubstantiated.

The falsehoods are not limited to mainstream media outlets. Social networks and blogs are flooded with fake photos generating hate for Israel and the Jews.[w] Consider one of dozens that went viral in 2012. In it a bloodstained, limp-bodied toddler was clutched in the arms of her grief-stricken dad. The caption read, "Little Girl in Gaza Is Casualty of Israeli Airstrikes." In response to the heart-wrenching picture, hundreds of comments were posted online, cursing the Jewish state. Weeks later, investigators found the photo was actually several years old, and the girl had been killed in a car accident having nothing to do with Israeli airstrikes.[x]

Later that year, during Operation Pillar of Cloud/Defense in Gaza, an international audience was treated to video footage of Gazans decrying Israeli brutality, mourning over a corpse and dragging it away from the site of an apparent missile attack. Seconds later they watched the corpse stand up, brush himself off and walk away with his comrades.[y] When Palestinians became aware of the gaffe, the video came down but a panoply of photos went up. Some of them, attempting to evidence excessive Israeli force, were later proved to have been shot years earlier—some inside Israel and actually depicting *Jews* injured in *Palestinian* terror attacks.[z]

Sadly, you and I live in an information-saturated Digital Age in which truth is an increasingly rare commodity. What may be sadder is that many people do not seem to care. Famed investigative journalists of the twentieth century Bob Woodward and Carl Bernstein comment on the reality: "We had a readership that was much more open to real fact than today. Today there is a huge audience only looking for information to confirm their already held political, cultural and religious prejudices, beliefs and ideologies."[22]

Lawfare

As a result of the world's diminished value on truth, 21st-century Palestinian and other anti-Israel leaders have made extensive use of what is called lawfare. Lawfare is warfare not by customary military means, but by manipulating or changing the laws of traditional Western civilization for otherwise unobtainable political goals. As such, it is an abuse of the law for disingenuous means.[23] Because it has little regard or respect for the law it employs, lawfare can gradually give way to lawlessness. Real-life examples of lawfare include claims filed according to an Al-Qaeda manual that instructs captured militants to file false charges of torture in order to portray themselves as victims; and hate speech lawsuits based on speaking peaceably but publicly about fundamentalist Islam and terror funding.[24]

In practical effect, lawfare usually seeks to take advantage of Judeo-Christian–based democracy-style laws to achieve Islamist or extreme secularist goals. It has been associated with the spread of universal jurisdiction, in which a nation or international organization may prosecute individuals or leaders of any other nation for committing crimes against humanity.[25] Because Israel is on the front lines in the battle against Islamism, her right to exist is now being assailed through lawfare and universal jurisdiction at precedent-setting levels.

Anti-Israel Lawfare at the UN

A major victory (or defeat, depending on your view) for the use of lawfare occurred when the UN upgraded Palestinians' status to that of nonmember observer state in 2012. The upgrade was approved at the expense of violating several preexisting international agreements. Most critically, the upgrade breached a major provision of the Oslo Accords, the formal peace agreement signed in 1993 between Israel and the PA. In the agreement, both parties pledged not to take any actions apart from direct negotiations with each other to establish a Palestinian state. Sidestepping direct negotiations could void the Accords and cause the peace process to self-destruct.[aa]

By the UN's precedent-setting upgrade of Palestine,[bb] its people have arguably gained standing to move forward until they get a sovereign state, jumping through loopholes in international law.[cc] In the process, they may seek—as other nations do—to file charges against Israel in the International Criminal Court at The Hague.[dd] They may submit complaints to the General Assembly, Security Council and other UN agencies, where for decades they have held "automatic majorities" (defined momentarily).

The UN General Assembly that approved the Palestinian status upgrade was not necessarily interested in respecting the preexisting rule of law. The UN is heavily influenced by *shari'a*-oriented Arab and Islamic states. The Arab League alone boasts a membership of 23 nations, counting Palestine. They are connected closely to the Organization of Islamic Cooperation, presently comprised of 56 states.[26] Consistently aligned with them are several dozen other countries highly dependent on oil from the Middle East. This unified bloc is typically unconcerned with traditional Western values of freedom and moral justice. Collectively, it has long constituted an automatic majority against Israel on issues relevant to the Jewish state.[cc]

As far back as 2002, former US ambassador to the United Nations Jeane Kirkpatrick spoke of her "very deep shock" over extreme anti-Semitism pervading the UN. Concerned about the potential for another Holocaust worse than the first, Kirkpatrick described the world's treatment of Israel as "nearly unbelievably insulting and outrageous."[27] She pointed out that in the history of the UN and its agencies, more than one thousand resolutions condemned Israel—but not one resolution had ever passed specifically condemning Arab terror against the Jewish state. Successive American ambassadors to the UN have made similar observations.[28] Today Israel stands as the only member state of the UN repeatedly—and illegally—threatened with genocide by another member state (Iran).

Of the United Nations and its automatic majority, former Israeli diplomat Abba Eban said, "If [an Arab country] introduced a resolution declaring that the earth was flat and that Israel had flattened it, it would pass."[29] Mr. Eban did not exaggerate.

Please pray for Israel as she is forced every day to defend herself from distortions and lies in the realms of media and lawfare. Pray also for Palestinians who need to know truth and deserve a better life. God is grieved for those suffering on both sides of the conflict, and we should be, too. At the same time, He knows the story ends well. As "the nations conspire and the peoples plot in vain," as "the kings of the earth rise up and the rulers band together against [Him] . . . the One enthroned in heaven laughs" (Psalm 2:1–2, 4). If we do not conform to the pattern of this world, we will be optimistic, too. In the next chapter we see how, concerning the Arab/Palestinian–Israel conflict, we can avoid conforming to the world by the renewing of our minds.

Israeli Statehood
and the Arab/Palestinian Plight

Be transformed by the renewing of your mind.

Romans 12:2

A true story opens on May 14, 1948, as the Jewish people prepare to declare a state. The air is electric. After two thousand years of exile, the sons and daughters of Jacob have come home. High-pitched excitement circles the globe.

That morning, Israel's founding father and first prime minister, David Ben-Gurion, pores over maps showing the array of Arab armies poised to attack. The Jews are outnumbered 100 to 1.[1] "I feel like a mourner at a wedding," he writes in his diary.[2]

In a few hours Ben-Gurion will deliver Israel's Declaration of Independence. He scribbles down notes for his speech on the only writing material at hand—sheets of toilet paper.[a]

At exactly 4:00 p.m., he steps to the podium in an overcrowded hall in Tel Aviv, before a hushed audience. This is the moment for which millions of Jews have lived and died. As Ben-Gurion reads the Israeli Declaration of Independence, those present cling to his every word. He speaks of Bible history and the Jews' undying hope to return to their ancestral home. Then with prophetic clarity Ben-Gurion decrees: "By virtue of the natural and historic right of the Jewish people . . . we hereby proclaim the establishment of the Jewish state in Palestine, to be called the State of Israel . . . for the fulfillment of the dream of generations—the redemption of Israel."

At once, cheers and tears resound. Golda Meir, who would later serve as prime minister, cannot stop crying. Her sobs, she explains, are for the many who should have been there, but are no more.[3] According to the nation's chief rabbi, "The dawn of redemption has broken."[4]

Euphoria erupts in Jerusalem and Tel Aviv, where traffic stops as streets swell with singing and dancing. But the party is soon interrupted. Sirens wail to warn of Egyptian bombers overhead. Joining them are the armies of Syria, Jordan, Lebanon and Iraq, together with militants from throughout the Arab world. All have a common goal: to annihilate the Jewish state in Allah's name.[5] The War of Independence has begun. *Happy birthday, Israel.*

Since 1948, tomes have been written on the history of Israel's restoration, and the Islamist/Arab/Palestinian resistance against it. Time and space permit us to summarize only basic facts. (For more detail, please refer to the notes at www.whystillcare aboutisrael.com.) I think you will discover a surprising perspective on today's conflict emerges when you consider the context from which it arose. You will see that Israel is not so much in a fight for land as for her life—and that changes everything.

Palestinian History: The Back Story

In the first century AD, Israel was renamed Palestine by the Romans who conquered her. This was done in derisive remembrance of the Jews' former—and extinct—enemy, the Philistines. The Philistines had by then already died out, so despite the similarity in name, they are not related to the Palestinians of today.[b] Collectively, Palestinians have no traceable ancient tie to the land of Israel and never identified as a self-governing people group. Like other Arabs in the Middle East, most of their ancestors dwelt as scattered family tribes on lands they often did not personally own. Generally, they coexisted alongside Jews who had, in small numbers, lived in Palestine since biblical times on inherited or legally purchased land.[6] But periodically, Islamic terror would erupt[7] and *jihadi* expropriation of Jewish real estate took place.[8]

From the 1500s up until World War I, the entire Middle East was ruled by the Ottoman Turkish Empire, a type of Muslim caliphate. No autonomous Arab state was on the map; most Arabs belonged to nomadic tribes wandering all over the Middle East.[c] At the same time, hundreds of thousands of Jews also lived in the region under Ottoman rule. According to a census taken in 1882, approximately 25,000 of them lived in Palestine, along with 260,000 Arabs.[9] As tourists and pilgrims testified, Palestine was by then mostly desolate and depopulated,[10] a far cry from the land of milk and honey it had once been for millions of Jews.

By the early 1900s, Palestinian Arab identity was said to be extremely mixed.[11] Persons counted as indigenous Palestinian Arabs included ethnic Balkans, Greeks, Syrians, Latins, Turks, Armenians, Italians, Persians, Kurds, Germans, Afghans, Circassians, Bosnians, Sudanese, Samaritans, Algerians, Tartars and others.[12] An official British document published in 1920 stated the majority of people living in Palestine were not indigenous Arabs but only Arabic-speaking.[13]

When Zionist pioneers began arriving in the early twentieth century, the number of Arabs immigrating to Palestine also sharply increased. With Jews from the West came new job opportunities, vastly improved medical care and a higher standard of living, all of which attracted their tribal neighbors.[14] Once inside Israel, most Arab immigrants continued living as bedouin, built simple villages or served for decades as tenants on farmlands owned by others. Later, countless more poured in from surrounding countries—not to carry on normal lives but to fight the formation of a Jewish state.[15] Together with the small indigenous Arab population, these individuals and their descendants comprise the Palestinian people of today.

Palestinians are not, as some have rather unkindly said, "an invented people." They are flesh-and-blood human beings created in God's image, with inherent dignity and worth. Though most of their ancestors came from across the Middle East and even beyond, they did form an identifiable collective by the mid–twentieth century. Palestinians are not the first people group formed by the force of history. They are, however, the only modern group whose creation and self-definition, as one Palestinian journalist writes,[16] rests largely on the planned elimination of another, namely Israel—or as they prefer to call her, "the Zionist entity."

Zionism and the Reestablishment of a Jewish State

Zionism is defined, in a broad secular sense, as the national liberation movement of the Jewish people. The Zionist movement contends that the Jewish nation, like every other indigenous people, is entitled to live autonomously in its ancestral home-land. As such, Zionism cannot be viewed as something separate from the Jewish people and nation-state. To be anti-Zionist is akin to being anti-Israel and, to a degree, anti-Jewish.

Zionism is not and has never been entirely secular; a strong religious element has always underlain it.[d] Officially launched in 1896, modern-day Zionism involves the return of the Jewish people to their God-given ancestral homeland.[e] The name of the movement derives from the Bible, where *Zion* is used over 150 times. "You will arise and have compassion on Zion; for it is time to show favor to her; the appointed time has come. . . . For the LORD will rebuild Zion and appear in his glory" (Psalm 102:13, 16). Zionism precipitates His Kingdom glory.

In rebuilding Zion, Sovereign God has worked through nations and human beings. The modern story starts with World War I, when the Ottoman Turks aligned with Axis nations, and collectively they lost the war. As a result, the Allies dismantled the Ottoman Empire and created Syria, Lebanon, Iran and Iraq for the Arabs and Persians to inhabit.[f] In an international agreement known as the San Remo Resolution of 1920, they set Palestine aside for the Jews.[g] Great Britain was made responsible for implementing the resolution by unanimous vote of the League of Nations, predecessor organization to the UN. The League of Nations directive, called the Mandate for Palestine, reserved explicitly for the Jews not just present-day Israel, but all of Judea, Samaria, Gaza and Jordan.[17]

The Mandate for Palestine was scarcely issued when Palestinian Arabs began rioting and conducting terror operations in protest of it. The deadly terror had nothing to do with occupation, settlements or allegedly disproportionate military force. From the beginning, Islamic terror had everything to do with opposing the existence of a Jewish state.

In an effort to appease Palestinian Arabs—and although international law forbade such an action[h]—Great Britain unilaterally took back 78 percent of the land allotted to the Jews. She then gave it to Palestinian Arabs—*specifically to create a Palestinian state*. Today that state is known as Jordan. Palestinian Arabs were expected to move to Jordan, and any Jews living in Jordan would relocate to the 22 percent of land remaining from the San Remo and Mandatory allotments. A smaller section of land in the Golan Heights, originally designated for the Jews, was also given away by Britain to Syria. But appeasement did not work—which we would do well to remember. Those who forget history, it is said, are doomed to repeat it. The acts we engage in for appeasement today, Britain's Winston Churchill presciently forewarned, we will have to remedy at far greater cost and remorse tomorrow.[18]

Not surprisingly, after Jordan was established, Palestinian rioting and terror killings of Jews persisted.[i] An exasperated Great Britain finally turned the political foray over to the UN. (When the League of Nations failed to prevent World War II, the UN was formed to replace it.) The UN's charter required that it adopt all laws and resolutions passed by the League of Nations. So when it inherited the Mandate for Palestine, the UN became responsible for creating a Jewish state.

As you can see, plans for the reestablishment of Israel were underway well before the onset of World War II. Israel's right to exist by international law is not fundamentally based on the Nazi Holocaust, as compelling a cause as that is from a humanitarian point of view. Certainly, the Holocaust demonstrated the need for a Jewish state to protect Jewish lives. But if we believe Israel's right to exist is rooted in a compassionate response to the Holocaust, when that compassion wears off, so will our belief that Israel has a right to exist. Israel's fundamental right to exist under international law rests on the recognition of the Jews' ancestral, sovereign control over identifiable land that, since their forced removal from it, remained sparsely occupied and mostly undeveloped.

Notwithstanding Israel's historical and legal right to the land, and dismissing international commitments to the Jews, the UN continued with a policy of Arab appeasement. In 1947, it partitioned the remaining 22 percent of the original Mandate for a Jewish homeland into two proposed states: one for Jews and yet another, second state for Palestinian Arabs. The Partition Plan, also called UN Resolution 181, recognized the Jews' right to sovereign control over a sliver of space amounting to a mere 10 percent of the original British Mandate. It offered the Arabs who lived within Mandate territory a state—in addition to Jordan—consisting of Judea, Samaria and Gaza.

Zionist pioneers felt it best to accept the UN's offer. Ten percent of the Promised Land after nearly two thousand years was better than zero. Moreover, they had no political clout or practical means with which to resist whatever the world community told them to do. The Arabs, however, thoroughly rejected the Partition Plan, which legally voided the offer to them. Ninety percent of the land, they insisted, was not enough. They wanted it *all*—an empire spanning the entire Middle East, leaving no place on earth for the Jews. They mobilized for a war against Israel they felt certain they would win. The world wondered, much as it does today, *Will Israel survive?*

Israel's Rebirth—Into War

Israel did not want the War of Independence to occur and tried extremely hard to prevent it.[19] When her every effort toward peace was rebuffed, Ben-Gurion extended a final appeal to the Arabs in his Declaration of Independence speech:

> We yet call upon the Arab inhabitants of the State of Israel to preserve the ways of peace and play their part in the development of the State, on the basis of full and equal citizenship and due representation in all its bodies and institutions. . . . We extend our hand in peace and neighborliness to all the neighboring states and their peoples, and invite them to cooperate with the independent Jewish nation for the common good of all.[20]

The same invitation had been offered daily for weeks.[i] British Mandate authorities who were stationed on the ground testified: "Every effort is being made by the Jews to persuade the Arab populace to stay and carry on with their normal lives . . . and to be assured that their lives and interests will be safe."[21] Most, however, chose to flee, creating a local refugee crisis that would upend history. A Palestinian priest who watched the events unfold stated, "[The Arabs] fled in spite of the fact the Jewish authorities guaranteed their safety and rights as citizens of Israel."[22]

Arab-Nazi Alliance

Why did so many Palestinians run from their homes and livelihoods? An overlooked historical fact is perhaps one of the most pivotal and still fuels the conflict today. An unshakeable Islamic/Arab–Nazi alliance predated World War II, and as a result of it, many Arabs vehemently despised and feared the Jews.

Early in his career, Hitler formed a pact with Jerusalem's grand mufti, Haj Amin al-Husseini. The notoriously anti-Semitic mufti held religious and political sway over Muslims throughout

Palestine and the larger Middle East. He and Hitler schemed together to annihilate the Jewish people worldwide. The fuehrer would focus on Europe and the extraordinarily influential mufti would target Palestine's growing Jewish population.[23]

Building on fundamental Islam's anti-Jewish ideology, Husseini mobilized an Arab militia, which served as a formal Nazi brigade. Supplied with German weaponry, the brigade murdered Palestinian Jews in acts of heinous terror throughout World War II.[24] To keep the violence going, Husseini saturated the Middle East with lies about the Zionists via propaganda broadcasts radioed in from Berlin.[k] So after the Holocaust ended in Europe, he and other Arab leaders hoped to immediately start another.

Creating a Refugee Crisis

When, to their profound dismay, Israel declared statehood, Palestinian Arabs panicked. An estimated 600,000 to 700,000 fled.[25] [l] Approximately 150,000 to 160,000 chose to remain inside the Jewish state.[26] Today, they and their descendants enjoy full democratic rights of Israeli citizenship, including a standard of living much higher than that of their brethren anywhere else in North Africa or the Middle East.

Under the influence of Muslim/Nazi anti-Semitism, the majority of Arabs who left their homes did so because their leaders told them to. Evacuations were ordered to make way for approaching armies that would quickly destroy the Jewish state.[m] Arab leaders boasted that Israel would be "driven into the [Mediterranean] sea" within a few days. Accordingly, the Higher Arab Executive gave Palestinians a choice: Quit and run, or accept Jewish protection and be regarded as a renegade in the Arab world that would imminently take over. The Arab

National Committee in Jerusalem ordered its constituency out of their homes, adding, "Any opposition to this order . . . is an obstacle to the holy war . . . and will hamper the operations of the fighters in these districts."[27]

The Arab Legion and Arab Liberation Army directed wholesale civilian flight from entire villages. Leaders like Iraqi prime minister Nuri Said warned, "We will smash the country with our guns and obliterate every place the Jews seek shelter. The Arabs should conduct their wives and children to safe areas until the fighting has died down."[28] To ensure compliance, some leaders planted rumors of Israeli terror operations and nonexistent atrocities.[29][n] Shortly after the war—which to their deep humiliation they did not win—Arab leaders freely admitted to having created the refugee crisis.[o] Mahmoud Abbas,[p] who would later serve as president of the PA, confessed:

> The Arab armies entered Palestine to protect the Palestinians from the Zionist tyranny, but instead they abandoned them, forced them to emigrate and leave their homeland, and threw them into prisons similar to the ghettos in which the Jews used to live.[30]

Palestinian Injustice

A sad reality is that the War of Independence was not fought without collateral damage to both Palestinian and Jewish civilians. For the sake of perspective, no war can be fought without collateral damage—and in this instance, there would not have been a war if the Arabs had not insisted on starting one. Nevertheless, some Arab families and villages were wrongly expelled or inexcusably overrun by Jewish soldiers.[q] In at least one such raid at Deir Yassin, genuinely innocent victims were massacred.[31] Upon learning of the sordid event, Israel denounced it and sought to compensate the victims.[r]

The Palestinian narrative claims that since 1948, Israel has stolen or destroyed over four hundred Arab villages. This figure, based on a recently created map of dubious veracity, cannot be objectively verified. Israeli historians point out that many Arab families who were forced to leave their homes did not actually own the lands or homes they left. Some were long-term renters—for generations—of lands sold legally, but without their knowledge, to the Jews.[s] Moreover—and without diminishing the loss some Arabs have suffered—a large Palestinian state (Jordan) existed just across the border. Those who might be displaced were expected to seek refuge there, just as 800,000 Jewish refugees were forced to leave their homes and wealth behind and relocate to Israel.[t] (More on this momentarily.)

Lacking objective documentation of their plight, Palestinians have amassed global sympathies through a narrative that inverts history.[u] Many share tragic personal tales—that prove either unverifiable or outrageously embellished.[v] Their stories tend either to romanticize Arab tribal-village life or misrepresent it as a bustling society.[w] Sadly, some of these accounts are presented by Christians as honest-to-God facts. Their pitiable tales tug at the heartstrings of any hearer. *It's their personal story*, we reason. *How can it not be true—and how can we not be deeply moved?* Emotions are stirred, then inflamed—against Israel. Gradually, hearts are hardened against the Jewish people and what God is doing with them today.

Jesus loves and died for the Palestinian people: He does not want us to disparage them. We must compassionately acknowledge their suffering and seek a right response to it. But even genuine suffering must be viewed in context to rightly ascertain truth and transform realities justly.

Palestinian—and Jewish—Refugees

Palestinians were not the only refugees to result from the War of Independence. According to official UN figures, over 800,000 Jewish refugees were forced to flee homes and lands in North Africa and the Middle East where they had lived for generations.[32] Unlike some Palestinians, they were in no sense "voluntary refugees." Jews were expelled, stripped of citizenship or both in retaliation for Israel's declaration of statehood. Arab nations have persistently refused to compensate these refugees for their confiscated properties, valued today at billions of dollars.[33]

Meanwhile, during the War of Independence, unincorporated areas proposed by the Partition Plan for a second Palestinian Arab state were illegally annexed and occupied—*not* by Israel but by Jordan and Egypt. Jordan seized Judea and Samaria, including East Jerusalem, while Egypt staked claim to Gaza. Now, the Arabs' publicly stated goal for the war had been to liberate Palestine. But neither Jordan nor Egypt ever gave the territories they annexed back to the Palestinians to liberate them. Instead, the latter were compelled—by their own brethren—to stay put indefinitely in refugee camp limbo.[x] *Why?* you may ask. They would not talk about it; let me explain.

Israel began offering, as early as 1949, to negotiate for the refugees' return—and full repatriation—back into the Jewish state. But no Arab leader was willing to negotiate with the Jews. Transacting with Israel, they said, would involve an implicit recognition of her existence. This they had vowed never to do.[34] Further, by refusing either to negotiate for the refugees' return or to absorb them themselves, they could continue the war against Israel in the political realm.[y] This they had vowed never to *cease* doing.

In 1949 the UN established a relief fund (United Nations Relief and Works Agency or UNRWA) to provide for the refugees' basic needs. Soon thereafter, UNRWA acceded to Arab demands to grant refugee status—for the first time in history—not only to those who fled but to their descendants, *indefinitely*. This redefinition of "refugee" guaranteed the Palestinian population would dramatically increase over time.[35] By 2013, of an estimated Palestinian population of five million, only 30,000—or approximately half of 1 percent—actually ever left a home in Israel.[36] Meanwhile, many billions of dollars have been given to Palestinians by Israel and other nations to provide for their "basic needs."[z] At this writing, UNRWA remains the largest employer in the West Bank, with thousands of Palestinians on its payroll and, according to some, padding the personal fortunes of Palestinian leaders.[37]

Former UNRWA director Ralph Galloway concluded early on:

> The Arab States do not want to solve the refugee problem. They want to keep it as an open sore . . . *as a weapon against Israel*. Arab leaders don't give a damn whether the refugees live or die.[38]

Israeli Prime Minister Benjamin Netanyahu similarly noted:

> The consistent refusal of Arab leaders to solve this problem is particularly tragic because it would have been so easy to do. . . . That the fifty million Arabs in 1948 could not absorb 650,000 Arab refugees—and have not finished the job even after half a century, and even after the fantastic multiplication of their oil wealth—is an indication of [how] the Arabs have manipulated the refugee issue to create reasons for world censure of Israel.[39]

Of the situation an Arab American journalist comments:

> What are the real roots of this [Palestinian-Israeli] conflict? . . . That Palestinians want a homeland and Muslims want control over sites they consider holy? . . . These two demands are nothing more than strategic deceptions, propaganda ploys. They are nothing more than phony excuses and rationalizations for the

terrorism and murdering of Jews. The real goal of those making these demands is the destruction of the State of Israel.[40]

Palestinian Statehood and the Phased Plan

In 1964, Yasser Arafat assumed leadership of the Palestine Liberation Organization (PLO), a terror group with the stated purpose to liberate all of Palestine. It was not, however, created to liberate the West Bank and Gaza; this was never the "Palestine" to which it referred. Recall that in 1964, Gaza still belonged to Egypt and the West Bank was governed by Jordan. Since 1964 the Palestinian agenda has been to liberate a Palestine that includes, by definition, every square inch of land between the Mediterranean Sea and the Jordan River—that is, all of Israel.[41] [aa]

Shortly after the PLO published its goals, Israel fought for her life in the Six Day War of 1967. To the world's surprise, she defensively acquired Gaza from Egypt and the West Bank, including East Jerusalem, from Jordan. Then, in 1973, Egypt and Syria launched another unprovoked attack, the Yom Kippur War. Again Israel prevailed. As a result of these mounting Arab defeats, the PLO announced its "Phased Plan" the following year. *The Phased Plan has never been revoked and still represents Islamist/Arab/Palestinian strategy today.*

The Phased Plan refers to the slightly revised goal of liberating Palestine not all at once, but in stages. Phase One is the establishment of an independent, combatant national authority consisting of Gaza and the West Bank. This was to a large degree accomplished by developing the PLO into the PA and by Israel's withdrawal from Gaza. Phase Two is the reconfiguration of Gaza and the West Bank into launching pads for provoking an all-out regional war, in which Israel is wiped off the map.[42]

This is to be accomplished by military operations, lawfare diplomacy, cyberattack or any combination thereof.

On the Occupation

When Israel pushed back her attackers in the Six Day War and gained Gaza and the West Bank, she acquired land that had been originally allotted to her in 1920. By 1967, however, the areas were inhabited by over a million Jew-hating Palestinians and angry insurgents.[43] Israel had no desire to "rule over" them.[44]

The Six Day War ended with UN Security Council Resolution 242, a truce that purposefully did not define borders. Resolution 242 authorized Israel to remain in possession of newly acquired territories until peace was established and final borders secured. It was meticulously and explicitly worded so that Israel would not be forced to withdraw from *all* the newly acquired territories, back to the boundary lines from which she had just been attacked.[45] Those boundaries, the 1949 armistice lines ending the War of Independence, were never meant to be permanent. Nor were they intended to substitute for negotiations to determine final borders. In less than twenty years, the lines had proved indefensible,[46 bb] leaving the middle and most populous section of the country only nine miles wide. With Palestinians having shown themselves unwilling or unable to make peace, some Israeli leaders have termed the 1949 lines "Auschwitz Borders," referring to a notorious Nazi death camp. Nevertheless, by 2011 the international community would euphemistically call them "pre-1967 borders" and urge Israel to retreat to them—with no enforceable guarantee of peace in return.

After the Six Day War, Egypt and Jordan eventually signed peace treaties with Israel. These nations refused, however, to take back either Gaza or the West Bank. Reclaiming these territories would have betrayed the pan-Arab plan, notoriously reaffirmed after the war,[47] to leave in place a local population to help destroy Israel. As a result, Gaza and the West Bank remained in a state of perpetual war with Israel, ruled by the increasingly militant PLO. That being the case, Israel was authorized by international law to administratively govern the territories, with quasi-military powers of enforcement, until peace could be achieved. The administration of law and order in a hostile, enemy population in such circumstances is called an occupation.

Some Israelis say, however, that they have not occupied any of these areas because the land rightfully belongs to them under customary international law. Customary international law refers to the body of international law and policy that Western nations have traditionally practiced and followed.

In either case, Israel's quasi-military administration known as the "occupation" is not illegal. The term "illegal occupation" is a pejorative mischaracterization, intended to conjure up images of oppression and abuse. Admittedly, Israel has not always acted fairly or justly during the difficult course of governing people dedicated to her demise. But to brand her lawful jurisdiction "illegal" or "oppressive" obscures the reality that if Palestinians sincerely accepted Israel's right to exist as a Jewish state, the war and the occupation would be history. Allow me to explain.

Peace Negotiations

In 1993, the PLO morphed into the Palestinian Authority under an agreement called the Oslo Accords. At that time Palestinians gained the right to negotiate peace with Israel for themselves.[cc] Sadly, rather than pursue a peaceful coexistence alongside Israel, history records how they proliferated terror instead. Nevertheless, in 2000, Israel offered the Palestinians full sovereignty over 95 percent of the disputed territories, including East Jerusalem, with secured geographic contiguity. There was virtually nothing left for the Jews to give away. But the Palestinians said no. Offering no counterproposal to the offer, they literally walked out on negotiations[48] and immediately launched a violent *intifada* ("uprising") of deadly terror lasting several years.[dd] US Middle East envoy Dennis Ross, who was present, said the Palestinians' main objection was the insertion of one critical clause in the agreement: "This is the end of the conflict."[49] [ee] The Palestinians could not end the conflict with anything less than ending Israel.[ff]

Yasser Arafat, who signed the Oslo Accords and walked out on the offer of a sovereign state, said (in Arabic): "I do not consider the [Oslo] agreement any more than the agreement which was signed by our prophet Muhammad and the Qurayish."[50] Arafat referred to an agreement that established the right, called *hudna*, for Muslims to fake peace when they are weak so they can wait for better timing to fight when they are strong.[gg] Thus an Arab saying goes like this: "When your enemy is strong, kiss his hand and pray that it will be broken one day."[51]

Faisal Husseini, a moderate Palestinian leader, compared the whole peace process to a proverbial "Trojan horse."[52] From the Arab perspective, it had been designed to fool Israel into letting the Palestinians arm themselves in order to destroy it. Said Husseini, "If you are asking me as a pan-Arab nationalist what are the Palestinian borders according to the higher strategy, I will immediately reply, from the [Jordan] river to the [Mediterranean] sea."[53]

Perhaps that would explain why, in 2008, when Israel offered Palestinians 93 percent of the territory they desired—including 98 percent of the West Bank—they again said no.[54] And why, in 2009, PA leaders said they would resume negotiations on the precondition that Israel stop all settlement construction—but still refused to talk when Israel complied with their demand. After that, with one perceived betrayal following another, Israelis were not so willing to believe Palestinians were sincere about peace.[hh]

In 2011, Israeli Prime Minister Netanyahu tried to restart peace talks and pleaded at the UN with PA President Abbas to meet face-to-face, without preconditions. Abbas refused, demanding that Israel first agree to an expanded list of preconditions.[ii] Under the Oslo Accords and other agreements, however, these preconditions were in fact supposed to be the subject of the negotiations. By agreeing to all the preconditions first, there would be very little left to negotiate. So Netanyahu replied with one precondition of his own. He demanded that Palestinians recognize Israel's right to exist as a Jewish state. If the PA would agree to the one precondition, Israel would agree to their whole list of them. But the Palestinians refused.[jj]

In 2012, Palestinians sidestepped negotiations, and thus breached the Oslo Accords, by seeking to forge a path for statehood in the UN. At the same time, they launched a war from Gaza and a terror wave in the West Bank. In 2013, Israeli Defense Minister Moshe Ya'alon commented on the situation:

> This is our history: Every time a proposal was raised to partition the land, the other side started a war. Every time we expressed willingness to give up territory, terror rose to new heights.[55]

Palestinians often say they resort to terror because Israeli proposals do not offer them a universal "right of return." Israelis reply this is because Palestinians are unwilling to limit the "right" to refugees who personally left Israel; they insist on extending it to every Palestinian in Gaza, the West Bank or anywhere else in the world. Therefore, when Israel has expressed willingness to give them land, Palestinians have sometimes agreed to recognize a country named Israel—but never as a *Jewish* state.[kk] The difference is critical. If Palestinians acknowledge Israel's right to exist as a Jewish state, they relinquish a strategy for turning it into a Palestinian/Islamist one by flooding it with millions of Arabs "returning" there.[ll] The right of return has remained, at this writing, uncompromisable—even though "homeland" is only a few miles away, and even though Palestinians would finally be getting a second sovereign state. From Israel's perspective, granting several million Muslims, many of whom are murderously militant, permission to immigrate and repopulate the country is tantamount to committing national suicide.

Israeli Settlements

In 2012, the PA began claiming that Israeli settlements were the main reason for the failure of the peace process. In fact, settlements represent only 1.6 percent of the disputed territories,[56] and 70 percent of settlers live in suburbs adjacent to major Israeli cities, not deep inside the West Bank.[57] Settlements do not disrupt Palestinian geographic contiguity. Despite public opinion to the contrary, settlements officially authorized by the Israeli government are not illegal under standards of customary international law.[mm] To be sure, settlements have been built on lands whose ownership is disputed. But in this dispute, Israel actually possesses the best claim to lawful—if not politically feasible or practical—ownership.[nn]

Recall that when Israel acquired the West Bank, no state or political entity held legal title to it. The last rightful owner of the land had been Israel, and historically, a Jewish presence has been maintained in Judea and Samaria for thousands of years. After World War I, Britain obtained the land and, through international agreements, returned recognized legal title to the Jews. When the UN offered the land to Palestinian Arabs in 1947, it wrongfully tried to take that title away. But the Palestinians rejected the offer, thereby rendering it null and void. Years later, Jordan illegally annexed the West Bank, but Israel defensively—and therefore, legally—acquired it from Jordan in the Six Day War. Under international law, the land has been technically "disputed" since 1967.[oo] In the future, international bodies may decide to rule on the legality of the territories and settlements built on them. Given the nations' collective stance toward Israel, it would likely take an act of God for a ruling in her favor to result. Which of course we cannot rule out.

Meanwhile, Israel's settlement policies are not necessarily perfect. Growing numbers of extremist settlers (and Palestinians) have turned violent, and the violence must be stopped. Some Israelis have tried to stake claim to biblical lands by erecting self-declared, unauthorized outposts. Usually these are dismantled by Israel within a short time. Jewish settlement construction has resulted in genuine hardship for some Bedouin and other Arabs, not always handled properly by Israeli courts.[pp] But these proportionately few unfair cases do not make all the settlements illegal. Nor do they provide a reason to suspend peace negotiations, if the parties sincerely desire peace.

Future Palestine

Repeatedly, Israel has demonstrated her willingness and even desire to accept Palestine as a new sovereign state. But as this book goes to print, Palestinians still insist (in Arabic) their state must stretch from the "river to the sea" and encompass all of Israel.[58] Surveys consistently reveal that a solid majority of Israelis would agree to live alongside a peaceful Palestinian state. (The operative word is *peaceful*.) But similar surveys consistently show the majority of Palestinians say they would never accept peaceful coexistence with a Jewish state.[qq] In 2011, 66 percent of West Bank Palestinians said that while they would accept a two-state solution as a "first step," they wanted to eventually replace Israel with a single Palestinian state.[59] In 2012, 88 percent of all Palestinians preferred a strategy of terror, or another *intifada*, over diplomacy to achieve it.[60] In 2013, similar polls yielded similar results.[61]

As you can see, the root of the Palestinian plight is well hidden beneath the surface tension exposed to public view. Deep-seated realities that will not change unless faced forthrightly are disguised and distorted. I do not minimize the genuine suffering, frustration and injustice that affects some Palestinians. But fundamentally, these conditions are not the *cause* of Arab and Islamist enmity toward Israel; they are the *result* of it. Moreover, injustices have repeatedly come about at the hands of Arab, not Israeli, leaders betraying their own people. That the world faults Israel—and threatens her survival—for a Palestinian plight that is Islamist/Arab generated, is highly unjust.

God wants transformational justice for both Israelis and Palestinians. But justice must be pursued and attained His way—according to righteousness based on truth—however His enemies try to obscure it. He wants us to "test and approve what [his] will is—his good, pleasing and perfect will" (Romans 12:2) as He restores His ancient covenant people. Toward them we must "not be arrogant, but tremble" (Romans 11:20).

The next chapter focuses on some of the questions we must ask along the way. Our answers could help shape the definition of social justice for years to come.

11

Israeli Injustice?

Be able to test and approve what God's will is—his good, pleasing and perfect will.

Romans 12:2

For three years I lived with my family in an apartment in the heart of West Jerusalem. It was a small place by American standards, but one that came with a panoramic cityscape. From my living room I looked daily upon the Israeli security wall, a sprawling, high and impenetrable concrete barrier. No doubt about it, the wall was ugly. The gray concrete was ugly. The reason it got built was ugly. The suffering resulting from it was ugly. I could not look at the thing without praying for both the Arabs and Jews on either side of it.

Israel built its security wall in response to the Palestinian Second Intifada of 2000–2005. At the time, suicide bombers could easily find their way from the West Bank into Jewish population centers, where they would murder and maim innocent civilians en masse. The bombings came to an abrupt halt, however, once the security wall was built.[a] The wall has saved countless lives, including those of potential *jihadi* martyrs. But it has led to many problems, too.

Precisely because the wall immediately quelled the terror, within a few years people around the world forgot why it had ever been built. No longer was it seen for what it is: a wall of protection and safeguard of life. Instead, the wall morphed into a flashpoint for accusations of oppression, racism and "apartheid" (described later in this chapter).

Admittedly, the wall has resulted in inconvenience and even hardship for some Palestinians. Time-consuming checkpoints—where, sporadically, inexcusable instances of humiliation or abuse have occurred—are associated with it. Sadly, innocent civilians sometimes suffer because of a minority of militant extremists whom their leaders are unable or unwilling to control.

Palestinians understandably want the wall torn down, the UN wants it down, social justice activists want it down and even a few left-wing Israelis want it down. Called at times a separation barrier, the wall separates two people groups that I believe will come together someday through the love, forgiveness and peace that only Jesus can offer them. Meanwhile, does justice require, as much of the world insists, that this life-saving structure be dismantled and the grisly killing of Israeli civilians resumed? Is that God's good, perfect and pleasing will?

Testing and approving God's will is an essential component of social justice from a Christian perspective. God's will flows from His righteousness, and biblical justice is founded on righteousness. The two concepts are so connected that the same words in both Hebrew and Greek for *justice* are often translated "righteousness."[1] Now, righteousness is that which is right—which means it must also be true. A simple working definition for *justice*, then, is the administration of righteousness according to truth.[2] As we have seen, to ascertain the truth about a controversial situation (like the security wall), its context must be considered. Only then can we seek to make an apparent wrong right. In other words, biblical social justice is *moral* justice.

From that perspective, we will address in this chapter some of the questions commonly asked about real-life Israeli injustice. But instead of focusing on alleged injustice to Palestinians, about which plenty of material already exists, we will ask if injustice might actually be suffered by *Israel*. To start, please revisit with me the issue of disproportionate military force.

Does Israel Use Disproportionate Military Force?

From 2005 through 2012, Israel endured approximately 12,000 terror attacks from Gaza in the form of rockets and other projectiles.[3] For the sake of perspective, based on population ratios, this would compare to roughly 480,000 violent acts of terror committed during the same period inside the United States. The raining down of rockets at the end of 2012 was such that life practically came to a standstill for half the country. Day upon day, offices, schools and businesses were forced to shut down in southern Israel. When the crisis could not be solved through diplomatic means, Israel assassinated the terror mastermind responsible for the onslaught. As a result, Gaza launched a full-scale retaliation. Rockets intentionally aimed at maximizing civilian casualties targeted high population cities as far as Tel Aviv and Jerusalem.

An Israeli response of proportionate force would have meant hurling thousands of deadly projectiles directly into Palestinian civilian population centers. But this, Israel chose not to do. Instead, the Jewish state determined to respond disproportionately. So in Operation Pillar of Cloud/Defense in Gaza, Israel undertook efforts to minimize civilian casualties of war rather than maximize them. Whenever possible, before striking targets, the army sent text messages to civilian cell phones, dropped mass leaflets over neighborhoods and aired broadcasts to warn of attacks, urging noncombatants to leave targeted zones.[4] Then Israel used surgical strikes to pinpoint just the militants and their weapons stores. If any civilians were spotted in a strike zone, meticulously planned operations were aborted, even at the last second.[5] But war is war; despite all the precautions, some collateral damage proved inevitable.

Much of the collateral damage occurred because Palestinian terror organizations have changed the rules of conventional warfare in order to maximize civilian casualties. Rocket launch pads and weapons caches are intentionally placed inside or adjacent to homes, schools, hospitals, mosques, sports arenas and other public sites.[b] For militants this serves two purposes: First, any outside attack is discouraged altogether; second, if an attack resulting in casualties does take place, the incident can be used to score a public relations victory against Israel.

Sometimes, to further enhance the appearance of Israeli brutality, *jihadists* summon families with children to sneak back into or around a target Israel has just warned them to leave.[6] The hope is that Israel will learn of the human shields and fail to attack. But Israeli military intelligence is not perfect; sometimes accidents take place and civilian deaths occur. When they do, Islamists may view such deeds among themselves as laudable acts of martyrdom, but publicly to the world they protest with rage.[c] Evidence of excessive force is displayed that may or may not include fake photos and scripted video footage. *The recurring and bizarre—yet tragic—scenario is like the story in which a man murders both his parents, and then pleads to be pardoned because he is an orphan.*

From the Israeli perspective, chronic charges of excessive military force or war crimes against humanity, based on death tolls she deliberately tries to minimize and her enemies intentionally maximize, are patently unjust.[d] From a Christian perspective, how can we not fall to our knees in prayer for all involved?

Is Israel an Apartheid, Racist State?

In 2001, at the UN Conference on Racism in Durban, South Africa, an international movement was formally launched to delegitimize Israel, or undermine the legality of her existence. Known as Durban I, the UN conference called for dissolution of the Jewish state.[7] Israel—not any of several extant totalitarian, tyrannical regimes—was accused of crimes against humanity, ethnic cleansing and genocide. During the proceedings, the World Council of Churches proposed that Zionism be equated with racism.[e] Jewish delegates were sought out, spat upon, physically pushed around and pressured to leave public sessions.

Durban I condemned Israel for being an apartheid state, comparable to former white South Africa, because of its insistence on remaining predominantly Jewish. But South African apartheid was a governmentally legislated and brutally enforced system of racial segregation between blacks and whites. Somewhat like the word *holocaust*, the use of *apartheid* conjures up emotional associations of systematic, violent abuse. Any fair-minded person who has spent a few days in Israel would recognize the apartheid charge as absurd.[f]

Israel is a robust democracy in which Israeli Arabs legally integrate with Jews and enjoy full rights of citizenship. Recall that Israeli Arabs are Palestinian Arabs who did not flee when the Jewish state was born. Today, some of their children and grandchildren hold public office, serving at the highest levels of legislative and judicial authority. All professions are open to them, and some are quite prosperous. Not surprisingly, polls consistently indicate that, if given a choice, most Israeli Arabs would prefer to live in Israel as a minority than in any presently existing Arab country as a majority.[8] This does not mean all Israeli Arabs harbor great love for their country; some actively aspire to replace the Jewish state with a Palestinian one.[9] But their right to speak out against Israel is protected—precisely because Israel is not an apartheid state.[g]

Durban I gave impetus to "Israel Apartheid Week," which is now observed annually in most nations around the world.[h] Israel Apartheid Week is marked by anti-Israel rallies and programs designed to stir sympathy and support for the Palestinian cause. Sponsored by affiliates of wealthy Islamist groups,[i] the programs particularly target young, impressionable future leaders on college campuses. Rousing outdoor speeches are made and demonstrations held. Alleged Israeli abuse is acted out in street theater that typically depicts uniformed soldiers beating Palestinian women and children. University students and faculty alike testify that these deceptive tactics incite irrational hate for Israel and Jews. Even on North American campuses, Jewish students have been made to fear for their safety.[10] Professor Alan Dershowitz of Harvard Law School, who speaks on Israel at universities across America, writes of the "passionate hatred, ecstatic hatred," even "orgasmic hatred" he sees in the eyes and actions of students toward Israel and those who support her.[11] [i] I have personally witnessed similar reactions among students at colleges where I have spoken in the US.

Dershowitz points out that challenging Israel's identity as an apartheid/racist state simply because it is Jewish might *possibly* be acceptable if all countries with official state religions or ethnicities were similarly challenged. But no such accusation is hurled at any Islamist *shari'a* state—including the putative state of Palestine, with its official religion of Islam.[12] Nor is any other state denounced as racist because of its law of return[k] based on national ethnicity. Countries such as Russia, China and Germany have had laws of return extending automatic citizenship to ethnic Russians, Chinese and Germans, not unlike Israel's law of return for ethnic Jews.[l] Only Israel, however, is globally censured for favoring and granting citizenship to its people returning home.

Ironically, while "apartheid" Israel is committed to protecting its Muslim, Christian and other minority populations, Palestinians are not. They insist no Jew will ever be allowed to live—let alone gain citizenship—in Palestine.[13]

In 2009, the UN sponsored its second official Durban Conference on Racism. Like the first, it was primarily dedicated to denouncing, demonizing and delegitimizing Israel. Durban II showcased plenary session speaker Mahmoud Ahmadinejad, who first denied the Holocaust ever took place, then called for another to finish the job. In 2011, Durban III morphed into a UN-sponsored Islamist/Arab tirade, largely unattended by Western officials. Participants strategized on fomenting anti-Israelism in the West through alternative means, such as the "BDS" movement.

Do Boycotts, Divestments and Sanctions Promote Justice?

An international Boycott, Divestment and Sanctions (BDS) movement against Israel is observed, to varying degrees, by countries and organizations around the world. Birthed at Durban I, the movement advocates the boycott of Israeli goods, products and sometimes people. Israeli professionals, from academics to athletes and artists, have found themselves targets of the boycott. They have been singularly excluded from professional organizations, international competitions and other events.

Within BDS, the boycott of Israeli academics is particularly baffling. More Nobel and other international academic prizes have been awarded to Israelis than to all Arab and Muslim nations combined.[14] Whereas the tiny Jewish state has long been on the cutting edge of medical, scientific and technological advance, the most significant academic contribution of the collective Arab world is in the proliferating field of Islamic studies. Arab regimes and political lobbies have established Islamic studies programs with hundreds of millions of dollars donated to top universities such as Harvard, Princeton, Columbia, Georgetown, Cornell, Oxford and Cambridge.[15]

The BDS campaign involves more than boycotts. It also pressures public and private institutions to divest from Israeli companies and from any companies that do business with Israeli enterprises—particularly in the West Bank. The stated goal of the movement is to economically isolate and thereby strangle the Jewish state.[m] Several large Christian denominations are among the most vocal advocates of BDS.

BDS pundits rarely mention that Israeli inventions include a burgeoning array of lifesaving pharmaceutical and medical interventions and devices, computer chips used in nearly every electronic device, cell phones, instant messaging, voicemail technology, drip irrigation, improved desalination techniques, the regional infrastructure to support electric cars and many other agricultural, environmental and counter-terror solutions beneficial to the world. Moreover, Israelis have for decades offered their inventions and humanitarian relief efforts at no cost to undeveloped nations and those hit by widespread disaster. To boycott these tangible blessings would seem to amount to the proverbial cutting off of one's nose to spite one's face. Does this achieve justice for either Israel or the nations? Does it reflect the good, pleasing and perfect will of God?

Does Israel's Military Violate Human Rights?[16]

The concept of human rights, in its purest expression, derives from the Bible. God's Word attributes inherent worth and dignity to every human being, for all are created in His image. The Bible advocates mercy and compassion for the needy and oppressed—but sometimes holds these in a "divine tension" with moral right and wrong. (To illustrate the tension, recall the story of the man who murders his parents, then pleads for mercy because he is an orphan.) Based originally on biblical values, an international human rights movement developed in the mid–twentieth century.

As the movement evolved, however, it gradually jettisoned the Judeo-Christian worldview for secularist goals. A new post-modern, humanistic and relativistic mind-set evolved. Soon, troubling ideologies[17] such as fundamental Islam appeared on the global scene. Without biblical moorings, universal-minded human rights organizations were unable or unwilling to withstand them. As might be expected, Israel has borne the brunt of today's new—and skewed—human rights movement.

We have already viewed, in previous chapters, a small sampling of invectives issued against the Jewish state for alleged violations of human rights. We have seen how these indictments stem from the reality that since her inception in 1948, Israel has existed under constant threat of terror, war and annihilation. Surrounded by enemies vastly outnumbering her, Israel has had to maintain a strong military defense simply to stay alive. What's more, that defense force has had to deal with enemies who do not conform to traditional Western standards of military conduct, fair play, reason or logic. In this context, Dershowitz points out that no nation in history that has faced comparable existential danger has tried so hard—and so successfully—to require its military to operate within the rule of law.[17]

Most of the world does not know that Israeli defense forces have adopted what is probably the highest ethical standard of any modern army.[18] To be sure, in the heat of conflict, individual troops cannot always abide by those standards—as is true of any army. But Israelis themselves are outraged when, even in a tense military situation, soldiers respond with genuinely excessive force.° Public outcry upbraids the incident, discipline is meted out and military procedures may be changed to prevent similar mistakes. Even the courts get involved.

Most of the world does not know the Jewish state extends fair judicial access to Palestinians so they may file complaints in court about the Israeli military. The Israeli Supreme Court has taken what is probably the most active role of any high court in any democracy in order to strike the balance between state security and individual freedom. Most of the world does not know that the court often overrides the military to protect the rights of both Palestinian noncombatants and terrorist prisoners—at considerable risk to Jewish civilians and soldiers.[19] In a practical sense, Israel has attempted to protect Palestinian human rights much more than Palestinian leaders themselves have tried to do.

Sometimes, charges of human rights abuse do not come in the context of a military operation, but from checkpoints designed to prevent militants from sneaking into Israel.[p] Checkpoint procedures can be difficult and complex. It is not uncommon for potential terrorists to disguise themselves as pregnant, sick or injured women. Some have tucked explosive devises in their underwear or private body parts; as a result, strip searches may be necessary. (What is a checkpoint soldier to do when he or she has reason to suspect a Palestinian man, woman or child is a deathtrap in disguise?) Even apparent humanitarian emergencies have been used to stage terror operations, such as booby-trapping ambulances with explosives. At times, checkpoint passage can be tedious, tensions can run high and both sides can overreact. But does justice require that Israel bear full blame for the dilemma?

How Do Human Rights Organizations Treat the Conflict?

How do human rights organizations treat the Arab/Palestinian–Israeli conflict? The UN Human Rights Council has made the Jewish state the one and only permanent standing item on its agenda.[q] A portion of every session it holds is dedicated to examining and excoriating Israel. In 2003, the Council went so far as to pass a resolution that condones terror—if it is aimed at Israel.[r] In 2013 the Council declared that private companies around the world must consider boycotting and divesting from Israel because of its so-called criminal occupation.[s]

A prominent non-governmental organization, Human Rights Watch, issues condemnations almost monthly, and almost exclusively against Israel.[t] The NGO's original founder has rebuked it for sacrificing its vision and mandate because of what he calls an "unjust obsession with Israel, the only nation in the Middle East that genuinely strives to safeguard human rights."[20] In like manner, Amnesty International publishes regular reports that single out and uniquely chastise the Jewish state for her presumed treatment of Palestinians and other Arabs. It has not issued comparable reports on human rights abuses in any other nation, including regimes where people are systematically murdered for reasons having nothing to do with terror or existential threats.[21]

International human rights champion Natan Sharansky, once held prisoner by the former Soviet Union, cautions that human rights can be safeguarded only through clear moral criteria. He warns these criteria are rapidly eroding, evidenced by the double standard used against Israel and measures taken to delegitimize her by today's human rights activists.[22]

Former prime minister of Spain José Aznar also decries today's eroding moral criteria:

> To defend Israel's right to exist in peace, within secure borders, requires a degree of moral and strategic clarity that too often seems to have disappeared. . . . The West is going through a period of confusion . . . caused by . . . the rule of political correctness, by a multiculturalism that forces us to our knees before others, by a secularism which . . . blinds us even when we are confronted by jihadists promoting the most fanatical incarnation of their faith. To abandon Israel . . . would merely serve to illustrate how far we have sunk. . . . The West is what it is thanks to its Judeo-Christian roots. If the Jewish element of those roots is upturned and Israel is lost, then we are lost too. . . . Our fate is inextricably intertwined.[23]

By its treatment of Israel, is it possible the human rights movement is guilty of chipping away at the very rights it originally sought to protect?[u] Consider how, as a result of global censure of Israel, only in the Jewish state do the following phenomena occur: an entire civilian population endures foreign militant attack—regularly—without reprisal; proportionately large swaths of land are relinquished to enemy states, with no guarantee of peace in return;[v] terrorists convicted of mass murder publicly declare their intent to kill more Jews when they are released from jail as forced political "goodwill gestures"; a country of only eight million suffers more than a million cyber terror attacks—targeting electrical, water, communications, medical, financial and other essential civilian infrastructures[w]—*every day*; national borders are illegally breached on a semi-regular basis by masses of militants and "peaceful civilians" operating in cahoots with them;[24] a nation is pressured to shrink itself to suicidally narrow borders that cannot be defended from invasion—while at the same time being threatened with nuclear genocide. *Why?* A respected secular journalist (who is decidedly not pro-Israel) concludes, "Singling out Israel for opprobrium and international sanction—out of all proportion to any other party in the Middle East—is anti-Semitic, and not saying so is dishonest."[25]

When Is Criticism of Israel Anti-Semitic?

Most Westerners, including believers, would agree (at least publicly) that anti-Semitism is unjust and wrong. Not all criticism of Israel is anti-Semitic, however, and we ought not think that it is. We can care deeply for Israel while at the same time pointing out her specific wrongs. Every Israeli I know, including every Messianic believer, disagrees with certain Israeli policies and practices—sometimes quite strongly. In an era when criticism of Israel and Zionism[x] runs rampant, how do we discern when that criticism is fair and reasonable and when it is anti-Semitic?

Some nations and organizations have adopted guidelines for distinguishing between fair criticism of Israel and "the new anti-Semitism." Many Israelis and others around the world find those set forth by the US Department of State to be especially helpful. The State Department regards criticism of Israel to be anti-Semitic when any one of "Three Ds" is present: (1) an expression that *delegitimizes* Israel; (2) a *double standard* used for Israel vis-à-vis other states; or (3) an attempt to *demonize* Israel by using images associated with classic anti-Semitism, making comparisons with Nazism or putting all the blame on Israel for the Islamist/Arab/Palestinian–Israeli conflict.[y]

Sadly, across the nations and even in some churches, it seems the new anti-Semitism flourishes in full 3-D. Sometimes it is expressed blatantly, but other times it is subtle. To illustrate, in one widely circulated Internet video called "Freedom for Palestine,"[26] a church Gospel choir sings an impassioned hip-hop ballad about Israeli injustice and alleged crimes against humanity. Images depict dishonest and cruel caricatures of abuse committed against presumably peace-loving Palestinians. The victims are made to look like you and me, regular folk with whom we can easily identify. The subconscious message is that we are all Palestine; when the Jewish state "oppresses" Palestine, she "oppresses" us all. The video makes no mention of Palestinian human rights abuse, terror, the agenda to annihilate Israel or Israeli efforts to protect Palestinian human rights. Rather, it demonizes and delegitimizes Israel, rousing resentment against her by employing an underlying double standard.

A less subtle but puzzling phenomenon in the anti-Israel movement is that a small number of very left-wing Jews, including Israelis, comprise some of Israel's most viciously vocal critics. Almost always, they identify as secularists,[z] subscribing to a universalist worldview that downplays fundamentalist Islam. These commentators attract large, anti-Israel audiences in both the Arab world and the West.[aa] The fact they are Jewish—and probably sincerely mean well—does not necessarily exempt them from anti-Semitism, however they may deny it.[bb]

One of Israel's iconic, left-wing historian-activists, Benny Morris, spent decades denouncing Israeli actions toward Palestinians. Long regarded as an intellectual leader in the pro-Palestinian movement, Morris recanted much of his life's work in 2012. He disappointedly concluded that the core reason for the ongoing conflict and injustice was the Palestinians' peristent refusal to accept the existence of a Jewish state.[cc]

Morris joins a growing number of disillusioned liberals.[dd] They have been forced to rethink their idealism and face facts honestly. You and I will have to do the same if we want to align with moral justice. Without sacrificing compassion, we will have to engage our God-given intellect, ask Him to sharpen our discernment and stand for righteousness according to truth.

Pursuing Justice

Despite ubiquitous anti-Semitism around her, Israel wants desperately to make peace with her neighbors, especially the Palestinian people.[ee] It is aptly said that if the Arabs put their weapons down today, there would be no more violence; if the Jews put their weapons down today, there would be no more Israel. The issue is not a cycle of violence; it is about the survival of the Jews on a miniscule slice of their historical homeland.

Israelis say there are two possible solutions to the conflict: the realistic and the miraculous. The realistic solution, they quip, involves divine intervention; the miraculous, a voluntary agreement between the parties themselves.

As we near the end of the age and spiritual warfare heightens, underlying currents of anti-Semitism are bound to intensify. Secularism, Islamism and more will increasingly impinge on biblical values of moral justice. The Father is sovereignly allowing individuals and nations to make choices that will chart their destinies.

As darkness covers the earth, however, His glorious light rises and shines upon the Bride He is preparing for His Son. The corporate Bride includes His people from within the Palestinian Christian Church. Already, they impact the Arab-Israeli conflict and the world. To them we now turn.

Countering Christian Zionism: Christian Palestinianism

God's gifts and his call are irrevocable.

Romans 11:29

One of my personal joys is worshiping and fellowshiping with Palestinians who love and follow Jesus. In Messiah we are one family, healed and reconciled in the beauty of His grace. But Palestinian believers who carry God's heart for the Jews comprise a very small remnant within the Palestinian church. Because of their love for Israel, they not only endure persecution from Islamists, but real harassment from other Palestinian Christians.[a] They truly deserve and need our sacrificial love and support.

Sadly, the majority of Palestinian Christians do not claim a spiritual rebirth experience or intimate walk with the Lord. Instead, they identify as Christian mainly in a cultural sense.

Most Western evangelicals, Pentecostals and charismatics would consider them nominal in their faith. Political-nationalist aspirations are generally more important to them than intimate surrender to Messiah, personal study of His Word or sharing the Gospel. Increasingly, they are influenced by the Islamist world in which they live.

The Traditional Palestinian Church

In contrast to the small pure-hearted remnant, traditional Palestinian Christianity does little to quell the conflict with Israel. Church pulpits can spew scathing sermons against the Jews,[b] such as these:

> Palestine is from the [Mediterranean] sea to the [Jordan] river. . . . They [Jews] have no right to live or settle in it. . . . We encourage our youth to participate in the resistance, to carry out martyrdom attacks and participate in removing the occupation. . . . Martyrdom operations are an excellent and a good way to resist the Zionists.[1]

> Had we lived in the days when the church was a church . . . a Crusader war crueler than the Crusader wars of the past would have been waged against Israel. I, the Christian Palestinian, say in all rage and daring to the Christians of the world: You are loathsome! You are contemptible! . . . Our Jesus is not their Jesus. . . . Our God is not their God.[2]

The traditional Palestinian Christian view reflects the same anti-Jewish theology expressed by much of the Church throughout the Arab Middle East:

> This religion [Judaism] is the enemy of God, the enemy of people, and the enemy of Christianity. . . . As Jesus once said

to the Jews, "You are the sons of Satan, and you do the will of your father Satan."[3]

The existence of Israel is an historic sin. . . . Israel managed to drug the leaders of those Christian countries . . . because of their surly nature. Israel planted among them the spirit of hatred and rage. . . . If only God would intervene to defend the world from these enemies of peace.[4]

Terrorism . . . against Christians . . . has nothing to do with Islam. . . . It is actually a conspiracy planned by Zionists and some Christians with Zionist orientations, and it aims at undermining and giving a bad image of Islam.[5]

Are we to regard such rantings as a legitimate expression of Christianity? God says, "Anyone who claims to be in the light but hates a brother or sister is still in the darkness" (1 John 2:9). In the diatribes of these church leaders, I hear a crying need for the Gospel to reach a pained people still groping in darkness without the Savior's light.

Palestinian Evangelicals

Traditional, anti-Jewish teachings in the Middle East church have strongly influenced many who identify as Palestinian evangelicals. As a result, a new theology, with varying expressions, has emerged out of the Palestinian-Israeli conflict. Most Messianic Jews, along with many Gentile believers, keenly disagree with this new theology in all its forms. It is not wrong to disagree, but we must do so humbly, in a gracious spirit toward brothers and sisters with whom we differ.

Given the difficult religious and political climate in which they live, Palestinian evangelicals are confronted with a dilemma:

Should they side with Palestinian nationalism or with a biblical view supportive of the Jewish state? Most have resolved the issue by denying God's present restoration of Israel. They interpret the Scriptures symbolically, so that any Jewish ties to the land can be superseded by new developments and realities. These realities are sometimes said to be the Church, sometimes Palestinians or sometimes Jesus Himself. At the core of their reasoning is a hermeneutic of the Bible virtually the same as that used in replacement theology. Accordingly, a Christian Palestinian spokesman concludes: "[The] concept of a promised land is expired to give way to the new concept of the kingdom of God, which resides in every believer's heart."[6] The result is a new variant of so-called fulfillment theology.

Many Palestinian evangelicals believe that all Old Covenant promises, especially those about land, have been fulfilled in the Person of Messiah. These promises, they say, are now expressed *exclusively* in the kingdom that exists inside believers' hearts.[7] As we saw in chapter 3, this perspective rightly reflects that God's promises find *consummate* fulfillment in Jesus (see Ephesians 1:22–23) and have *a* fulfillment for all believers in the spiritual realm. But the perspective is highly incorrect insofar as it denies these promises find their fundamental fulfillment in Israel, in the physical realm. So while Palestinian fulfillment doctrine differs slightly from classic replacement theology, its practical effect is the same: It teaches that Israel's calling is superseded and done away with, leaving no biblical justification for her existence today.

To those in the Western Church, Christian Palestinians often claim something like this: "I am not against the Jewish people and I am not anti-Semitic. I do not believe in replacement theology. But the Bible does not justify the existence of a Jewish state today. Don't you want to hear how your Christian brothers and sisters are suffering due to Israeli injustice and abuse?" Sadly, what follows is a litany of unforgiving accusations against Israel—but *not* fundamentalist Islam. Strands of liberation theology (defined below) are often woven into their presentations, along with narratives of history preserved in dour, personal pain. I believe Palestinian Christians' theology must be addressed, their pain recognized and healed and their destiny in God restored. By His grace, let's try to begin.

Christian Palestinian Fulfillment Theology

Frequently, Palestinian evangelical views on Israel incorporate into fulfillment theology what is known as liberation theology. Liberation theology esteems justice for the oppressed as a foremost—typically *the* foremost—theme of Scripture. Social justice becomes the lens through which the entire Bible is read. At all times, God is seen as taking the side of the oppressed.[c] Uniquely applying liberation with fulfillment theology to the Palestinian plight,[d] the most popular of the emergent theologies has been termed Palestinian fulfillment theology or Christian Palestinianism.[e]

Palestinian theology teaches that Old Covenant prophecies concerning Israel and the Kingdom "vanish in Jesus Christ, who has fulfilled them."[8] As one scholar writes: "The New Testament relocates the properties of the Holy Land and discovers them in Christ Himself."[9] Because Jesus fulfilled the Old Covenant, its original meaning to its original hearers and readers is now practically irrelevant. Promises and prophecies originally made to them must be reinterpreted and applied exclusively to Jesus—because they were fulfilled in Him.[f] With all due respect, the reasoning is not scripturally based and the logic is rather circular.

211

With every Old Covenant passage having been fulfilled in the Person of Messiah, it is not the Church that disinherits or replaces Israel this time, but Jesus Himself. This belief permits fulfillment advocates to distance themselves from classic replacement theology. Christians only indirectly supersede Israel as recipients of Old Covenant promises because Jesus has already transferred the promises into Himself.

A key passage pertaining to Israel's restoration illustrates the quandary caused by this interpretive scheme. In its original context, Zechariah 14:3–4 refers to the apocalyptic battle in which Jesus returns to Jerusalem. The passage reads, "Then the LORD will go out and fight against those nations, as he fights on a day of battle. On that day his feet will stand on the Mount of Olives, east of Jerusalem." Taken to its logical conclusion, Palestinian fulfillment theology would teach that Jesus fights in a battle taking place inside of Himself, where the Mount of Olives has now relocated. In the process, His feet (perhaps symbolically) stand inside of His own divine Person. But this interpretation makes no sense, as some supersessionists themselves admit. The passage can only be fairly understood as a prophecy yet to be fulfilled, on the ground of the physical Mount of Olives.

As you might suspect, Palestinian fulfillment theology interprets the Bible allegorically. Recall that an allegorical approach rejects the Hebraic-based interpretation of Scripture taught by the Scriptures themselves (see chapter 3). It disregards the plain understanding, or the literal-grammatical-historical level of interpretation. Because the allegorical method is primarily symbolic and subjective, "Israel" is not seen as referring prophetically to the physical land or people of Israel, the Jews or their restoration. Such an approach to Bible interpretation is intrinsically disposed toward delegitimizing Israel's existence today. It denies that "God's gifts and call are irrevocable" (Romans 11:29).

Some Christian Palestinians adopt a less symbolic hermeneutic but hold to a preterist theological view. Preterism teaches that some prophecies, including those of Jesus, do have literal fulfillments, but those fulfillments have already entirely occurred.[g] Preterist doctrine denies any future for national Israel or a last days restoration of the Jews. Unlike classic replacement theology, preterism can allow Israel to be superseded by any group presenting a supposedly valid claim, including militant Muslims. If liberation theology is added to the mix, God's favor is disposed to whoever is the perceived victim. The reason for the perceived victimization is not necessarily relevant. (Remember the orphaned killer?)

Sympathizing with Islam

Like other Arab Christians in the Middle East, many Palestinian evangelicals confess they rarely, if ever, read the Old Covenant. They say politics and pain make it difficult—if not impossible—for them to study it, much less use it as a source of theology.[10] Many dismiss it as a Jewish book based largely on myth, not the inspired Word of God.[11][h] Those who do read the Old Covenant often selectively delete personally troubling words such as "Israel" and "Zion."[12] Accordingly, the Jewish state is rarely, if ever, viewed through the lens of Scripture. For some Christian Palestinians, only one aspect of the Hebrew Scriptures still has major significance—the link between Israel's sin and her exile from the land.

Accordingly, Palestinian believers admit they do not study prophecy or think much about the end times.[13] Most do not expect Jesus to physically return to Jerusalem.[14] This expectation, they say, has resulted in tremendous injustice to them because it encourages a Jewish restoration to the Holy Land and the "oppressive occupation."

Sadly, to the extent Christian Palestinians avoid or reinterpret the Old Covenant, they will likely lack a solid foundation in the Scriptures. As a result, they may be prone to harbor undue sympathy for Islam.[i] A small minority within an Islamist majority, they can be desperate to prove their patriotism—which necessarily involves resistance against Israel. Seeking to gain their countrymen's respect, some have consciously or unconsciously embraced anti-God and anti-Jewish dispositions reflective of fundamental Islam.[15][j] Consequently, while most Christian Palestinians insist their problems are due to Israeli occupation, they almost never mention Islam. They dismiss the connection between Palestinians' relentless campaign to destroy the Jewish state and the "oppressive occupation" existing as a result.

Privately, a Palestinian pastor once confessed to me he had some concern for the future of his very much hoped for, free and sovereign state. He acknowledged that when Israeli administration in the West Bank ends, an Islamist government could easily come to power. In that event, he and others suspect life for Christians may be much worse than it already has been. But, he said, Palestinian believers want their state and will deal with the Islamist problem if it happens. *How*, I wondered, *will they deal with the problem once they are forced by shari'a law into dhimmi, second-class citizen status?*[k] Sadly, their brethren in Gaza are now dealing with it through intimidation, harassment, forced conversions and martyrdom.[l] Under Gaza's Islamist regime, the Christian population there rapidly plummeted by almost 50 percent[16]—and some have actually sought political asylum in Israel.[17]

Justice for the Foreigner

Christian Palestinians often argue that Israel fails to follow her own code of moral justice. The Hebrew Scriptures, they point out, require that Jews not mistreat or oppress a stranger or foreigner in the land (see Exodus 22:21; 23:9). They say Israel has wrongly violated this command for decades, and they suffer greatly as a result.

To be sure, God tells Israel to extend compassion, protection and the equivalent of human rights to the stranger sojourning among her (see Jeremiah 7:6–7). But in context, the Scriptures presuppose the stranger has first submitted to the God of Israel and the covering of His people. In so doing, such an individual (called a *ger*) was placed, like Ruth, under the protection of Israel and her God.[m] A *ger* inevitably acknowledged Israel's existence as a Jewish nation-state. Consequently, he or she was given privileges not accorded to other foreigners. Fully equal status could then be obtained by circumcision, which placed a male foreigner, along with his family, in direct covenant relationship with God. It is the same today, with conversion to Judaism qualifying a foreigner for Israeli citizenship.

Israel was never to tolerate, however, a violent stranger not submitted to the ways of Yahweh. Especially repugnant to Him was the idolatrous foreigner who polluted the land by worshiping false gods—such as the Islamist Allah (see Exodus 23:32–33a). The foreigner who despised God's people and whose aim was their annihilation could never claim protection as a *ger*. Such a person was considered an enemy.

Collectively, Palestinians do not qualify as *ger*-type foreigners, and it would be unjust to require Israel to treat them as if they did. Nonetheless, it is my prayer that more and more Palestinian believers will embrace God's heart for the Jewish nation. When, someday, they align with Israel in the spirit of Ruth (or Rahab or Jethro), I believe the Jews will welcome them with deep affection and appreciation. Perhaps even the *ger* policy, with its accompanying right to dwell in the land, will be renewed and extended to them.

The Christian Palestinianist Movement

Meanwhile, the following represents a small sampling of what evangelical Christian Palestinianist leaders teach:

- Jesus was a Palestinian, His Jewish identity merely a misconception of Western Christianity.[18]
- "Real Christianity exists only in Palestine."[19]
- Christian Zionism "is not connected to Christianity in any way."[20]
- "Jesus is on the cross again with thousands of crucified Palestinians around Him. . . . Palestine has become one huge Golgatha. The Israeli government crucifixion system operates daily."[21]
- "Zionism is just another form of racism."[22]
- "The notion that God has purposes for the Jewish people is at best deeply flawed and at worst heretical. . . . Those who insist that this is the case . . . are no different from white South Africans who still try to justify apartheid on biblical grounds."[23]
- The New Covenant cancels any plans for the Jewish people.[24]

Christian Palestinianists often express strong resentment toward Christian Zionists or any believer who supports the Jewish state.[n] Conferences are convened, personal tales poignantly told, books published and videos produced—specifically to quench evangelical love for Israel. Unique strategies exist to target justice-minded charismatic and Pentecostal believers.[o] Participants, sponsors and spokesmen in the movement include leading Western theologians and seminary professors, many of whom are known for their anti-Israel, even anti-Semitic, disposition.[p] As a result, Israel now faces international opposition in the form of Christian Palestinianism.

A Christian Palestinian Manifesto was released in 2012.[25] The purpose of the Manifesto is to challenge evangelicals to bring "peace, justice and reconciliation in Palestine and Israel." At the same time, it denies the covenantal inheritance of the Jewish people to the land of Israel. It declares that "the occupation" is the "core issue" of the Palestinian-Israeli conflict. There is no mention of the historical and ongoing Palestinian agenda to annihilate the Jewish state, which, from Israel's perspective, is the core reason—and perhaps the only reason—for the conflict. The document is silent about any legal or moral right Israel may have to exist. The Manifesto does include a statement suggesting that anti-Semitism and delegitimization of Israel are wrong, the implication being that Christian Palestinian criticism of Israel is not anti-Semitic. Most Jewish believers do not regard the Manifesto as a fair call to peace, justice or reconciliation.

The Christian Palestinian Manifesto is a product of recurring, and increasingly influential, evangelical conferences in Bethlehem called "Christ at the Checkpoint." Cosponsored by theologians from the West, the gatherings use security checkpoints to symbolize alleged Israeli oppression.[q] In 2012, Christ at the Checkpoint speakers included a head representative of the World Evangelical Alliance, parent group for the largest evangelical network in the US, the National Association of Evangelicals,[r] and Dr. Stephen Sizer, one of the most vocal anti-Israel Western theologians in the world. Dr. Sizer has been accused by Jewish and Christian leaders, including some ministers in his own, resolutely not pro-Israel denomination, of blatant anti-Semitism.[26] Other presenters consistently shared perspectives that were perceived as anti-Israel by Jewish believers who attended the conference.[s] However, in what some termed a hollow gesture, but others saw as a sincere step toward reconciliation, two Israeli Messianic leaders were invited to speak; they attempted to defend the Jewish state.

Other Christian Palestinian decrees parallel Christ at the Checkpoint's Manifesto. A prominent example is Kairos, written in 2009 and released by an international organization of the same name. Endorsed by leaders of thirteen mainline denominations, Kairos concludes that "Israel's occupation of Palestinian land is a sin against God and humanity." It makes no mention of any sin on the part of Palestinian terrorists and Islamists in prolonging the occupation. Written in strident terms used historically by Christians to stir violence against Jews, it claims that any theology legitimizing Israel's presence in the West Bank is not Christian.[27] In a 2012 interview televised across America, a Kairos spokesman insisted their document was not anti-Semitic—because the piece of paper on which it is written is nonviolent![28]

Joining the Christian Palestinian movement are many Arab denominational leaders from Israel. Collectively, they make no secret of their aim to overturn any pro-Israel stance within the international Body of Christ. Quite openly, they seek to counteract Christian Zionism, or as it is sometimes called, Biblical Zionism.[t] As a result of their efforts, Bible schools and seminaries throughout the West, including America, teach Christian Palestinianism as a valid grid through which to view the Palestinian-Israeli conflict. The movement's impact on secular Western society is also rapidly increasing.

Western Responses to Christian Palestinianism

Many Western Jews and Christians believe that Christian Palestinianism aggressively promotes anti-Semitism, replacement theology and the delegitimization of Israel.[29] They say it represents a dangerous resurgence of the Church's historical, anti-Jewish doctrine that has led in the past to the widespread murder of Jews. At a minimum, it is appropriate to ask if the Palestinian Church has heeded the exhortation of Romans 11:17–25 not to be ignorant or arrogant toward Israel, but to tremble in humility.

A Christian Zionist leader from the UK pointedly comments:

> The big lie is Christian Palestinianism, the anti-Israel, pro-Palestinian crusade going on in the Church today that will say from one corner of its mouth, "We love the Jewish people" and from the other corner of its mouth, "We hate Israel." That is not possible. You cannot love the Jewish people and hate Israel.[30]

In 2012, a highly regarded rabbi in the US stated that Christian Palestinianism had so influenced the Church that relations between mainline Protestants and Jews in America had hit its lowest point. He did not know if the relationship could recover.[31] Israeli Rabbi Shlomo Riskin, a leader in the Jewish-Christian interfaith movement, explains:

> As long as you believe in replacement theology . . . and that the Jews no longer stand in covenantal relationship to God, then [you believe] we have no right to be in Israel and you join our enemies.[32]

As a follower of Jesus, an Israeli and a mother, I am sobered to realize how many evangelical brothers and sisters are attempting to compel the world to take action that, apart from divine intervention, could lead to the slaughter of millions of my people—including my own family. Now, to my knowledge, none of them is suggesting outright that any of us be killed. But as Rabbi Riskin remarks, some have unwittingly joined forces with the enemies of Israel who aim at nothing less.

In no small part, the spread of Christian Palestinianism is related to the current Western trend to dismiss the concept of absolute truth. Today, more and more Christians say the Bible cannot be read according to any objective hermeneutical standard—because there *are* no objective standards. Each individual and each culture perceives reality differently, so any given standard is as valid as the next. Palestinian victimization, therefore, provides a framework for Scripture interpretation just as sound as any other. Israeli Messianic scholar Lisa Loden describes the dilemma:

> The question of whether or not the [Bible] text has meaning in and of itself, [or] if meaning is derived from the interaction between the reader and the text, is a crucial question in contemporary hermeneutical studies. The primacy of the text has been the gold standard of biblical scholarship . . . but is currently under examination and attack.[33]

Forgiveness at the Cross

Palestinian believers freely share that their theology stems in large measure from personal pain and offense. To be sure, some have suffered much and are in need of compassionate help. God does not want us belittling or ignoring them. At the same time, let us remember that they are not the first Christians through history to feel offended or victimized. Countless believers have unjustly suffered extreme, prolonged pain. But they did not seek to reinvent the message of the Scriptures to accommodate their suffering. To the contrary, those who identified intimately with Messiah in their deep distress often gave the world a lasting witness of the Gospel.

Please do not misunderstand: I am not suggesting that Palestinian believers stay silent in the face of injustice. I merely point out that Jesus is greater than any of our circumstances—and can give us the love, peace and joy with which to overcome them. Personally, when I have unjustly suffered prolonged, seemingly unbearable pain, I have heard the Lord lovingly ask: *Are unforgiveness and self-pity going to limit your response to My ways? If you meet Me at the cross with your pain, I will transform it.* Some of my most intimate, life-changing encounters with Yeshua have been at the cross as I released forgiveness toward those who deeply mistreated or offended me. Is it possible the cross of Yeshua could offer our Palestinian brothers and sisters some of the same overcoming grace and comfort? I recently asked a Palestinian pastor this question, after spending hours listening to him and his church members share personal grievances about the Jewish state. He replied that Palestinian preachers generally did not discuss taking pain and offense about Israel to the cross. With his next breath, he said they probably should start.

A New Christian Zionism

Some Christian or Biblical Zionists attribute the new Palestinian theology to a demonic force opposing God's promises to the Jews. As we have seen, the devil works in many ways to discourage Israel's restoration. I believe, however, we must forthrightly hear our brothers and sisters. We must embrace them with prayerful love, discernment and practical help. In the process, God might even use them to point out areas in *us* that He wants to mature.

What might we learn from Palestinian believers and how can we best respond to them? First, we can acknowledge that certain Israeli policies, forged in the context of the state's struggle to survive, have caused unwarranted suffering and, sometimes, abuse. We must not ignore or excuse Israel's disobedience, reflected in those policies, to God's ethical commands. We can focus support on Israeli policy makers who advance biblical righteousness.

Second, some Christian Zionists have in the past expressed little concern for Palestinians due to an emphasis on Israel's fulfillment of Bible prophecy. Because Palestinian believers usually reject the idea of Jewish covenant election, they do not regard Israel's existence as anything prophetic at all. They feel they have been marginalized by the Western Church—and many deeply resent it. To rectify the past, we must seek the Lord for His compassionate, honest and wise response. We can pray for Spirit-led opportunities to engage with Palestinian believers. We can also pray for reconciliation efforts between Christian Palestinians and Israeli Messianic Jews to deepen and expand.

Third, we are to intentionally remember that being pro-Israel does not—and must not—mean being anti-Palestinian. It has been aptly said that if our love for Israel means we cannot love Palestinians, then something is wrong with our love for Israel.[34] If we lack love for Palestinians because we have been offended or injured by them, we must take that to the cross.

Last but certainly not least, we must remember the Lord does not want our ultimate focus on either Israel or putative Palestine, but on *Him*. Those who care passionately for the Palestinian people may be tempted to confuse love with unsanctified mercy. Unsanctified mercy seeks to alleviate suffering at any cost, regardless of the injustice that may result. It does not align with God's will or His Word. It does not flow from a focus on Him.

Therefore, Christlike love for Palestinian Christians will not be expressed by aligning with them against Israel. It will be expressed by aligning with them for Jesus and His heart for the Jews. When Palestinians understand God's love, mercy and grace for Israel, they will experience it at new levels for themselves. Healing from heaven will flow to them. Palestinian Christians will begin to walk in the manifest power of the Gospel of the Kingdom as never before. Could God even use them, together with Israeli believers, to help minister peace to both peoples?

A leading pro-Palestinian theologian has stated that Christians must choose one side or the other: Israel's or Palestine's. He writes: "The question is, am I as a Christian going to view the Middle East through the lens of prophecy or the lens of justice?"[35] In response, I propose the time has come to drop the dichotomy. God does not choose between presumably pro-Palestinian justice and presumably pro-Israel prophecy. His immense love, expressed in His Word, beautifully reconciles prophecy and justice. It is not a matter of either/or, but both/and. In the end, each evidences the reality of the Gospel. But neither is itself the Gospel.

The Gospel of the Kingdom revolves around Jesus and His restoration of all nations in mercy and grace. Which gives Palestinians, Israelis and everyone else a bountiful future and a hope.

A Future and a Hope

The deliverer will come from Zion; he will turn godlessness away from Jacob. And this is my covenant with them when I take away their sins.

Romans 11:26–27

Long ago, when the Jewish people were exiled from the Promised Land, their prophets received spectacular visions of hope. Jeremiah foresaw a time of blessed restoration and peace:

I know the thoughts that I think toward you, says the LORD, thoughts of peace and not of evil, to give you a future and a hope. . . . I will gather you from all the nations and . . . bring you back . . . to the place from which I cause you to be carried away captive.

Jeremiah 29:11, 14 NKJV

Ezekiel previewed the Jewish people regathered and revived from around the world. They would be restored physically to the land, and then spiritually to the Lord:

> "These bones are the people of Israel. They say, 'Our bones are dried up and our hope is gone; we are cut off.' . . . 'My people, I am going to open your graves and bring you up from them; I will bring you back to the land of Israel. Then you, my people, will know that I am the LORD, when I open your graves and bring you up from them. I will put my Spirit in you and you will live, and I will settle you in your own land. Then you will know that I the Lord have spoken, and I have done it.'"
>
> Ezekiel 37:11–14

> "For I will take you out of the nations; I will gather you from all the countries and bring you into your own land. I will sprinkle clean water on you, and you will be clean; I will cleanse you from all your impurities and from all your idols. I will give you a new heart and put a new spirit in you; I will remove from you your heart of stone and give you a heart of flesh."
>
> Ezekiel 36:24–26

Israel's reestablishment after the Holocaust—with its thousands of mass graves into which Jewish corpses were piled—strikingly parallels Ezekiel's vision of restoration. The prophet saw a valley of dry bones, physically and spiritually dead. But God miraculously revived the dry bones. Then He settled His people back in their land (see Ezekiel 37:1–14). Israel's restoration would have nothing to do with righteousness on her part. It would be—and in fact has been—solely by mercy and grace.

God's grace is so great that, as we have seen, some of us are tempted to stumble over it. We see Israel's shortcomings and her sin. We wonder why, if He is truly restoring her, she is not walking more in His holy ways. We hear some Christians who oppose the Jewish state insist her rebirth was not a miracle but a mistake—a strictly human and sorely misplaced endeavor. What are we to think? Does Israel's modern-day restoration fulfill Bible prophecy or not?

Does Israel's Restoration Fulfill Bible Prophecy?[1]

The tension that can appear to exist between Israel's restoration and her present condition of spiritual unbelief is resolved when we read the Bible according to proper interpretive principles (see chapter 3). Ezekiel says God will return the Jewish people to their land before He fully restores their faith. First, He will "gather them from all countries"; after that, He will "sprinkle clean water" on them and "put a new spirit" in them. Other Hebrew prophets confirm this sequence of events. They describe a Jewish regathering to the land before the end of the age, contested by the nations and culminating in apocalyptic warfare. After they are back in the land, Jews collectively turn to Messiah in the context of a military assault (see Zechariah 12). The Second Coming of Jesus follows (see Zechariah 14).

The New Covenant describes a similar end times scenario. Yeshua declares, "Jerusalem will be trampled on by Gentiles until the times of the Gentiles are fulfilled" (Luke 21:24). Messiah foresees that when the times of the Gentiles are fulfilled, the trampling of Jerusalem ends. First, a predominant Jewish presence is restored to Jerusalem—and after that, the city welcomes Him back (see Matthew 23:39). Likewise, Romans 11:26–27 reveals that in the future, the Jewish people are living in the land when "the deliverer will come from Zion" and "turn godlessness away from Jacob." None of these events can be interpreted with biblical integrity as having already occurred in the past. The reality we see today reflects their last days' unfolding.

To understand how it is that God regathers Israel to her land in unbelief and then allows her to sin in it, recall the interplay between the Abrahamic and Mosaic covenants. The promise of land ownership[a] to Israel in the Abrahamic covenant is unconditional. In the Mosaic covenant, however, Israel's ability to physically inhabit the land is conditioned on her obedience to God. To the extent she disobeys Him, she may lose land or even be exiled from it. But if exile occurs, it is only temporary, not permanent (see Deuteronomy 28–30). On account of God's covenant promise with Abraham, Isaac and Jacob, He will eventually return the Jews to their home.

God promised a singular time would come in which Israel would be regathered to her land, then follow in His ways and never again be uprooted (see 2 Samuel 7:10–16; Jeremiah 31:21–40; Amos 9:11–15; Romans 11:26–27). This is the promise He has been prophetically working out over the past hundred years. But the process is not instantaneous; it is progressing gradually over time. Now, will God have to dissolve the Jewish state because, during the period of her restoration, many are not yet following Him? Of course not; that would undermine the whole process. So as He regathers the Jews, He is also saving and growing a remnant among them that loves and follows Yeshua. They are preparing the nation for spiritual revival in the future.

Not just today, but for much of her history, Israel sinned grievously while living in the Promised Land. She was not walking in perfect, holy obedience when Joshua led her into Canaan (see Joshua 7:1, 11). Many years later, after her first exile, she was not collectively faithful to God when He regathered her. Ezra was part of this regathering. He told the Jews their return to the land had nothing to do with their righteousness. They had come back because "grace has been shown from the LORD our God" (Ezra 9:8; see also 9:1–15 NKJV). After Ezra, the Jewish people lived in the land for five hundred years, with only a remnant faithfully serving the Lord. Israel's spiritual condition then was comparable to her condition today. For better or worse, her collective unbelief at this phase of her restoration is consistent with the Scriptures. This does not excuse Israel's sin, but demonstrates God's extreme mercy and grace that sustains her today.

Twice Cursed and Divinely Reversed

Israel's present regathering parallels Bible prophecy in still other ways. God's Word describes two—and only two—exiles and returns to the land (see Isaiah 11:11). The first exile occurred from 723 to 586 BC. The Jews who returned from it under Ezra's guidance came from just one place (Babylon). The second exile, which took place in AD 70, dispersed the Jews all over the earth. This is the dispersion that would end when God regathered His people "from all the countries" (Ezekiel 36:24). So unlike the first, the second regathering is global in nature. Not just Ezekiel, but other prophets were shown a similar worldwide return in the last days (see Isaiah 11:10–12; Jeremiah 16:15; 23:3; 29:14). The Zionist movement, starting in the late 1800s, represents the only global Jewish regathering in history. It reflects the second regathering described in the Hebrew Scriptures and affirmed by the New Covenant.

The Zionist movement, though certainly imperfect, is consistent with the ways of God. It is not, as some allege, a coincidental mistake of history in which the Jewish people regathered themselves. Our God is sovereign over the rise and fall of nations (see Acts 17:26–27). He alone can remove His covenant people from their land or return them back to it. As Messianic scholar Michael Brown points out,[2] God describes Israel's exile from the land as His curse upon her,[b] and the Church has historically regarded it as such. If He does not reverse His own curse, then, as the Church has taught for nearly two millennia, it cannot possibly be lifted.[c] No human enterprise can withstand the decree of our omnipotent King. If the Jews are regathered to their land, He is ultimately responsible for it.

To be sure, God uses human beings in the process, just as He used King Cyrus, Artaxerxes and others to bring about Israel's first regathering (see Ezra 1:1–4; Nehemiah 2:4–9). In the process of Israel's restoration today, the loving support of believers from the nations is a sign that the "time to show favor" to Zion has come (Psalm 102:13; see Isaiah 49:22). Their blessing and succor points presciently to the fullness of the Gentiles. The fullness of the Gentiles, in turn, suggests that the times of the Gentiles are coming to a close.

If we insist that Israel's present restoration does not align with God's will, it seems we must accuse Him of doing a sloppy job with His curses, and use a faulty hermeneutic to seriously misinterpret the Scriptures. The Almighty has not been outwitted by zealous Zionists, Holocaust-guilty Western countries or anyone else. He has merely and magnificently done what He said He would do, reversing His curse and fulfilling His Word.

Israel Is a Work in Progress

Some prophecies are fulfilled in the blink of an eye, but others take decades or centuries or longer. Israel's restoration to the land and to the Lord is not an instantaneous event. The Jewish state is very much a work in progress.[3] Beginning over a century ago, the process could take much more time than we expect. During this period, human beings exercise free will and demonic opposition exists. As a result, temporary setbacks occur. Sometimes it looks like Israel takes two steps forward, followed by one step backward.

At this writing, for example, the Jewish state has relinquished most of the land she acquired in wars she was forced to defensively fight. In addition, the nation is beset by much of the same sin affecting the rest of the world—and also the Church. There is sexual and ethical immorality, drug addition, human trafficking, widespread abortion and more. But if we deny the prophetic truth of Israel's restoration because Jews still sin, to be fair, we ought to also deny the prophetic truth of the Gospel because Christians still sin. (Just to be clear: I suggest neither!)

Israel's restoration will not reach perfected fulfillment until after the Lord returns.[d] Meanwhile, those who doubt her regathering is genuinely from Him because it is taking so long might consider Yeshua's advice to people of His day who were similarly perplexed. A group of Jewish messengers once approached Him to ask if He was the "Coming One," or if they should expect another. Yeshua told them to go back and report what they had seen and heard: The lame walked, the blind received sight, the deaf could hear and the poor got good news (see Luke 7:20–22). He added, "Blessed is he who is not offended because of Me" (verse 23 NKJV).

What have we seen and heard about modern Israel? For the first time in two thousand years, Jews have returned from the ends of the earth to their ancestral home. Their ancient language has been revived. Against all odds, Israel has defended herself from millions of mortal enemies surrounding her. In many ways the nation has thrived, rebuilding ancient cities and making deserts bloom. Fruit from the Promised Land blesses every continent, from oranges and grapes to biomedical/technological breakthroughs. Jerusalem is mostly not trampled down. Since the city was returned to Israel in 1967, more Jews have come to faith in Yeshua than in the previous 1,900 years combined. Indigenous believers now worship Messiah in every city and town. Some go out to the nations ministering the Gospel. Blessed is he who is not offended because of what God is doing in our day!

Can We Be Neutral Bystanders?

To those tempted with offense, the one-chapter book of Obadiah practically shouts with prophetic advice. Obadiah writes originally to Edom, Esau's descendants: "Because of the violence against *your brother* Jacob, you will be covered with shame; you will be destroyed forever" (Obadiah 10, emphasis mine). The prophet reminds Edom—and us—that we will be treated according to how we have treated the Jews (see Genesis 12:3). Obadiah's message applies uniquely to Christians because they have been embraced like brothers into a Jewish-rooted family of faith.

According to the prophet, ignoring Israel's assault or exploitation by others is the same, in God's eyes, as aggressively attacking her: "On the day you stood aloof while strangers carried off his wealth and foreigners entered his gates and cast lots for Jerusalem, you were like one of them" (Obadiah 11).

The Living Bible says more pointedly: "For you deserted Israel in his time of need. You stood aloof, refusing to lift a finger to help him when invaders carried off his wealth and divided Jerusalem among them. *You were as one of his enemies*" (emphasis mine).

Obadiah uses a Hebrew term for *stood aloof* that speaks powerfully to us today. The word refers to a posture of intentionally abstaining from positive action. The idea is that of bystanding, or purposely distancing oneself from a problem. When Israel's enemies act violently against her, God does not want us staying silent, ignoring her plight or neutrally standing by. If we do not get involved—or at least pray—we may ourselves be counted by Him as her enemies.

Consider how Israeli foreign minister Abba Eban described the nation's quandary at the inception of the Six Day War: "As we looked around us we saw the world divided between those who were seeking our destruction and those who would do nothing to prevent it."[4] Dr. Martin Luther King Jr.[e] similarly remarked that in the end, those who are treated unjustly remember not the words of their enemies, but the silence of their friends.[5]

Obadiah admonishes even more seriously those who go beyond neutrality and take open delight in Israel's defeat. The next time you see Islamists or social activists celebrate or sneer at Israeli suffering—and appeal to Christians for support—remember these piercing words:

> You should not gloat over your brother [Israel] in the day of his misfortune, nor rejoice over the people of Judah in the day of their destruction, nor boast so much in the day of their trouble. You should not march through the gates of my people in the day of their disaster, nor gloat over them in their calamity in the day of their disaster, nor seize their wealth in the day of their disaster. You should not wait at the crossroads to cut down their fugitives, nor hand over their survivors in the day of their trouble.
>
> Obadiah 12–14

Finally, Obadiah issues a clarion call to every generation:

> The Lord's vengeance will soon fall upon all Gentile nations. As you have done to Israel, so will it be done to you. Your acts will boomerang upon your heads.
>
> Obadiah 15 TLB

God takes note of how we treat Israel in her time of distress. Neutrally standing by while the world curses and assails her is not an option. What would you like to "boomerang upon your head"? Send it to Israel, and in one form or another you will get it back.

Is Arab Palestine in Prophecy?

When God gave Ezekiel visions of a Jewish restoration, He included a sobering message for those seeking to overrun "the mountains of Israel" or her "ancient heights" (Ezekiel 36:1–3). The mountains and ancient heights include Judea and Samaria, also known as the West Bank. Some believe that prophecies about the mountains and heights of Israel apply today to putative Palestine.[f]

God decrees judgment for those staking claim to these territories for their "ancient hatred" and for shedding Jewish blood (see Ezekiel 35:5 NKJV). Then He chastises other nations joining in the fray:

> The enemy said of you, "Aha! The ancient heights have become our possession." Therefore prophesy and say, "This is what the Sovereign LORD says: Because they ravaged and crushed you from every side so that you became the possession of the rest of the nations and the object of people's malicious talk and slander . . . I have spoken against the rest of the nations, and against all Edom, for with glee and with malice in their hearts they made my land their own possession so that they might plunder its pastureland. . . . But you, mountains of Israel, will produce branches and fruit for my people Israel, for they will soon come home."
>
> Ezekiel 36:2–3, 5, 8

God's "jealous wrath" is roused and He "swears with uplifted hand" these nations will suffer great scorn (verses 6–7). As for the mountains and heights of Israel, they will be returned to the Jewish people with blessing and favor.

The Scriptures indicate that despite many warnings, the nations impose ill-intended divisions of Israel's land. For this they are severely judged: "At that time, when I restore the fortunes of Judah and Jerusalem, I will gather all nations and . . . enter into judgment against them concerning my inheritance, my people Israel, for they scattered my people among the nations and *divided up my land*" (Joel 3:2 NIV1984, emphasis mine). In modern times, the nations have divided up Israel's land over and over again, going all the way back to the British Mandate. And today, the world has slated the city of Jerusalem for a slicing.

Jerusalem: Pray for the Peace or Prey for the Piece

Psalm 122:6 gives us a succinct and enduring prayer request: "Pray for the peace of Jerusalem: 'May those who love you be secure.'" God is passionate about His city and her future. The gospels recount that Yeshua wept on only two occasions in His earthly ministry, one being over Jerusalem (see Luke 19:41). But God is also passionate about *you*; your own security is connected to Jerusalem. Events taking place in the holy city ripple in the Spirit and rumble on the ground to all nations. And whether we pray or not, God's enemies prey mendaciously for their piece of Jerusalem.

Because I live in the Jerusalem area, I am often asked how best to pray for the city. My answer always starts out the same: Pray for the Prince of Peace to be welcomed into the hearts of those who live here. He alone—no international community or coalition—can bring lasting peace to Jerusalem. Pray that His Kingdom will come and His will be done in Jerusalem as it is in heaven. Then, listening to the leading of the Spirit, go on to the specific and critical issues of the day. Realize that praying for Jerusalem means not just lifting up Israel's capital city, but beyond that, the whole Jewish state. It includes praying for Jerusalem's large Arab population, too.

Jerusalem is destined to serve as the flashpoint of Kingdom conflict on earth. Entities and empires will prey for their piece of the place where God's name has been put. Meanwhile, as events unfold, He will note our hearts' response to them. Will we resign from responsibility or stand up and speak out? At minimum, He wants us to care and to pray.

To help you pray for the peace of Jerusalem, I have condensed hundreds of Scripture-based points into a broadly defined few. The ten categories below provide a flexible framework into which specific details can be added as the Holy Spirit leads and circumstances change. I encourage you to pray for:

- The outpouring of "a spirit of grace and supplication" (Zechariah 12:10), leading to the salvation of Jews, Arabs and others in Jerusalem (Isaiah 30:19; Romans 10:1; 1 Timothy 2:3–4);

- Strengthening and maturing of the Body of Messiah (John 17; Acts 4:29–31; Romans 15:26–27), including laborers for the harvest (Luke 10:2);

- Righteousness and wisdom for all spiritual, governmental, social, military and other authorities (1 Timothy 2:1–2; Proverbs 21:1);

- Domestic and internal unity, accord and peace within Jerusalem (Psalm 122:3, 8);

- Physical restoration through God's regathering of the Jewish people (aliyah) and material prosperity (Psalm 147:2; Jeremiah 30:17; Psalm 122:9);

- Security, protection and defense from attack (Psalm 91; Psalm 125), including salvation for Israel's enemies who seek to overtake her (Psalm 83:18);

- The outworking of prophetic events according to the ideal timing of God (Ecclesiastes 3:1–8; Matthew 24:22);

- Your church's and nation's blessing of Jerusalem (Genesis 12:3; Obadiah);

- Intercessors who give God "no rest till he establishes Jerusalem and makes her the praise of the earth" (Isaiah 62:6–7); and

- Fulfillment of Jerusalem's destiny as the City of the Great King (Matthew 5:35) that blesses all nations (Psalm 48; Isaiah 2:2–3; 62:1–2).

Praying for Jerusalem's Temple

Some believers are intrigued by the rebuilding of Jerusalem's Temple and earnestly desire to pray for it. If you are among them, please bear in mind that the Jewish people preparing to build a third Temple hope to reconstruct not just an edifice, but a whole system designed to substitute the blood of animals for Messiah's atonement. Resumed animal sacrifice will render the Crucified One, in their eyes, more irrelevant than ever. At the same time, some of these zealots anticipate that the Temple, once up and running, will herald the coming of their messiah—a *man,* definitely *not* Yeshua, who establishes world peace. Certainly, Yeshua may completely cleanse this Temple when He returns, then rule and reign from that purified place. Though worthy of anticipation, the project is mentioned in Scripture only in connection with its desecration (see Daniel 9:25–27; Matthew 24:15; 2 Thessalonians 2:3–4; Revelation 13:14–15).

The Bible also describes a fourth Temple wherein only the true Messiah will be worshiped in holy splendor (see Ezekiel 40–48). This Temple will be enormous in size, many times larger than the entire Temple Mount as it now exists (see Ezekiel 42:15–20). Whether the sacred structure pertains to the coming Messianic Age, whether it exists in the new heaven and earth—or both—we cannot yet be sure.

We can, meanwhile, be certain and supportive of another kind of temple-building taking place in Jerusalem. Yeshua died for *living temples* He would, by the Holy Spirit, indwell (see 2 Corinthians 6:16). We can invest wholeheartedly in those living temples: Jewish, Arab and other believers in Jerusalem who love and follow the Lord. They carry the presence of the Prince of Peace wherever they go.

Psalm 83 Conspiracy

To align with God's heart and Kingdom plans, those who pray for Israel need to have at least a general understanding of end times prophecy concerning her. As you probably know, different believers hold different interpretations of specific end times events and details. Some Christians even insist the events will not occur at all because they have been fulfilled spiritually in Jesus. But I believe the Lord wants us to have some idea of the future, or He would not have given us hundreds of Scriptures concerning it. In previous chapters, we have looked at some of the blessings and glories that lie ahead for Israel and the nations. We turn now to a distilled macro-view of some of the battles that will also come to pass.

Psalm 83 describes a besetting Middle East campaign against a beleaguered Jewish state. A military operation based on the alignment of nations in this passage has never historically taken place. For that reason, some Bible scholars say Psalm 83 is merely hyperbolic. Because it had no ancient, initial fulfillment, we should not expect one in the future.

Others believe the psalm literally relates how every nation in her neighborhood unites against Israel: Edom and the Ishmaelites (now Jordanian and Palestinian areas, together with Saudi Arabia), Moab (Jordanian and Palestinian areas), the Hagrites (Syria, Saudi Arabia and possibly Egypt), Gebal (north Lebanon), Ammon (Jordanian and Palestinian areas), Amalek (Sinai desert), Philistia (Gaza), Tyre (southern Lebanon), Assyria (areas of Syria, Iraq and possibly Turkey) and Lot (Jordanian and Palestinian areas).[6] Verse 4 sounds their bellicose cry: "Come . . . let us destroy them as a nation, so that Israel's name is remembered no more."

Since the moment she became a modern state, Israel's enemies have rallied to this refrain. The call to destroy her as a nation is echoed, practically nonstop, throughout the Middle East. Psalm 83 could describe a unified Islamist operation undertaken in the future. But note that it is not necessarily limited to a military campaign in the traditional sense. The weapons used against Israel here refer mainly to a conspiracy of spoken words. As we have seen, a war of words now wages relentlessly against the Jewish state by all the people groups described above. It seems we are already experiencing a limited prophetic fulfillment of Psalm 83.

The psalm closes with a prayer I strongly encourage you to make your own. Amid the treacherous onslaught, the psalmist petitions God to exalt Himself—for the sake of the nations attacking: "May they ever be ashamed and dismayed. . . . Let them know that you, whose name is the LORD—that you alone are the Most High over all the earth" (verses 17–18). Yahweh's overarching goal in end times warfare is to manifest His supremacy. He will ultimately use the Islamist/Arab/Palestinian–Israeli conflict to do it.

Ezekiel's Vision of War

Ezekiel 38–39 describes a cataclysmic war that has not yet taken place. "Gog, of the land of Magog," spearheads a military coalition seeking to destroy Israel (see Ezekiel 38:2). But God actually instigates the attack:

> "I am against you, Gog, chief prince of Meshek and Tubal. I will turn you around, put hooks in your jaws and bring you out with your whole army. . . . In future years you will invade a land . . . whose people were gathered from many nations to the mountains of Israel, which had long been desolate . . . and now all of them live in safety."
>
> Ezekiel 38:3–4, 8

This "great horde" descends from the "far north" (verse 15), joined by Persia, Cush, Put, Gomer and Beth Togarmah (see verses 5–6). The Jewish people are living in their land but are not yet following the Lord. His purpose in the war is to draw both Israel and the nations to Himself.

The passage indicates that Israel experiences a significant—but not lasting—period of peace and prosperity before the assault. Some Bible scholars believe this has already been achieved, and so the war could occur any moment, or at least very soon. Others believe the war may not take place until the Great Tribulation (described later in this chapter). They interpret the peace as resulting from a false peace treaty brokered by the Antichrist. Gog is either aligned with the Antichrist, they say, or he *is* the Antichrist.

For many years, prophecy teachers identified Russia as leading the Ezekiel 38 invasion. With the rise of fundamentalist Islam, some now theorize the onslaught will be led by either Iran or a revived Turkish-based caliphate. Other than Russia and part of Turkey, the nations and peoples listed in Ezekiel 38 appear to be located in the Middle East, North Africa and Central Asia.[7] Notably, every state in that region is now Islamic and none is friendly toward Israel.

Yahweh plans to pulverize this coalition that invades Israel when she is enjoying relative calm and rest. He decimates her enemies with a monstrous earthquake, accompanied by lightning, fire and brimstone, torrents of bloodshed and a plague (see Ezekiel 38:19, 22). The destruction resembles that of a horrific nuclear blast. Displaying His awesome power, God stuns the world in His defense of the Jews:

> "And so I will show my greatness and my holiness, and I will make myself known in the sight of many nations. Then they will know that I am the LORD."
>
> Ezekiel 38:23

> "I will display my glory among the nations, and all the nations will see the punishment I inflict and the hand I lay upon them. From that day forward the people of Israel will know that I am the LORD their God. . . . I will no longer hide my face from them, for I will pour out my Spirit on the people of Israel."
>
> Ezekiel 39:21–22, 29

Zechariah's Prophecy of Jerusalem

The prophet Zechariah describes a scenario in which God pours out His wrath on a cohort of nations invading Jerusalem. In chapters 12–14, he foresees a series of events leading to the Second Coming and Millennial Age:

> "I am going to make Jerusalem a cup that sends all the surrounding peoples reeling. . . . On that day, when all the nations of the earth are gathered against her, I will make Jerusalem an immovable rock for all the nations. All who try to move it will injure themselves. . . . On that day I will set out to destroy all the nations that attack Jerusalem."
>
> Zechariah 12:2–3, 9

Today the nations have aligned against Jerusalem as never before. In Zechariah 12, however, those trying to conquer or divide her get crippled in the process. God makes the city an "immovable rock" they cannot lift or push around. In this context, Jerusalem recognizes her Messiah, repents and returns to God:

> "And I will pour out on the house of David and the inhabitants of Jerusalem a spirit of grace and supplication. They will look on me, the one they have pierced, and they will mourn for him as one mourns for an only child, and grieve bitterly for him as one grieves for a firstborn son. . . . On that day a fountain will be opened to the house of David and the inhabitants of Jerusalem, to cleanse them from sin and impurity."
>
> Zechariah 12:10; 13:1

In His physical body, Yeshua arrives with His armies and defends Jerusalem. "On that day his feet will stand on the Mount of Olives, east of Jerusalem" (Zechariah 14:4). He unleashes cataclysmic judgments against those who attacked His city and His people. Then, ushering in the Messianic Age, He assumes glorious kingship over all the earth (see Zechariah 14).

Spiritual dynamics that crescendo in the battle for Jerusalem have already begun to manifest. Israeli sovereignty over the city is threatened by the nations. Simultaneously, a spirit of grace and supplication is drizzling over Jerusalem, where some Jewish people report they are receiving entirely supernatural revelations of Yeshua. The more the world comes against Jerusalem, the more God wants us contending for her to "look on me, the one they have pierced," and see Messiah, His Son.

When Do the Battles Occur?

Not just Ezekiel and Zechariah, but practically all the prophets record glimpses of cataclysmic end times battles waged against Israel. Joel 3:2 speaks of the Valley of Jehoshaphat. The War of Armageddon is referenced in Revelation 16:16. The Day of the Lord, with all its devastating warfare, is described in Amos 5:18 and Malachi 4:5. Isaiah and others foresee similar attacks against Zion.

The prevailing view is that these eschatological battles are completely and chronologically distinct from each other. The invasion led by Gog of Magog is thought to describe something entirely different, and years apart, from the assault on Jerusalem, or the battle in the Valley of Jehoshaphat, and so on. Commentators have had various interpretations on the timing and order of Israel's future wars.

An alternative view is supported by some traditional rabbinic writings and contemporary Christian scholars. According to their understanding, the prophets were shown different battles all taking place during the same colossal, years-long military campaign. Together, they describe a single gargantuan war that is fought on different battlefronts shortly before the Messianic Age.

It is honest and fair to say that God has not yet clearly disclosed to His people all the details of these end times battles.

Even the prophets who wrote down their revelations of the events did not always fully understand them (see Daniel 12:8–9). However matters unfold, there is much suffering during this time—but also a magnificent move of God's Spirit. When darkness covers the earth, His brilliant glory rises upon His people (see Isaiah 60:1–2). Our response to Him, in both prayer and deed, may profoundly affect how realities play out.

Israel's Future Suffering and Sanctification

In the context of end times battles, certain prophetic Scriptures portray Israel as devastatingly overrun, nationally shattered and partially rescattered amid the fighting.[g] At first glance, these verses can seem inconsistent with Israel's present regathering and restoration. As a result, some Christians have concluded that the Jewish nation exists today only for her "necessary failure" in the future. Is this a stance the Bible teaches we should take?

First and foremost, we must remember that God grieves over the suffering of His people. When they suffer He suffers, too. Concerning Israel's distress, "in all their affliction He was afflicted" (Isaiah 63:9 NKJV). Therefore, the prospect of Israel's future suffering should cause us to grieve rather than harden our hearts. God wants us praying passionately for the Jewish nation in her day of trouble and caring for her needs (see Matthew 25:34–40). The expectation of peril and plight should not lead us to cease supporting her. If anything, we should be moved toward even greater expressions of His covenant love for Israel.

Second, verses about Israel's future suffering can be properly understood only in connection with other related passages. As we have seen, Israel's restoration is gradual and progressive. In the process, she appears to take some steps backward instead of forward. This does not, however, change the big picture, the overall trajectory of what Yahweh is doing with her (see Acts 3:17–21). The Jewish people are being fully restored to their land and their Lord.

On the one side, prophetic passages in the Bible indicate severe distress lies ahead. International opposition to God and His people will reach its zenith during a unique span of seven years, just before the onset of the Messianic Age. The Hebrew Scriptures refer to this as the "time of Jacob's trouble" or "the day of the Lord" (Jeremiah 30:4–7; Joel 1:15; 3:14 NKJV). The New Covenant describes it as a period of "great tribulation," so Christians generally call it the Great Tribulation.

But on the other side, the Great Tribulation is not limited to the Jewish state. The entire earth convulses under the heinous rule of the Antichrist and outpouring of God's judgments.[h] Military conflagrations erupt in many places other than Israel. Not only Jews, but all who follow Yahweh are fiercely persecuted during this time.[i] In the end, every nation—*not just Israel*—is broken and laid low. These years prove so devastating that half of all humankind is killed (see Revelation 6:8; 9:15–18). No person or nation would survive if not for a divine shortening of the time (see Matthew 24:22; Joel 2:11). In that sense, we could say that *every* nation is doomed and exists for its "necessary failure" apart from Yeshua.

As horrific as it will be, the Great Tribulation represents a relatively brief period of history. Those few years do not upend God's everlasting covenants. They do not undermine the trajectory of His love or mercy and grace toward Israel. During the Great Tribulation, many Jews turn to faith in Yeshua and proclaim the Gospel, in the power of the Spirit, to nations abroad. A great harvest of souls is reaped.[j] (At a certain point related to the Great Tribulation, believers are caught up in the air to be with Yeshua in what is known as the Rapture [see 1 Thessalonians 4:15–17; 1 Corinthians 15:51–52][8]).

At the Second Coming, Yeshua arrives "with thousands upon thousands of his holy ones" and spectacularly defeats the Antichrist (Jude 14). The devil and his hordes are banished from the planet for a thousand years (see Revelation 20:2–3). Messiah judges all nations, based in part on how they responded to Jewish suffering in the Great Tribulation. He tenderly and completely regathers Jews who are not in the land.[k] Then, as His heart has long yearned to do, He restores His Jewish "brothers and sisters" to Himself, their Savior and King, with unmatched loving-kindness (Matthew 25:40; Romans 11:26). Israel's consummate restoration follows, as well as that of the nations—and even the earth itself. Under Messiah's thousand-year leadership, the planet is rehabilitated to a resplendent, Eden-like condition. It is in effect brought back to "life from the dead" (see Romans 11:15). Then, after more testing, comes the glorious new heaven and earth.[l]

From Here to Eternity

God has graciously given us a broad outline in His Word of that which is to come. But He does not intend for us to compromise our expression of His love, mercy and grace because of our expectation of "inevitable" prophecy (see Jeremiah 18:7–10; Jonah 3:10). A key reason we are told about future events is so we will pray proactively concerning them, and not wait passively to be evacuated out of them. Through prayer, the nature and severity of suffering can be greatly diminished. Recall that ancient Nineveh received a firm prophecy from Jonah, but when the city repented in prayer, the prophecy did not come to pass quite as predicted (see Jonah 3). For even in wrath, God desires to remember mercy. Usually, however, someone must stand in the gap and wholeheartedly ask Him to release it.

As the apocalyptic hour approaches, God wants our hearts aligned with His, postured to weep with those who weep. He wants us ministering the Gospel of the Kingdom in the power of the Spirit. He wants us caring about and comforting the Jewish people in their distress—just like past heroes of the faith, as we see in the next chapter.

14

Altar of Sacrifice

> Therefore, I urge you, brothers and sisters, in view of God's mercy, to offer your bodies as a living sacrifice, holy and pleasing to God—this is your true and proper worship.
>
> Romans 12:1

I love stories about heroes of the faith. Not only Bible accounts, but biographies of tried-and-true saints through history who have stood valiantly for God despite the cost. Their courage convicts and inspires me. I am convicted because I want to be so in love with Yeshua that nothing deters me from taking up my cross and following Him. He is wholly worthy of all I am, or have, or could possibly ever offer Him. I am inspired because I know all believers are called, to varying degrees, to the sacrament of suffering for the Kingdom's sake. "All who desire to live godly in Christ Jesus will suffer persecution" (2 Timothy 3:12 NKJV).

The story of Pastor Richard Wurmbrand[1] was known throughout the twentieth-century Christian world. Wurmbrand was a Romanian Jewish believer imprisoned by Nazis, then Communists, for fourteen years. For his faith in Yeshua, he endured excruciating, repulsively inhumane tortures. During that time, he said, he also experienced unspeakable joy in the Savior's abiding presence and intimate love. After a miraculous release from prison, Wurmbrand founded a ministry to support persecuted believers around the world.

I met Pastor Wurmbrand long ago, when he was in his eighties and living in the US. His face was weathered with crevices and grooves that bore witness to previous pain, and he limped from his former lashings. But Wurmbrand's eyes sparkled with life and his countenance glowed. Every word he spoke rippled supernatural love and otherworldly peace into the atmosphere. The aged Jewish saint had offered his body a living sacrifice as his spiritual act of worship. That his offering had been holy and pleasing to God was strikingly evident.

I once asked Pastor Wurmbrand if he felt profound spiritual depth and Messiah-likeness could be attained only through severe suffering. I will never forget his humble reply. I would have liked it so much more if he had simply said no. But instead he fixed his eyes on mine with fatherly compassion and, after a brief silence, assured me that opportunities to die to self in order to live for Yeshua were not limited to dank Romanian prisons. "Each day," Pastor Wurmbrand said, "wherever you are and whatever you do, you can choose to offer your body as a living sacrifice—or not."

Living Sacrifices

The apostle Paul was well acquainted with suffering and sacrifice for Messiah's sake. Not by accident does he refer to them immediately after sharing his cornerstone message on Israel. In

Romans 9–11 the Spirit has just given him—and us—revelation of God's covenant mercy and grace. His plan of redemption for humankind involves one nation through which all others are eternally blessed. That nation has sacrificed much. Now, through the Church, Israel may receive mercy as a result of how God has used her to release mercy to the Gentiles (see Romans 11:31). Paul cannot help but exuberantly praise Him for His unparalleled plan. God's merciful ways are "unsearchable" and "to him be the glory forever!" (Romans 11:33, 36).

The apostle continues in Romans 12:1, "*Therefore*, I urge you, brothers and sisters, in view of God's mercy, to offer your bodies as a living sacrifice, holy and pleasing to God—this is your true and proper worship" (emphasis mine). The Amplified Bible puts it like this:

> I appeal to you *therefore*, brethren, and beg of you in view of all the mercies of God, to make a decisive dedication of your bodies—presenting all your members and faculties—as a living sacrifice, holy (devoted, consecrated) and well pleasing to God, which is your reasonable (rational, intelligent) service and spiritual worship.
>
> (emphasis mine)

You have probably heard it said that when we see *therefore* in the Scriptures, we need to ask what it is there for. In this instance, we are plainly told: In light of all we have just read about Israel and God's mercy, worship Him properly by offering our bodies in living sacrifice.

Bible scholar Mark Nanos interprets Romans 12:1 as a call for Christian sacrifice in view of Israel's sacrifice on behalf of the Gentiles:

> They [the Romans] are somehow, in God's unsearchable judgments and unfathomable ways, benefiting from the "stumbling"

on the part of Israel, whom they are so quick to condemn for not believing what they now believe. Certainly, this is cause for humility where arrogance had once been tempting, laying the groundwork for the commitment Paul urges from 12:1 onward . . . in the tradition of the suffering of Christ Jesus.[2]

Wouldn't it have been nice if, instead, God had said to worship by offering up our songs, hymns and high-tech church services? Such worship would certainly be more consistent with today's Western concept of "proper." But the Almighty said to offer up more—our bodies—even as Yeshua did.

> Follow God's example . . . and walk in the way of love, just as Christ loved us and gave himself up for us as a fragrant offering and sacrifice to God.
>
> Ephesians 5:1–2

> "Whoever desires to come after Me, let him deny himself, and take up his cross, and follow Me. For whoever desires to save his life will lose it, but whoever loses his life for My sake and the gospel's will save it."
>
> Mark 8:34–35 NKJV

In the days ahead, the call to sacrificial worship and Christlikeness, or the "fullness of the Gentiles," will be linked more and more with Israel. As this present age draws to a close, saying yes to the call will not be easy. Some will be willing—but some will not.

The Choice

God uses Israel to expose the intents of our hearts. It has always been so, even for the One we follow, Yeshua crucified and resurrected. "Greater love," He said, "has no one than this: to lay down one's life for one's friends" (John 15:13).

In God's hand and plan, Israel will prove a point of division among humankind—a last days' great divide. The Church will not be exempt. Lies will arise about the Jewish people obscured in a worldly reasonableness that will persuade and pervert many. Slowly and subtly, as in the past, devilish deceptions about Israel/Zionism/the Jews will overtake the nations, including many Christians. As you know from this book, it is already happening.

Professor Robert Wistrich is regarded by many as the world's foremost scholar on anti-Semitism. In his 2010 tome, *A Lethal Obsession,* Wistrich concludes that less than seventy years after the Holocaust, "the politics of genocidal anti-Semitism—and the indifference that made it possible—are still with us."[3] Wistrich is not an alarmist; he is a clear-thinking academic.

Basilea Schlink wrote decades ago that future generations of Christians who support anti-Semitism may suddenly find themselves on the wrong side, just as many German believers failed to recognize Nazism and its theology as an enemy of God. She warns that anti-Semitism reflects the anti-Christ spirit:

> As God's plan of salvation nears its final consummation . . . and hatred flares up against Him more than ever, there will be a bringing together of those who belong together because they fear the living God and give Him glory—Jews and Christians.[4] . . . But if all the time we have been opposing God's people or else condoning the attacks made on them by powers hostile to God, woe betide us later when the whole world is caught up in a rebellion against God! Then, even without noticing it, we shall suddenly find ourselves on the side of the antichristian kingdom, whose prime target will be the Jews. . . . [For] our relationship with them is indicative of our true relationship to the Lord Jesus, showing whether it is a relationship of love. If we love Jesus, we

shall love the people whom He loves and always will love and who will yet be the centre and blessing of all nations.[5]

During the lifetime of many readers of this book, Israel's overt battles have been fought mostly with Palestinians and terrorist groups. But signs point to a change. The slightest spark could ignite regional conflagration in the tinderbox of the Middle East. Expect Israel to be at the center of it—along with the Commander of the armies of heaven.

The Jewish nation will remain a testing ground in years to come. But our God does not test us in order to torment us. His tests are designed to conform us to the image of His Son, refining us for outrageous blessing and destiny. He wants us shining as beacons of light to a dark, perplexed world in the throes of kingdom conflict. In the process, He is grooming His Bride.

Jesus cautions that in the last days, because of the increase of wickedness—a significant degree of which will revolve around Israel—the love of most will grow cold. Both good and evil will simultaneously increase. Nations, organizations and individuals will polarize over the controversy of Zion. Unprecedented dimensions of heaven—and hell—will impact the earth. Riptides of revival will meet with reprisal. Many may be persecuted for righteousness' sake. But in the end, the Bride of Christ—those fervidly loving Him, radically obeying Him and denying themselves for Him will align with the Jews. Will that include you?

Are you waiting to get a personal word from God before you decide? Friend, you may never hear it. You see, this is about *your* choice, based on *your* heart and the Word that is already in you.

Are you holding out until a major stand must be taken? Are you waiting until your Jewish neighbor shows up one day on your doorstep, suddenly in need of a hiding place? In case you have not realized it, the test has already begun. You are already taking a stand each time you choose how to access and process the news, or how to pray, or how to study the Scriptures, or how to speak within your personal sphere of influence, or how to promote social justice—or how to respond to this book. As an Israeli ambassador once told the UN about actions destructive to the Jewish state, "God is watching."[6]

The Remnant in Revelation

Will you be part of the joining of God's Old and New Covenant people in a shared last days' Kingdom destiny? He is preparing the way for Yeshua's return by preparing hearts. He is looking for those willing to learn to love unconditionally, whose heartbeats resonate to His own. He will join them together with like-minded Messianic Jews as one new humanity. Together, we will joyfully set the stage for the greatest revival—and revelation—on earth. Thrilling times are ahead.

The book of Revelation, with its mystifying and pulsating prophetic symbolism, also foretells of some down-to-earth, seemingly soon-coming events. One of these involves "the 144,000" (see Revelation 7:3–17; 14:1–5). Coming from "all the tribes of Israel," with 12,000 per tribe, they are distinct from a larger group, called the "great multitude" (see 7:4–9). The great multitude comes from every nation, tribe, people and language; they are not necessarily Jews. A subgroup of the great multitude, the 144,000 stand on Mount Zion, "follow the Lamb wherever he goes" and are "offered as first fruits to God and the Lamb" (14:1, 4). Apparently, they are gathered from within the Jewish state, Messianic Jews awaiting Yeshua's return. But offered as first fruits, many may be martyred.

A sacrament of suffering may await us. You and I may have opportunity to worship in total self-sacrifice to the Worthy One.

If so, we will be in very good company. We will join countless courageous saints of the past, like the valiant family of Corrie ten Boom.

Heroes of the Holocaust

The beloved and unforgettable Corrie ten Boom, together with her family, took up a cross of self-sacrifice for the Jews of Holland during the Holocaust. Like Ruth in the Bible, the ten Booms were extravagantly blessed. But not as you or I might expect.

When the Nazis overtook Holland, Jews came knocking, one by one, on the ten Booms' door. "In this household," Corrie's father had said, "God's people are always welcome."[7] The ten Booms loved the Jewish people ultimately for one reason: They loved God. Their home quickly became a hiding place for Dutch Jews with nowhere else to go—until one horrifying day, German soldiers knocked on the door.

What was this family's reward for their blessing of Israel, their kneeling to enrich the Jews? Imprisonment and sentencing to a concentration camp, where they all, except Corrie, died. Did the ten Booms know what they were getting into? Indeed. Losing their lives for the Jews, Corrie's father said from the start, would be "the greatest honor that could come to my family."[8]

Corrie was miraculously released from prison one day before her scheduled execution, the result of a "clerical error." In years to come millions around the world would hear her story. They would learn of a woman who lived extraordinarily beyond a place of blessing; they would encounter in her the Blesser Himself.

Corrie is but one of a righteous remnant of twentieth-century Christians who sacrificially cared for the Jews. Archbishop

Stefan of the Bulgarian Orthodox Church saved virtually all of Bulgaria's 50,000 Jewish citizens from the Holocaust. No other church in any other country resisted Hitler as did the church under Stefan's leadership. The archbishop effectively persuaded the Bulgarian government to refuse German orders to deport Jews. When Nazi troops arrived, some priests stood alongside intended victims as human shields. Said one to the frightened Jewish people of his town, "Where you go I will go." Echoing the vow of Ruth, it is reported that he meant every word.[9]

Jewish-Catholic nun Edith Stein was offered a way of easy escape in the Holocaust. Instead she chose to accompany and comfort the Jewish people up to the end. Leaving her convent in Europe for a concentration camp, she took a sister's hand and, according to witnesses, said, "Come, let us go for our people."[10] She was not heard from again.

Such heroes were the exception, however, to the collective Christian response to World War II. Martyred for his own stand against Hitler, Rev. Dietrich Bonhoeffer wrote, "The Church . . . has been unwilling to suffer for what she knows to be right. Thus the Church is guilty of becoming a traitor to the Lordship of Christ."[11]

The Joy of the Cross

Standing for God and sharing His heart for Israel means sacrifice of self—and for some, perhaps even martyrdom—in the spirit of Romans 12:1. But those who bless Israel are blessed. They bless God who blesses bountifully of Himself in return. If He uses the Jewish nation to summon us *to* the cross, the cross summons to *us* the Blesser Himself.

Famed missionary-martyr Jim Elliot said, "He is no fool who gives what he cannot keep to gain what he cannot lose."[12] I have learned that the more a sacrifice costs, the more blessing it tends to release. The more I give myself to Messiah, the more He gives Himself to me. I discover that whatever was to my profit is loss for the sake of His presence. I am told to consider everything as rubbish compared to the surpassing greatness of knowing Yeshua my Lord. If I am willing to share in the fellowship of His sufferings, becoming like Him in His death, I may know Him in the glorious power of His resurrection (see Philippians 3:7–11).

Our Messiah is coming for a pure and spotless Bride whose love for Him is stronger than death. She will gladly lay down her life for the One who offered Himself up for her. She will not run from the cross; in adoring love she will embrace that altar of atonement which binds her heart to His. She will take up her cross to follow Him. This will be her most powerful act of worship, intercession and identification with the Infinite One.

Yeshua endured the cross for the joy set before Him. So, too, will those who wholeheartedly follow Him. When their crosses are borne for loving Israel, they can expect lavish and blessed delight. "Rejoice with Jerusalem and be glad for her, all you who love her; rejoice greatly with her, all you who mourn over her" (Isaiah 66:10). As you pour yourself out for God's Jewish nation, prepare to exult in the King of Glory and His infinite splendor, forever. Because in the end, it is all about *Him*.

יברכך יהוה מציון עשה שמים וארץ.

May the Lord bless you from Zion, he who is the Maker of heaven and earth.
Psalm 134:3

Notes

Chapter 1: Why Still Care about Israel?

1. See John F. Walvoord, *The Prophecy Knowledge Handbook* (Wheaton, Ill.: Victor Books, 1990), 398; Dan Gruber, *The Church and the Jews: The Biblical Relationship* (Hagerstown, Md.: Serenity Books, 1997), 199–200.

2. *The NIV Study Bible: New International Version* (Grand Rapids: Zondervan, 1985), see note for Matthew 25:31–46.

Chapter 2: God's Inseparable Love

1. C. E. B. Cranfield, *A Critical and Exegetical Commentary on the Epistle to the Romans, International Critical Commentary* (Edinburgh: T & T Clark, 1979), 2:446–48.

2. A. W. Tozer, *The Knowledge of the Holy* (San Francisco: Harper & Row, 1961), 97.

3. Cranfield, *Romans*, 2:448. Cranfield uses the word *mercy* here in connection with the doxology of God's mercy in Romans 11:30–36.

4. Merril C. Tenney, *Zondervan Pictorial Encyclopedia of the Bible,* vol. 3 (Grand Rapids: Zondervan, 1975), 989.

5. James Strong, *The Exhaustive Concordance of the Bible* (Nashville: Abingdon, 1977), #2836.

6. Francis Brown, *The New Brown-Driver-Briggs-Gensenius Hebrew and English Lexicon* (Boston: Houghton Mifflin, 1983), 888.

7. J. H. Laenen, *Jewish Mysticism: An Introduction* (Louisville: John Knox, 2001), 255–58; Bruce K. Waltke and M. O'Connor, *An Introduction to Biblical Hebrew Syntax* (Winona Lake, Ind.: Eisenbrauns, 1990), 45; Ellen Frankel and Betsy Platkin Teutsch, *The Encyclopedia of Jewish Symbols* (Northvale, N.J.: Jason Aronson, 1995), 4–5.

8. Frank I. Seekins, *Hebrew Word Pictures* (Phoenix: Living Word Pictures, 1994), 14–19, 28–29; Edward Horowitz, *How the Hebrew Language Grew* (New York: Ktav Publishing House, 1960), 14, 312–13; Frankel and Teutsch, *Jewish Symbols*, 5.

9. J. I. Packer, *Knowing God* (Downers Grove, Ill.: InterVarsity Press, 1973), 112.

Chapter 3: The Sanctity of Covenant

1. Nahum M. Sarna, *Genesis*, vol. 1 of *The JPS Torah Commentary* (Philadelphia: The Jewish Publication Society, 1989), 114–15.

2. John Piper, *The Justification of God: An Exegetical and Theological Study of Romans 9:1–23* (Grand Rapids: Baker, 1993), 24, 33.

3. Cranfield, *Romans*, 2:446–47; Mark Nanos, *The Mystery of Romans: The Jewish Context of Paul's Letter* (Minneapolis: Fortress Press, 1996), 239.

4. Arnold G. Fruchtenbaum, *Israelology: The Missing Link in Systematic Theology* (Tustin, Calif.: Ariel Ministries Press, 1993), 343; Sarna, *Genesis*, 114–15.

5. J. Dwight Pentecost, *Things to Come: A Study in Biblical Eschatology* (Findlay, Ohio: Dunham Publishing Company, 1958) as quoted in Fruchtenbaum, *Israelology*, 343.

6. Grateful acknowledgment is given to Barry Horner, *Future Israel: Why Christian Anti-Judaism Must Be Challenged* (Nashville: B&H Academic Books, 2007), Kindle edition, and Michael Vlach, *Has the Church Replaced Israel?* (Nashville: B&H Academic, 2010), Kindle edition, for some of the ideas expressed in the rest of this chapter.

7. See Cranfield, *Romans*, 2:867–68; James D. G. Dunn, "Romans 9–16," in David A. Hubbard and Glenn W. Becker, ed., *Word Biblical Commentary*, vol. 38B, (Dallas: Word, 1988), 678; Joseph Shulam, *Hidden Treasures* (Jerusalem: Netivyah Bible Instruction Ministry, 2008), 12; Jacob Prasch, "Apostolic Jewish-Christian Hermeneutics and Supersecessionism," in Calvin L. Smith, ed., *The Jews, Modern Israel and the New Supersessionism* (Lampeter, UK: King's Divinity Press, 2009), 54.

8. Roy B. Zuck, *Basic Bible Interpretation: A Practical Guide to Discovering Biblical Truth* (Wheaton, Ill.: Victor Books, 1991), 59–75.

9. See ibid., 27–55.

10. Ernest F. Kevan, "The Principles of Interpretation," in Carl F. H. Henry, ed., *Revelation and the Bible* (Grand Rapids: Baker, 1958), 291.

11. John F. Walvoord, *Every Prophecy of the Bible: Clear Explanations for Uncertain Times* (Colorado Springs: David C. Cook, 2011), Kindle edition, Introduction.

12. Marvin R. Wilson, *Our Father Abraham: Jewish Roots of the Christian Faith* (Grand Rapids and Dayton, Ohio: Wm. B. Eerdmans Publishing Co. and Center for Judeo-Christian Studies, 1989), 166–84.

13. Augustine, *City of God* [1886], reprint in Philip Schaff, ed., *Nicene and Post Nicene Fathers of the Christian Church*, vol. 2 (Grand Rapids: Eerdmans, 2009).

14. Horner, *Future Israel*, chapter 8.

15. Gruber, *The Church and the Jews*, 326–29.

16. Walter C. Kaiser Jr., "The Land of Israel and the Future Return," in H. Wayne House, ed., *Israel: The Land and the People* (Grand Rapids: Kregel, 1998), 219–20.

17. Horner, *Future Israel*, chapter 9. As Horner points out, classic theologians such as Jonathan Edwards, Horatius Bonar, J. C. Ryle, and C. H. Spurgeon believed likewise.

18. Dunn, "Romans," 527–28.

19. Horner, *Future Israel*, chapter 9; see also, Walter C. Kaiser Jr., "Kingdom Promises as Spiritual and National," in J. S. Feinberg, ed., *Continuity and Discontinuity: Perspectives on the Relationship Between the Systems of Old and New Testaments* (Wheaton, Ill.: Crossway, 1988), 302.

20. Walter C. Kaiser Jr., *Toward Rediscovering the Old Testament* (Grand Rapids: Zondervan, 1987), 49.

21. Vlach, *Has the Church Replaced Israel?* chapter 10.

22. Cranfield, *Romans*, 578.

23. Walvoord, *Every Prophecy*, chapter 11.

Chapter 4: Israel's Prophetic Destiny

1. Tenney, *Zondervan Pictorial Encyclopedia*, vol. 2, 540.

2. Merrill F. Unger, *Unger's Bible Dictionary* (Chicago: Moody Press, 1966), 367.

3. George Buttrick, gen. ed., *The Interpreter's Dictionary of the Bible*, vol. 2 (Nashville: Abingdon Press, 1981), 270–71.

4. See for example Dunn, "Romans 9–16," 533–34.

5. See George Eldon Ladd, *The Gospel of the Kingdom* (Grand Rapids: Eerdmans, 1990).

6. See Piper, *Justification*, 37–38, n14.

7. See for example Daniel C. Juster, *The Irrevocable Calling* (Gaithersburg, Md.: Tikkun Ministries, 1996), 13–26.

8. Abraham Cohen, *Everyman's Talmud: The Major Teachings of the Rabbinic Sages* (New York: Schocken, 1949), 63; Juster, *The Irrevocable Calling*, 21.

9. Walter C. Kaiser Jr., *Mission in the Old Testament: Israel as a Light to the Nations* (Grand Rapids: Baker, 2000), 56–57.

10. M. Basilea Schlink, *Israel: My Chosen People* (Radlett, England: Evangelical Sisterhood of Mary and Kanaan Publications, 2000), 40.

11. See for example Robert S. Wistrich, *A Lethal Obsession: Anti-Semitism from Antiquity to the Global Jihad* (New York: Random House, 2010); Chaim Potok, *Wanderings: Chaim Potok's History of the Jews* (New York: Fawcett, 1990); Max I. Dimont, *The Indestructible Jews* (New York: Signet, 1973); Fr. Edward Flannery, *The Anguish of the Jews: Twenty-three Centuries of Antisemitism,* rev. ed. (New York: Paulist Press, 2004); Michael L. Brown, *Our Hands Are Stained with Blood* (Shippensburg, Pa.: Destiny Image, 1992).

12. *Merriam Webster Collegiate Dictionary*, 11th ed., s.v. "scapegoat," http://www.merriam-webster.com/dictionary/scapegoat.

13. Melanie Phillips, *The World Turned Upside Down: The Global Battle Over God, Truth and Power* (New York: Encounter Books, 2012), 71, 195.

14. *Merriam Webster*, s.v. "racism," http://www.merriam-webster.com/dictionary/racism.

15. Reuven Doron, *One New Man* (Cedar Rapids, Iowa: Embrace, 1993), 81.

Chapter 5: The Contention of Election

1. Abraham Twerski, *Twerski on Chumash* (New York: Shaar Press, 2003), 42.

2. C. F. Keil and F. Delitzsch, "Genesis," trans. James Martin, *The Pentateuch,* vol. 1, *Commentary on the Old Testament* (Grand Rapids: Eerdmans, 1983), 220, as cited in Hal Lindsey, *The Everlasting Hatred: The Roots of Jihad* (Murietta, Calif.: Oracle House Publishing, 2002), 58.

3. Grateful acknowledgment is given to Avner Boskey for some of the ideas expressed in this and preceding paragraphs.

4. Benjamin Netanyahu, *A Durable Peace* (New York: Warner Books, 2000), 462.

5. D. Guthrie, ed., *The New Bible Commentary Revised* (Grand Rapids: Eerdmans, 1981), 742.

6. Cranfield, *Romans*, 2:471–74; Dunn, "Romans," 551–69; David Stern, *Jewish New Testament Commentary* (Clarksville, Md.: Jewish New Testament Publications, Inc., 1992), 389–90.

7. Strong, *Concordance*, see *bless* in Main Concordance, see *barakh* in Hebrew and Chaldee Dictionary; Francis Brown, S. R. Driver and Charles A. Briggs, *A Hebrew and English Lexicon of the Old Testament* (Oxford: Clarendon Press, 1980), see *barakh*.

8. Allen P. Ross, *Creation and Blessing: A Guide to the Study and Exposition of the Book of Genesis* (Grand Rapids: Baker, 1988), 263.

9. Andrew Murray, *Humility* (Springdale, Pa.: Whittaker House, 1982), 28.

10. Strong, *Concordance*, see *curse* in Main Concordance, see *alah, arar, qalal* in Hebrew and Chaldee Dictionary. See also, Ross, *Creation and Blessing*, 264.

11. See Ross, *Creation and Blessing*, 263–64; Kaiser, *Mission*, 19.

12. Eric Solsten and Sandra W. Meditz, eds., "A Country Study: Spain," Library of Congress, http://lcweb2.loc.gov/frd/cs/estoc.html.

13. Iain H. Murray, *The Puritan Hope: Revival and the Interpretation of Prophecy* (Edinburgh: Banner of Truth Trust, 1991), 41–48; Jack Padwa, ed., *You Don't Have to be Jewish to be a Zionist* (Jerusalem: ICEJ, 2000), 38–54.

14. Ibid.

15. Claude Duvernoy, *The Prince and the Prophet,* trans. Jack Joffe (Jerusalem: Christian Action for Israel, 2003), 7–13.

16. Joan Peters, *From Time Immemorial: The Origins of the Arab-Jewish Conflict Over Palestine* (New York: Harper & Row, 1984), 384–90.

17. See generally William Koenig, *Eye to Eye: Facing the Consequences of Dividing Israel* (McLean, Va.: About Him, 2008); John McTernan, *As America Has Done to Israel* (Longwood, Fla.: Xulon Press, 2006); John McTernan and Bill Koenig, *Israel: The Blessing or the Curse* (Oklahoma City: Hearthstone Publishing, 2002), 103–4, 212–18; Doyle Rice in "Weather Disasters Target N. America," *USA Today*, October 12, 2012, referring to a 2012 study documenting America's increase in natural disasters since 1980.

Chapter 6: The Salvation of Israel

1. Jonathan Bernis, *A Rabbi Looks at the Last Days* (Minneapolis: Chosen, 2013), Kindle edition, chapter 4; Yoaz Hendel, "Jesus Lives on in Jerusalem," YnetNews .com, August 19, 2010, http://www.ynetnews.com/articles/0,7340,L-3939336,00. html; Edmund Sanders, "US Broadcasters Ready for Messiah in Jerusalem," *LA Times*, October 1, 2012, http://articles.latimes.com/2012/oct/01/world/la-fg-israel -evangelical-20121001. Exact numbers are impossible to obtain because many Israeli Jewish believers do not openly reveal their faith.

2. See for example Bernis, *A Rabbi Looks at the Last Days*, chapter 4.

3. Cranfield, *Romans*, 2:531; Michael L. Brown, *60 Questions Christians Ask about Jewish Beliefs and Practices* (Minneapolis: Chosen Books, 2011), 233–38.

4. The Christian Scholars Group on Christian-Jewish Relations, "A Sacred Obligation: Rethinking Christian Faith in Relation to Judaism and the Jewish People," September 1, 2002, http://www.bc.edu/dam/files/research_sites/cjl/sites/partners/ csg/Sacred_Obligation.htm.

5. See Walter Bauer, *A Greek-English Lexicon of the New Testament and Other Early Christian Literature*, 2nd ed. (Chicago: University of Chicago Press, 1979), 672; W. E. Vine, *A Comprehensive Dictionary of the Original Greek Words with*

Their Precise Meanings for English Readers (Iowa Falls: Riverside Book and Bible House, n.d.), 477.

6. Nanos, *Romans*, 265–66.

7. See Ruth Eglash, "Messianic Jews Ousted 'Illegally' in Mevaseret Zion," *Jerusalem Post*, September 2, 2011; Calvin L. Smith, "Faith and Politics in the Holy Land Today," in Calvin L. Smith, ed., *The Jews, Modern Israel and the New Supercessionism* (Lampeter, UK: King's Divinity Press, 2009), 132–34.

8. Ruth Eglash, "Reaching Out," *Jerusalem Post*, October 19, 2010, quoting Yehiel Eckstein of the International Fellowship of Christians and Jews.

Chapter 7: Rejected Roots and Broken Branches

1. As pointed out in Michael L. Brown, *60 Questions*, 233–38, the term "spiritual Israel" is never used in the Bible. The concept would refer, however, only to Israelites or Jews who believe in Jesus.

2. Wilson, *Our Father Abraham*, 88–89, 94.

3. James Carroll, *Constantine's Sword: The Church and the Jews* (Boston: Houghton Mifflin, 2001), 144–48.

4. As quoted in Malcolm Hay, *The Roots of Christian Antisemitism* (New York: Freedom Library Press, 1981), 27–28.

5. Martin Luther, *The Jews and Their Lies*, part III (1543), Martin H. Bertram, trans., http://www.humanitas-international.org/showcase/chronography/documents/luther-jews.htm. Contemporary Lutheran denominations have renounced Luther's diatribes against the Jewish people.

6. Daniel Juster, acknowledging Peter Hocken, John Dillon and Catholic University research for *Toward Jerusalem Council II,* in "Anti-Messianic Judaism: A Brief Summary," http://bethhamashiach.com/AntiMessianicJudaism.htm.

7. Elwood McQuaid, *The Zion Connection* (Eugene, Ore.: Harvest House Publishers, 1996), 42. Most Messianic Jews expelled from German churches perished in the Holocaust.

8. Daniel Johnson, "Catholics, Jews, and Jewish Catholics" Jewish Ideas Daily, June 18, 2012, http://www.jewishideasdaily.com/content/module/2012/6/18/main-feature/1/catholics-jews-and-jewish-catholics.

9. James W. Goll, *Exodus Cry* (Ventura, Calif.: Regal Books, 2001), 76.

10. F. F. Bruce, "The Epistle of Paul to the Romans" in R. V. G. Tasker, ed., *The Tyndale New Testament Commentaries* (Grand Rapids: Eerdmans, 1963), 217–18.

11. "Study: Global Anti-Semitism Rises by 30 Percent," *Jerusalem Post*, April 7, 2013, http://www.jpost.com/Jewish-World/Jewish-News/Study-Global-anti-Semitism-rises-by-30-percent-308970?rz=n_07Apr13.

12. "Who Are We?," World Council of Churches, http://www.oikoumene.org/en/who-are-we.html; "Member Churches," World Council of Churches, http://www.oikoumene.org/en/member-churches.html; "About Us," World Council of Churches, http://www.oikoumene.org/en/about-us.

13. Giulio Meotti, "The Churches Against Israel," YnetNews.com, July 3, 2011, http://www.ynetnews.com/articles/0,7340,L-4090528,00.html.

14. World Council of Churches, http://eappi.org/en/about/overview.html.

15. Manfred Gerstenfeld, "The WCC Anti-Israel Policies," Israel National News, December 29, 2011, http://www.israelnationalnews.com/Articles/Article.aspx/11053#.T_smtpGvjbV.

16. Ibid.

17. National Council of Churches USA, http://www.ncccusa.org/about/about_ncc
.html.

18. Teresa Watanabe, "Christians Split Over Conflict in the Mideast," *Los Angeles Times,* May 5, 2002.

19. See "Interfaith Groups Caution Candidates: Mid East Peace 'More Urgent Than Ever,'" National Council of Churches USA, March 15, 2012, http://www
.ncccusa.org/news/120305mideast.html.

20. Josh Tapper, "United Church Members Vote for Boycott," August 16, 2012, http://www.thestar.com/news/canada/politics/article/1242391—united-church
-affirms-israeli-settlements-boycott.

21. See for example the Charter of Hamas, http://www.acpr.org.il/resources/
hamascharter.html; "Hamas in Their Own Words," Anti-Defamation League, May 2, 2011, http://www.adl.org/main_israel/hamas_own_words.htm.

22. "Letter to President Obama Urging Bold, Concrete, and Immediate Action for Peace," Churches for Middle East Peace, June 27, 2011, cmep.org/content/
letter-president-obama-urging-bold-concrete-and-immediate-action-peace.

23. Protestant Consultation on Israel and the Middle East, November, 2012, http://www.pcime.org/Declaration.aspx.

24. Moshe Aumann, "An Israeli Response," in Evangelical Sisterhood of Mary, ed., *Changing the Future by Confronting the Past* (Darmstadt, Germany: Evangelical Sisterhood of Mary, 2001), 28.

Chapter 8: The Islamic Middle East and Anti-Semitism

1. Alfred Guilaume, *The Life of Muhammad* (New York: Oxford University Press, 2001), 106, quoted in Joel Richardson, *The Islamic Antichrist* (Los Angeles: WND Books, 2009), 98–102; Lindsey, *Everlasting Hatred*, 103. See also "Who Was Muhammad," Contender Ministries, http://contenderministries.org/islam/muhammad.php.

2. Tony Malouf, *Arabs in the Shadow of Israel* (Grand Rapids: Kregel Publications, 2003), 25.

3. Countries and Their Cultures, 2012, http://www.everyculture.com/Africa
-Middle-East/Arabs-Religion.html.

4. http://muslimpopulation.com/World/. The present global Muslim population is estimated at 1.6 to 2.1 billion. (The Pew Forum on Religion and Public Life, http://
www.pewforum.org/The-Future-of-the-Global-Muslim-Population.aspx.)

5. The Pew Forum on Religion and Public Life, http://www.pewforum.org/The
-Future-of-the-Global-Muslim-Population.aspx.

6. Rabbi Berel Wein, *Echoes of Glory: The Story of the Jews in the Classical Era* (New York: Menorah Publications, 1995), 299.

7. John Foxe, *The Acts and Monuments of John Foxe*, vol. 4, 4th ed. (London: Religious Tract Society, n.d.), 19.

8. John Foxe, *Foxe's Annals of Martyrs* (Burlington, Ontario: Inspirational Promotions, 1960), 247–48; Foxe, *The Acts and Monuments,* 18–23; Paul Marshall, Roberta Green, and Lela Gilbert, *Islam at the Crossroads: Understanding Its Beliefs, History and Conflicts* (Grand Rapids: Baker, 2002), 49; Anis A. Shorrosh, *Islam Revealed: A Christian Arab's View of Islam* (Nashville: Thomas Nelson, 1988), 182–83.

9. John Foxe, *Annals of Martyrs,* 247–48.

10. David K. Shipler, *Arab and Jew: Wounded Spirits in a Promised Land* (New York: Time Books, 1986), 162–64, citing Quran, Sura 2:59, 83, 121–22; 3:60; 4:48; 58:15–16; 9:29–30; Avner Boskey, *Israel: The Key to World Revival* (Nashville: Final Frontier Ministries, 1999), 7, citing Quran, Sura 2:89, 105, 213; 9:30; 4:171; 5:72–75; 19:88–93; 5:116–18; 2:113, 120, 159; 4:46; 5:41; 57:27; 8:39; 9:5; 29:47; 47:4. See also Sura 4:157–8; 5:17, 75; 9:30.

11. Translation of the Inscriptions of the Dome of the Rock (Jerusalem) http://www.learn.columbia.edu/courses/islamic/pdf/Inscrip_Dome.pdf; Bernard Lewis, *The Crisis of Islam: Holy War and Unholy Terror* (New York: Modern Library, 2003), 44.

12. Richardson, *The Islamic Antichrist*, 24–28, 31–32, 48, 51–57, 63. Grateful acknowledgment is given to Joel Richardson for some of the ideas expressed in this chapter.

13. Richardson, *The Islamic Antichrist*, 57, 73–77.

14. George Otis Jr., *The Last of the Giants: Lifting the Veil on Islam and the End Times* (Tarrytown, N.Y.: Chosen Books, 1991), 214–18; see generally Richardson, *The Islamic Antichrist*.

15. See for example Ergun Mehmet Caner and Emir Fethi Caner, *Unveiling Islam* (Grand Rapids: Kregel, 2002), 105–7.

16. "Islamonline.net, 'Offensive Jihad Is Permissable to Secure Islam's Borders, to Extend God's Religion, and . . . to Remove Every Religion but Islam from the Arabian Peninsula,'" Translating Jihad, January 11, 2011, http://www.translatingjihad.com/2011/01/islamonlinenet-offensive-jihad-is.html, translating fatwa on offensive jihad issued in 2011 by Dr. Imad Mustafa of al-Azhar University; Richardson, *The Islamic Antichrist*, 138–143.

17. Foxe, *Annals of Martyrs*, 248–67; Quran, Sura 8:12–17, 60.

18. Sura 9:5, as stated by Dr. Mark Gabriel, *Islam and Terrorism* (Lake Mary, Fla.: Charisma House, 2002), quoted in Mychal Massie, "Peaceful Religion Is Not Spelled I-S-L-A-M—From My Vault," *The Daily Rant* (blog), September 15, 2012, http://mychal-massie.com/premium/peaceful-religion-is-not-spelled-i-s-l-a-m-from-my-vault/. The doctrine of abrogation teaches that Muhammad's later writings abrogate his earlier writings if there is any contradiction between them.

19. Raymond Ibrahim, "How Taqiyya Alters Islam's Rules of War," *Middle East Quarterly*, Winter 2010, 3–13; Richarson, *Islamic Antichrist*, 154–161; Ibn Taymiyah, *The Sword on the Neck of the Accuser of Muhammed*, quoted in Gabriel, *Islam and Terrorism*, 91.

20. Walid Shoebat, *Why I Left Jihad* (Los Angeles: Top Executive Media, 2005); Nonie Darwish, *The Devil We Don't Know: The Dark Side of Revolutions in the Middle East* (Hoboken, N.J.: John Wiley & Sons, 2012); Nonie Darwish, *Now They Call Me Infidel: Why I Renounced Jihad* (New York: The Penguin Group, 2007); Mosab Hassan Yousef, *Son of Hamas* (Carol Stream, Ill.: Saltwater Publishers, 2011); Susan Crimp and Joel Richardson, eds., *Why We Left Islam: Former Muslims Speak Out* (Los Angeles: WND Books, Inc., 2008); Sam Solomon and Elias Al-Maqdisi, *Al-Yahud: Eternal Islamic Enmity and the Jews* (Charlottesville, Va.: ANM Publishers, 2010); see also Brigette Gabriel, *Because They Hate* (New York: St. Martin's Griffin, 2006).

21. David Horowitz, "A Mass Expression of Outrage against Injustice," *Jerusalem Post*, February 25, 2011, quoting Bernard Lewis. See also, John Bradley, *After the Arab Spring: How Islamists Hijacked the Middle East Revolts* (London: Palgrave Macmillan, 2012).

22. Oren Kessler, "Democracy and Political Islam Can't Coexist, Says Key Witness in Congress Hearings," *Jerusalem Post*, March 18, 2011.

23. This phrase was used by Mahmoud Ahmadinejad at the United Nations in July 2012, as quoted in Joel Rosenberg, *Israel at War: Inside the Nuclear Showdown with Iran* (Carol Stream, Ill.: Tyndale House Publishers, 2012), Kindle edition, chapter 4.

24. David Lev, "IDF Chief: 200,000 Missiles Aimed at Israel," Israel National News, February 2012, http://www.israelnationalnews.com/News/News.aspx/152362#.UIDdxK4rysU.

25. Ibid.

26. Oren Kessler, "Egypt Islamist Vows Global Caliphate in Jerusalem," *Jerusalem Post*, May 8, 2012, http://www.jpost.com/MiddleEast/Article.aspx?id=269074; Nicole Gaouette and Flavia Krause-Jackson, "Egypt's Mursi Challenges Israel, Claims Arab Leadership," September 26, 2012, http://www.businessweek.com/news/2012-09-26/egypt-s-mursi-challenges-israel-claims-arab-leadership.

27. Haim Harari, *A View from the Eye of the Storm* (New York: Regan Books, 2005), 88; Wistrich, *A Lethal Obsession*, 313, 733; Anti-Defamation League, "Brotherhood of Hate," October 15, 2012, http://archive.adl.org/NR/exeres/57145DAE-F76E-46F6-9173-27EEFBBA69A4,DB7611A2-02CD-43AF-8147-649E26813571,frameless.htm; Sarah Schlesinger, "A History of Hatred: The Muslim Brotherhood and Anti-Semitism," Hudson Institute, December 19, 2011, http://www.hudson.org/index.cfm?fuseaction=publication_details&id=8596.

28. Oren Kessler, "Egypt Islamist Vows."

29. *Times of Israel*, "Mursi Mouths 'Amen,'" October 21, 2012, http://www.timesofisrael.com/in-morsis-presence-egyptian-preacher-urges-allah-destroy-the-jews/.

30. See Ezekiel 38–39; Daniel 7:23; and Joel Richardson, *Mideast Beast* (New York: WND Books, 2012), 205–21.

31. Sura 7:166; 5:60; 2:65 (Yusuf Ali trans.).

32. Sayed Kamran Mirza, "Did Muhammad Order Killing Surrendered Jews?" Islam Watch, July 7, 2007, http://www.islam-watch.org/SyedKamranMirza/Muhammad-Killing-Jews-of-Banu-Quraiza-and-Khaybar.htm; Lindsey, *Everlasting Hatred*, 117–21.

33. *The Book Pertaining to the Turmoil and Portents of the Last Hour* (Kitab Al-Fitan wa Ashrat As-Sa'ah) of Sahih Muslim Book 41.

34. Ibid., Sahih Muslim 41:6982–4; Sahih al-Bukhari 4:56:791; 4:52:177.

35. Richardson, *Islamic Antichrist*, 113–14.

36. "Egyptian Cleric Muhammad Hussein Ya'qoub: The Jews Are the Enemies of Muslims Regardless of the Occupation of Palestine," Al-Rahma TV, January 17, 2009, as translated by MEMRI TV Video No. 2042, 4:24, http://www.memritv.org/clip/en/2042.htm.

37. "Saudi Government Daily," MEMRI Special Dispatch No. 354, March 13, 2002, http://www.memri.org/bin/articles.cgi? Page=archhives&Area=sd&ID=SP35402.

38. Itamar Marcus and N. Jacques Zilberdick, "PMW Bulletins—PA Mufti: Muslims' Destiny Is to Kill Jews," Palestinian Media Watch, January 15, 2012, http://www.palwatch.org/main.aspx?fi=157&doc_id=6098.

39. "Friday Sermon on PA TV," MEMRI Special Dispatch No. 228, June 12, 2001, http://www.memri.org/report/en/0/0/0/0/0/76/467.htm.

40. Marcus and Zilberdick, "PMW Bulletins." The PA-appointed grand mufti of Jerusalem has repeatedly called for the murder of Israeli Jews as an Islamic duty.

Chapter 9: Discerning Truth about Israel Today

1. Israel Ministry of Foreign Affairs, "Terrorist Involved in Passover 2002 Netanya Park Hotel Arrested," http://www.mfa.gov.il/MFA/Terrorism-+Obstacle+to+Peace/ Terrorism+and+Islamic+Fundamentalism-/Terrorist+involved+in+Passover+2002 +Netanya+Park+Hotel+arrested+26-Mar-2008.htm, March 26, 2008.

2. Yehuda Kraut, "Palestinian Spokesmen, Jenin Lies and Media Indifference," *Committee for Accuracy in Middle East Reporting in America Media Report* 12, no. 1 (Winter 2003): 22, quoting Saeb Erekat interview with Jim Clancy of CNN, April 10, 2002, repeated with Wolf Blitzer, April 17, 2002.

3. Kraut, "Jenin Lies," 31–32, quoting CNN's Bill Hemmer interview with Saeb Erekat, April 14, 2002, and FOX News' Greta Van Susteren interview with Abdel Rahman, April 14, 2002.

4. As quoted by "Dishonest Reporting Award for 2002," HonestReporting.com, April 14, 2003, http://honestreporting.com/dishonest-reporting-award-for-2002/, citing *London Evening Standard* and *Guardian*.

5. United Nations General Assembly Report of the Secretary-General Prepared Pursuant to the General Assembly Resolution ES-10/10, July 31, 2002.

6. Kraut, "Jenin Lies," 32, quoting *Washington Post*, May 1, 2002, 33; Associated Press, "U.N. Report: Jenin Not Massacre," August 1, 2002, http://foxnews.com/ story/0,2933,59276,00.html.

7. Kraut, "Jenin Lies," 21–22, 31–35.

8. Joel Leyden, "Palestinian Sources Confirm No Massacre in Jenin," *Jerusalem Post*, July 14, 2003, http://www.mombu.com/culture/israel/t-palestinians-confirm -no-massacre-in-jenin-13723433.html.

9. Jerome Marcus, "Jenin's War Criminals," *Wall Street Journal*, April 30, 2002.

10. Ben Hartman, "Bakri, IDF Reservist Trade Barbs outside 'Jenin, Jenin' Hearing," *Jerusalem Post*, March 8, 2011; "Seven Lies about Jenin," Israel Ministry of Foreign Affairs, http://www.mfa.gov.il/MFA/Archive/Articles/2002/Seven+Lies +About+Jenin-+David+Zangen+views+the+fil.htm. *Jenin, Jenin* was produced by an Arab Israeli citizen.

11. "Rocket Attacks on Israel from Gaza," Israel Defense Forces, October 29, 2012, http://www.idfblog.com/facts-figures/rocket-attacks-toward-israel/; together with Jerusalem Center for Public Affairs, "Daily Alert," December 7, 2012, News Service Email.

12. Gabriela Shalev, "Letter to UN Secretary General and President of the UN Security Council," December 24, 2008, http://www.mfa.gov.il/MFA/Foreign+Relations/ Israel+and+the+UN/Issues/Israel_files_second_protest_UN_24-Dec-2008.htm.

13. Committee for Accuracy in Middle East Reporting, "The Goldstone Report: A Study in Duplicity," CAMERA, November 3, 2009, http://www.camera.org/index .asp?x_context=2&x_outlet=118&x_article=1736.

14. Richard Goldstone, "Reconsidering the Goldstone Report on Israel and War Crimes," *Washington Post*, April 1, 2011, http://www.washingtonpost.com/opinions/ reconsidering-the-goldstone-report-on-israel-and-war-crimes/2011/04/01/AFg111JC _story.html; "Updated: The Goldstone Report and the New York Times," CAMERA, April 14, 2011, http://www.camera.org/index.asp?x_context=2&x_outlet=35&x _article=2025; "US Agrees: Israel Did Not Commit Operation Cast Lead War Crimes," *Jerusalem Post*, April 6, 2011.

15. Israel Ministry of Foreign Affairs, "Behind the Headlines: The Goldstone Report Refuted—by Goldstone Himself," April 3, 2011, http://www.mfa.gov.il

/MFA/About+the+Ministry/Behind+the+Headlines/Behind-The-Headlines-The -Goldstone-Report-Refuted%E2%80%93By-Goldstone-Himself-3-Apr-2011.htm.

16. Hamas Charter, http://www.mideastweb.org/hamas.htm. Hamas' intent to destroy Israel has been repeatedly reaffirmed.

17. Israel Ministry of Foreign Affairs, "New Government policy Brings More Goods to Gaza," January 15, 2012, http://www.mfa.gov.il/MFA/HumanitarianAid/ Palestinians/New_government_policy_brings_more_goods_to_Gaza_June_2010 .htm. Figures used in this book represent daily and weekly averages for the year.

18. Yaakov Lappin, "Red Cross: There Is No Humanitarian Crisis in Gaza," *Jerusalem Post*, April 21, 2011, http://www.jpost.com/MiddleEast/Article.aspx?id=217460.

19. See for example Michael L. Brown, *Our Hands*, 60.

20. Josef Goebbels, "Die Juden Schuld!," *Das Eherne Herz* (Munich: Zentralverlag der NSDP, 1943): 85–91, as quoted in http://www.calvin.edu/academic/cas/ gpa/goeb1.htm.

21. Phillips, *World Turned*, 53, 71.

22. Bob Woodward and Carl Bernstein, in a panel discussion on "The Digital Age and Investigative Journalism," at the American Society of News Editors, April 3, 2012, http://www.c-spanvideo.org/program/305299-1. Woodward and Bernstein were responsible for exposing the Watergate scandal in 1972.

23. "Lawfare: The Use of the Law as a Weapon of War," The Lawfare Project, http://www.thelawfareproject.org/what-is-lawfare.html.

24. Ibid.

25. Jack Goldsmith, *The Terror Presidency: Law and Judgment Inside the Bush Administration* (New York: W. W. Norton, 2007), 53–64; Diane Morrison and Justus Reid Weiner, "Curbing the Manipulation of Universal Jurisdiction," Jerusalem Center for Public Affairs, 2010, http://jcpa.org/text/universal-jurisdiction.pdf.

26. Shaimaa Fayed and Paul Taylor, "Islamic Summit Opens with Calls for Syrian Dialogue," Reuters, February 6, 2013, http://www.reuters.com/article/2013/02/06/ us-syria-crisis-islamic-idUSBRE9150VN20130206.

27. Melissa Radler, "Kirkpatrick Blasts UN's Antisemitism," *Jerusalem Post*, October 29, 2002, http://www.internationalwallofprayer.org/A-111-Kirkpatrick -Blasts-UNs-Anti-Semitism.html.

28. See Joshua Hersh, "AIPAC: Susan Rice Emerges as Pro-Israel Courter in Chief," March 6, 2012, *Huffington Post*, http://www.huffingtonpost.com/2012/03/06/ aipac-susan-rice-obama-israel_n_1323398.html; Simon Wiesenthal Center, "SWC to UN Secretary-General," June 1, 2012, http://www.wiesenthal.com/site/apps/nlnet/ content2.aspx?c=lsKWLbPJLnF&b=4441467&ct=11778429.

29. "Abba Eban on the UN," Jewish Virtual Library, http://www.jewishvirtual library.org/jsource/Quote/ebanq.html.

Chapter 10: Israeli Statehood and the Arab/Palestinian Plight

1. *The Peace Encyclopedia: Palestine*, 2002, http://www.peacefaq.com/palestine .html.

2. Charly Wegman, "Friday May 14, 1948: Israel's Debut," *Agence France Presse— English*, 1998, as contained in LexisNexis Academic database, http://www.lexisnexis .com/hottopics/lnacademic; Benny Morris, *1948: A History of the First Arab-Israeli War* (New Haven: Yale University Press, 2008), 178–79.

3. Golda Meir, *My Life* (London: Futura Publications, 1989), 186.

4. Mark Laqueur, "The Struggle for a Jewish State," *The Palestine-Israel Journal*, http://www.pij.org/details.php?id=927.

5. *Palestine Post* [predecessor to the *Jerusalem Post*], May 16, 1948.

6. Jewish Virtual Library, "Demography of Palestine & Israel, the West Bank & Gaza," http://www.jewishvirtuallibrary.org/jsource/History/demograhics.html.

7. Peters, *From Time Immemorial*, 392.

8. Benzion Dinur, "From the Conquest of the Land of Israel by the Arabs to the Crusades," *Israel in the Diaspora*, vol. 1 (Tel Aviv: Dvir, 1960), 27–30, as cited in Netanyahu, *A Durable Peace*, 27.

9. Howard M. Sachar, *A History of Israel from the Rise of Zionism to Our Time*, 2nd ed. (New York: Knopf, 1996), 24, 167.

10. Michael Rydelnik, *Understanding the Arab-Israeli Conflict: What the Headlines Haven't Told You* (Chicago: Moody Publishers, 2004), 58–59. Israel consisted mostly of swampland, desert and barren wasteland due to the Ottoman policy of denuding forests through the centuries. Peters, *From Time Immemorial*, 221–68.

11. Peters, *From Time Immemorial*, 156–7, citing Jacob de Haas, *History of Palestine* (New York: Macmillan, 1934), 147, 258.

12. Peters, *From Time Immemorial*, 155–56, citing *The Encyclopaedia Britanica*, 1911 ed. While some of Peters' research is disputed, it has also been recently corroborated.

13. Peters, *From Time Immemorial*, 157.

14. Peters, *From Time Immemorial*, 223, 396; Shimon Apisdorf, *Judaism in a Nutshell: Israel* (Pikesville, Md.: Leviathan Press, 2003), 62–64; see generally Walter Lowdermilk, *Palestine: Land of Promise* (London: Victor Gollancz Ltd., 1944).

15. Netanyahu, *A Durable Peace*, 84.

16. Ray Hanania, "The Wandering Palestinians," *Jerusalem Post,* December 20, 2011.

17. See Howard Grief, *The Legal Founations and Borders of Israel Under International Law* (Jerusalem: Mazo Publishers, 2008); Martin Gilbert, *The Arab-Israeli Conflict: Its History in Maps* (London: Weidenfield and Nicolson, 1974), 10–11.

18. As quoted in Peters, *From Time Immemorial*, 412.

19. Efraim Karsh, *Palestine Betrayed* (New Haven and London: Yale University Press, 2010), 21–38.

20. *The New Palestine* 38, no. 18 (May 18, 1948): 1.

21. British Superintendent of Police Memo, Haifa, April 26, 1948, as quoted in Samuel Katz, *Battleground: Fact and Fantasy in Palestine* (New York: Bantam Books, 1973), 19.

22. Monsignor George Hakim, Greek Catholic Bishop of Galilee, *New York Herald Tribune,* June 30, 1949.

23. Wistrich, *A Lethal Obsession*, 662–683, referencing Joseph Schechtman, *Mufti and the Fuehrer* (London: Thomas Yoseloff Publishers, 1965), 139ff., 147–52; Karsh, *Palestine Betrayed*, 16–20, 30, 62–63.

24. Karsh, *Palestine Betrayed*, 62–63.

25. Peters, *From Time Immemorial*, 16; Benny Morris, *The Birth of the Palestinian Refugee Problem Revisited* (Cambridge, Mass.: Cambridge University Press, 2004), 603–04; Karsh, *Palestine Betrayed*, 264–72, see also 8–15.

26. See for example Morris, *Palestinian Refugee Problem*, 588–89; Gilbert, *The Arab-Israeli Conflict*, 57.

27. As reported in *Middle Eastern Studies,* January 1986, cited in Mitchell G. Bard, "The Palestinian Refugees," Jewish Virtual Library, accessed April 30, 2013, http://www.jewishvirtuallibrary.org/jsource/History/refugees.html.

28. Myron Kaufman, *The Coming Destruction of Israel* (New York: American Library, 1970), 26–27, cited in Bard, "The Palestinian Refugees"; Iraqi prime minister Nimr el-Hawari, *Sir Am Nakbah* (Nazareth, Israel: 1952), as cited in "Refugees Forever?," *International Jerusalem Post,* February 21, 2003, special supplement.

29. Karsh, *Betrayed,* 241–42.

30. Reported in *Falastin a-Thaura,* March, 1973, as cited by Mitchell G. Bard, "The Refugees," Myths and Facts Online, Jewish Virtual Library, accessed April 30, 2013, http://www.jewishvirtuallibrary.org/jsource/myths3/MFrefugees.html#7.

31. Bard, "The Refugees"; Karsh, *Palestine Betrayed,* 122.

32. Auguste Lindt, UN High Commissioner for Refugees, "Report of the UNREF Executive Committee, Fourth Session," Geneva, January 29 to February 4, 1957; Dr. E. Jahn, Office of the UN High Commissioner, "United Nations High Commissioner for Refugees, Document No. 7/2/3," Libya, July 6, 1967, as cited in Alan Baker, ed., *Israel's Rights as a Nation-State in International Diplomacy* (Jerusalem: Jerusalem Center for Public Affairs and World Jewish Congress, 2011), 50.

33. "Refugees Forever? Issues in the Palestinian-Israeli Conflict," *International Jerusalem Post,* February 21, 2003, special supplement; Bard, "The Refugees."

34. Terence Prittie, "Middle East Refugees," in Michael Curtis, Joseph Neyer, Chaim Waxman, and Allen Pollack, ed., *The Palestinians: People, History, Politics* (New Brunswick, N.J.: Transaction Books, 1975), 66–67.

35. Daniel Pipes, "Peculiar Proliferation of Palestinian Refugees," *Washington Times,* February 20, 2012, http://www.washingtontimes.com/news/2012/feb/20/peculiar-proliferation-of-palestine-refugees/.

36. Donna Cassata, "Defining a Palestinian Refugee," Associated Press, May 31, 2012, http://bigstory.ap.org/content/defining-palestinian-refugee-us-complication.

37. Jonathan Shanzer, "Chronic Kleptocracy: Corruption within the Palestinian Political Establishment," Hearing before House Committee on Foreign Affairs, Congressional Testimony, July 10, 2012, http://archives.republicans.foreignaffairs.house.gov/112/HHRG-112-FA13-WState-SchanzerJ-20120710.pdf.

38. As cited by Prittie, "Middle East Refugees," 71, emphasis mine.

39. Netanyahu, *A Durable Peace,* 155.

40. Joseph Farah, speech given at Messiah College, Grantham, Pennsylvania, July 3, 2003.

41. See for example Palestinian Media Watch, "PA Depicts a World Without Israel," 2012, http://palwatch.org/main.aspx?fi=466; "Mashaal: We Will Never Give Up Any of Palestine," *International Jerusalem Post,* December 14–20, 2011.

42. "Political Plan of the PLO Council," June 8, 1974.

43. Jewish Virtual Library, "Demography of Palestine & Israel, the West Bank & Gaza."

44. See for example Michael B. Oren, *Six Days of War: June 1967 and the Making of the Modern Middle East* (New York: Ballantine Books, 2002), 306–27.

45. Jewish Virtual Library, "The Meaning of Resolution 242," http://www.jewish virtuallibrary.org/jsource/UN/meaning_of_242.html; Dore Gold, *The Fight for Jerusalem: Radical Islam, the West and the Future of the Holy City* (Washington, D.C.: Regnery, Inc., 2007), 172–74; Israel Ministry of Foreign Affairs, "Disputed Territories— Forgotten Facts About the West Bank and Gaza Strip," February 1, 2003, http://www.mfa

.gov.il/mfa/mfaarchive/2000_2009/2003/2/disputed%20territories-%20forgotten
%20facts%20about%20the%20we.

46. Jerusalem Center for Public Affairs, *Israel's Critical Security Requirements for Defensible Borders* (Jerusalem: Jerusalem Center for Public Affairs, http://jcpa .org/book/israels-critical-security-requirements-for-defensible-borders/.

47. The Arabs' Khartoun Resolutions of 1967 solidified the notorious "Three No's": No peace with Israel, no recognition of Israel, no negotiations with Israel. Jewish Virtual Library, "The Khartoun Resolutions," http://www.jewishvirtuallibrary .org/jsource/Peace/three_noes.html.

48. Benny Morris, "Camp David and After: An Exchange (Interview with Ehud Barak)," *New York Review of Books* 49, no. 10, June 13, 2002, http://www.nybooks .com/articles/15501.

49. Ambassador Dennis Ross, in a Fox News interview, as reported by David Kupelian, "The Real Reason Arafat Rejected a Palestinian State," *Whistleblower* 12, no. 3 (March 2003): 7.

50. Speech by Arafat in Johannesburg, May 10, 1994 (while Oslo was in effect), as cited in Daniel Pipes, "Lessons from the Prophet Muhammad in Diplomacy," *Middle East Quarterly*, September 1999, http://www.meforum.org/article/480.

51. Kupelian, "The Real Reason," 8–9; Pipes, "Lessons."

52. "Faysal al-Husseni in His Last Interview," MEMRI Special Dispatch No. 236, July 6, 2001, http://www.memri.org/report/en/0/0/0/0/0/0/474.htm.

53. Ibid.

54. Reuters and Aluf Benn, "PA Rejects Olmert's Offer," *Haaretz*, August 12, 2008, http://www.haaretz.com/news/pa-rejects-olmert-s-offer-to-withdraw-from -93-of-west-bank-1.251578.

55. Mazal Mualem, "New Defense Minister No Threat to Netanyahu's Policies," Al-Monitor, March 13, 2013, http://www.al-monitor.com/pulse/originals/2013/03/ who-is-the-new-defense-minister-moshe-yaalon.html.

56. See Michelle Whiteman, "To the Media, Building Settlements in Israel's a Crime," *Huffington Post,* December 26, 2012, http://www.huffingtonpost.ca/michelle -whiteman/israeli-settlements-west-bank_b_2316941.html, and Mitchell G. Bard, "The Settlements," Myths and Facts Online, Jewish Virtual Library, accessed April 30, 2013, http://www.jewishvirtuallibrary.org/jsource/myths3/MFsettlements .html.

57. Bard, "The Settlements."

58. "Jerusalem-on-the-Line," Jerusalem News Network, Prayer Letter, April 3, 2013, http://www.jnnnews.com/jol_apr_03_13.htm, quoting Palestinian Hamas leader Khaled Mashaal's speech in Arabic at a rally in Gaza City, March 30, 2013.

59. United Press International, "Poll: Arabs Reject Two-State Solution," July 26, 2011, http://www.upi.com/Top_News/World-News/2011/07/26/Poll-Arabs -reject-two-state-solution/UPI-61891311710436/.

60. Elhanan Miller,"88 Percent of Palestinians Believe Armed Struggle Is the Best Way," *Times of Israel*, December 16, 2012, http://www.timesofisrael.com/ hamas-political-strategy-trumps-that-of-fatah-new-poll-finds/.

61. Palestinian Center for Policy and Survey Research, "Palestinian Public Opinion Poll No. 47," press release, April 1, 2013, http://www.pcpsr.org/survey/polls/2013/ p47epressrelease.html.

Chapter 11: Israeli Injustice?

1. See "Justice," *International Standard Bible Encyclopedia,* http://www.bible-history.com/isbe/J/JUSTICE/.

2. See W. E. Vine, *Vine's Expository Dictionary of New Testament Words* (Iowa Falls: Riverside Book and Bible House, n.d.), 623; James Strong, *The New Strong's Exhaustive Concordance of the Bible* (Nashville: Thomas Nelson, 1990), 119, on Strong's Hebrew Nos. 6662–6666.

3. See Israel Defense Forces, "Rocket Attacks on Israel from Gaza," October 29, 2012, http://www.idfblog.com/facts-figures/rocket-attacks-toward-israel/, as cited in "Daily Alert," December 7, 2012, News Service Email.

4. Israel Defense Forces, "IDF Carries Out Widespread Attack on Gaza Terror Sites," November 2012, http://www.idf.il/1283-17570-EN/Dover.aspx; Israel Defense Forces, "How Does the IDF Minimize Harm to Palestinian Civilians?," November 15, 2012, http://www.idfblog.com/2012/11/15/how-does-the-idf-minimize-harm-to-palestinian-civilians/.

5. Israel Ministry of Foreign Affairs, "Operation Pillar of Defense: Legal Points," November 19, 2012, http://www.mfa.gov.il/MFA/About+the+Ministry/Behind+the+Headlines/Operation_Pillar_of_Defense_Legal_points.htm; Israel Defense Forces, "IDF Carries Out Widespread Attack."

6. Alan Dershowitz, *The Case Against Israel's Enemies: Exposing Jimmy Carter and Others Who Stand in the Way of Peace* (Hoboken, N.J.: John Wiley and Sons, 2008), 143–80.

7. Simon Wiesenthal Center, "UN NGO Document Is a Call for Dismantling Israel," Wiesenthal Press Information, September 1, 2001, http://groups.yahoo.com/group/Support_Israel/message/2791.

8. Ahiya Raved, "Arab-Israelis Prefer to Live in Israel," YnetNews.com, June 6, 2012, http://www.ynetnews.com/articles/0,7340,L-4239288,00.html; "Poll: Jerusalem Arabs Would Prefer to Live in Israel," January 13, 2011, Australian Jewish News, http://www.jewishnews.net.au/poll-jerusalem-arabs-would-prefer-to-live-in-israel/18793; Hillel Fendel, "Why Jerusalem Arabs Don't Want to Live in PA," April 29, 2010, Israel National News, http://www.israelnationalnews.com/News/News.aspx/137281#.UKrJRWcrysU.

9. See generally Dan Schueftan, *Palestinians in Israel: The Arab Minority's Struggle Against the Jewish State* (Tel Aviv: Zmora Bitan, 2011).

10. Jordana Horn, "Jewish Student Files Anti-Semitism Complaint against York University," *Jerusalem Post,* March 30, 2011, 20; Liran Kapoano, "Anti-Semitism on College Campuses," *The American Thinker,* March 6, 2012, http://www.americanthinker.com/blog/2012/03/anti-semitism_on_college_campuses_video.html; Robert Wistrich, "Anti-Semitism and the American College Campus," *Jewish Daily Forward,* June 29, 2011, http://forward.com/articles/139195/anti-semitism-and-the-american-college-campus/.

11. Dershowitz, *Case Against Israel's Enemies,* 5–7.

12. Alan Dershowitz, *The Case for Israel* (Hoboken, N.J.: John Wiley and Sons, 2003), 156; see also James Bennet, "Letter from the Middle East: Arab Showpiece?," *New York Times,* April 1, 2003.

13. Sarah Honig, "No Jews in Judea," *Jerusalem Post Magazine,* June 10, 2011, 34, quoting Mahmoud Abbas, at Emergency Session of Arab League Ministers in Qatar, December 2010, stating he would never agree "that there will live among us even a single Israeli on Palestinian land."

14. Dershowitz, *Case Against Israel's Enemies*, 88, citing http://nobelprize.org /nobel_prizes/lists/all/.

15. Michael Curtis, *Should Israel Exist?*, Kindle edition, chapter 26.

16. Grateful acknowledgement is given to legal expert Alan Dershowitz, *The Case for Israel* and *The Case Against Israel's Enemies*, for some of the ideas expressed in this section.

17. Dershowitz, *Case for Israel*, 183.

18. See for example David Horowitz, "The Moralist," *Jerualem Post*, April 22, 2011, quoting Professor Asa Kasher, co-author of the IDF Code of Ethics, http:// www.jpost.com/Opinion/Columnists/Article.aspx?id=217479; see also Jewish Virtual Library, "The Spirit of the IDF: The Ethical Code of the Israeli Defense Forces," http://www.jewishvirtuallibrary.org/jsource/Society_&_Culture/IDF_ethics.html.

19. Dershowitz, *The Case for Israel*, 183–87.

20. Speech by Robert Bernstein delivered November 10, 2010, at the University of Nebraska at Omaha, reported in "Badly Distorting the Issues," *Jerusalem Post*, November 25, 2010.

21. Amnesty International, http://www.amnesty.org/en/region/israel-occupied -palestinian-territories.

22. Natan Sharansky with Shira Wolosky Weiss, *Defending Identity: Its Indispensable Role in Protecting Democracy* (Philadelphia: Persius Group, 2008), 92.

23. José Maria Aznar, "Support Israel: If It Goes Down, We All Go Down," *Times*, June 17, 2010, http://www.thetimes.co.uk/tto/opinion/columnists/article2559280.ece.

24. "Scores of Syrian Protesters Breach Israel Border," "IDF Concerned That Border Protests Just the Beginning," "Police Break Up Violent Demo near Lebanese Border," "Breach of Border with Syria Unprecedented Violation of Israeli Sovereignty," "One Day We Will Go Back to Jaffa," "Right-wing MIKs Speak Out against Nakba Day," all appearing in *Jerusalem Post*, May16, 2011.

25. Thomas Friedman, "Campus Hypocrisy," *New York Times*, October 16, 2002.

26. OneWorld, "Freedom for Palestine," video, 3:43, posted by FreedomOneWorld, May 23, 2011, http://www.youtube.com/watch?v=V28HnPTYz-I.

Chapter 12: Countering Christian Zionism: Christian Palestinianism

1. Archimandrite Theodosios Hanna, Greek Orthodox Patriarchate, excerpts from sermons delivered in Jerusalem in 2002, as translated in "Palestinian Christian Leader in Praise of Martyrdom Operations," MEMRI Special Dispatch No. 459, January 23, 2003, http://www.memri.org/report/en/0/0/0/0/0/0/797.htm.

2. Father Manuel Musalam (director, Latin Church, Gaza), excerpts from April 22, 2002, message on Palestine Television, as translated in MEMRI, "Arab Christian Clergymen Against Western Christians, Jews, and Israel," Inquiry and Analysis Series No. 93, May 1, 2002, http://www.memri.org/report/en/0/0/0/0/0/0/656.htm.

3. Bishop George Saliba (Assyrian Orthodox Church), excerpts from April 24, 2002 message on *Al-Manar* Television (Lebanon), as translated in MEMRI, "Arab Christian Clergymen."

4. Marcus Aziz Khalil (Egyptian Coptic priest), excerpts from April 22, 2002, article by Khalil in *Al-Maydan* (Egypt), as cited in *Al-Quds Al Arabi* (London), April 24, 2002, as translated in MEMRI, "Arab Christian Clergymen."

5. Gregory III Laham (Melkite Greek Catholic Patriarch, Syria), as quoted in Mohammed Zaatari, "Sidon Archdiocese Reopens Following Refurbishment," December

6, 2010, http://www.dailystar.com.lb/News/Local-News/Dec/06/Sidon-archdiocese
-reopens-following-refurbishment.ashx#axzz17KeYYrWe; see also Aymenn Jawad,
"Middle Eastern Christians and Anti-Semitism," *Jerusalem Post,* August 2, 2011.

6. Alex Awad, "A Palestinian Theology of the Land," in Salim Munayer and Lisa
Loden, ed., *The Land Cries Out* (Eugene, Ore.: Cascade Books, 2012), 86.

7. Lisa Loden, "Knowing Where We Start," in *The Bible and the Land: An Encounter*, Lisa Loden, Peter Walker, and Michael Wood, ed. (Jerusalem: Musalaha,
2000), 21–23; Colin Chapman, "Getting to the Point," in Loden, Walker, and Wood,
Bible and the Land, 147–59; Canon Naim Ateek, "Putting Christ at the Center," in
Loden, Walker, and Wood, *Bible and the Land*, 56–57, 60.

8. Vlach, *Has the Church Replaced Israel?*, quoting K. Riddlebarger, *A Case for
Amillennialism: Understanding the End Times* (Grand Rapids: Baker Books, 2003),
68–80.

9. Gary M. Burge, *Jesus and the Land: The New Testament Challenge to Holy
Land Theology* (Grand Rapids: Baker Academic, 2010), 129.

10. Mitri Raheb, "Biblical Interpretation in the Israel-Palestinian Context,"
112–16, in Torleif Elgvin, ed., *Israel and Yeshua* (Jerusalem: Caspari Center, 1993),
209–17; Elfar, "Dealing with the Scriptural Past," in Loden, Walker, and Wood, *Bible
and the Land*, 95–105; Munther Isaac, "Reading the Old Testament in the Palestinian
Church Today," in Munayer and Loden, *Land Cries*, 217–21, 227.

11. Elfar, "Dealing with the Scriptural Past," in Loden, Walker, and Wood, *Bible
and the Land*, 95; Colin Chapman, *Whose Promised Land? The Continuing Crisis
over Israel and Palestine* (Grand Rapids: Baker Books, 2002), 120.

12. Munther Isaac, "Reading the Old Testament in the Palestinian Church Today,"
in Munayer and Loden, *Land Cries*, 218.

13. Naim Ateek, *A Palestinian Cry for Reconciliation* (Maryknoll, N.Y.: Orbis
Books, 2009), 89; personal interview with an Arab Christian faculty member of a
Bible college in Nazareth in 2011.

14. Ibid.

15. See Mitri Raheb, *I Am a Palestinian Christian* (Minneapolis: Fortress Press,
1995); see also "Op-Ed: Sabeel Christian Anti-Zionist Organization Gains Power,"
Israel National News, April 3, 2013, http://www.israelnationalnews.com/Articles/
Article.aspx/13080.

16. Stand With Us, "Fact Sheet: Hamas," November 28, 2012, http://www.stand
withus.com/factsheets/?type=focus&wc=7.

17. RescueChristians.org, "Israel/PA Christians Ask to Move to Israel," January 6,
2013, http://www.rescuechristians.org/2013/01/06/israelpa-christians-from-gaza-ask
-to-move-to-israel-because-they-no-longer-feel-comfortable-living-among-muslims/.

18. As stated by Suhail Akel in *International Relations Magazine,* no. 22 (Argentina: University of LaPlata, 2002), as cited in Simon Wiesenthal Institute, "Wiesenthal
Center Protests Antisemitic Statements by the Palestinian Authority Representative
in Argentina," April 2, 2003, http://www.wiesenthal.com/site/apps/s/content.asp?c
=lsKWLbPJLnF&b=4442915&ct=5852537. See also Malcolm Lowe, "Palestinian
Theologian Trashes Palestinian Theology," Gatestone Institute, November 10, 2011,
http://www.gatestoneinstitute.org/2573/palestinian-theologian-theology, referencing
similar statements by Bethlehem pastor Mitri Raheb.

19. Bishop Alex (head of the Roman Orthodox Bishopric of Gaza), *Al-Quds* (PA),
April 24, 2002, as translated in MEMRI, "Arab Christian Clergymen."

20. "PA Conference Denounces Christian Zionists," Israel National News, July 4, 2003, http://www.israelnationalnews.com/News/News.aspx/46085#.UKwki2crysU.

21. David Parsons, "Background Briefing: Behind the Christ at the Checkpoint Conference in Bethlehem." International Christian Embassy, March 4, 2012, quoting Naim Ateek, http://int.icej.org/news/press-statements/behind-christ-checkpoint -conference; Phillips, *World Turned,* 382, quoting Naim Ateek, "An Easter Message from Sabeel," Sabeel Center, April 6, 2001, http://www.sabeel.org/pdfs/2001%20Easter %20Message.htm.

22. Stephen R. Sizer, "Where Is the Promised Land?" in Munayer and Loden, *Land Cries,* 307.

23. Ibid., 305–07.

24. See for example Alex Awad, *Through the Eyes of the Victims: The Story of the Arab-Israeli Conflict* (Bethlehem: Bethlehem Bible College, 2001), 14, 24–26, 54, 86–88, 96; and Joseph Farah, "The Truth About Christians in 'Palestine,'" February 28, 2003, http://www.wnd.com/2003/02/17513/.

25. Christ at the Checkpoint, http://www.christatthecheckpoint.com/.

26. *Archbishop Cranmer Blog,* "Stephen Sizer: Is This Behaviour Befitting the Leader of an Evangelical Church?," blog entry by Anglican Archbishop Cranmer, September 29, 2012, http://archbishop-cranmer.blogspot.com/2012/09/stephen-sizer -is-this-behaviour-of.html, regarding Vicar Dr. Stephen Sizer; Johnny Paul, "Group Says Church of England Vicar Anti-Semitic," *Jerusalem Post,* November 2, 2012, http://www.jpost.com/JewishWorld/JewishNews/Article.aspx?id=290233.

27. "A Moment of Truth," Kairos Palestine, 2009, http://www.kairospalestine .ps/sites/default/Documents/English.pdf.

28. CBS News, "Christians of the Holy Land," *60 Minutes,* April 12, 2012, http://www.cbsnews.com/video/watch/?id=7406228n.

29. See for example "Season of Good Will, but Not Toward Israel," Israel National News, December 22, 2012, http://www.israelnationalnews.com/Articles/Article .aspx/12628#.UNpKtWeL5XY.

30. Jeremy Sharon, "Leaders Call to Fight Wave of Anti-Israel Agitation," *Jerusalem Post,* November 6, 2012, http://www.jpost.com/JewishWorld/JewishNews/ Article.aspx?id=290739, quoting Rev. Dr. Paul R. Wilkinson.

31. Raphael Ahren, "At Interfaith Meet in Jerusalem, a Grim Picture of Jewish-Protestant Relations," *Times of Israel,* November 9, 2012, quoting Rabbi Eric Yoffe http://www.timesofisrael.com/at-interfaith-meet-in-jerusalem-a-grim -picture-of-jewish-protestant-relations/.

32. Sharon, "Leaders Call," quoting Rabbi Riskin.

33. Lisa Loden, "Where Do We Begin?," in Munayer and Loden, *Land Cries,* 43.

34. This comment is attributed to author and prophetic minister James Goll.

35. *With God on Our Side,* DVD produced by Porter Speakman Jr. (2010), quoting Dr. Gary Burge. For an exposé of this DVD, see Eliyahu Ben-Haim, *Setting the Record Straight,* (Jerusalem: n.p., 2010).

Chapter 13: A Future and a Hope

1. Grateful acknowledgement is given to Dr. Michael L. Brown for some of the ideas reflected in this section of this chapter.

2. As stated by Dr. Michael L. Brown in 2012–2013 personal correspondence and discussions with the author.

3. See for example Walvoord, *Every Prophecy*, chapters 6–7.

4. *Abba Eban: An Autobiography* (New York: Random House, 1977), 392.

5. "Quotations by Author: Martin Luther King Jr." The Quotations Page, http://www.quotationspage.com/quotes/Martin_Luther_King_Jr.

6. See Richardson, *Mideast Beast*, 227–28; Boskey, *Israel*, 158.

7. See Joel C. Rosenberg, "What Is the 'War of Gog and Magog'? Part One," *Joel C. Rosenberg's Blog*, May 9, 2011, http://flashtrafficblog.wordpress.com/2011/05/09/what-is-the-war-of-gog-and-magog-part-one/, and "What Is the War of Gog and Magog? Part Two," May 11, 2011, http://flashtrafficblog.wordpress.com/2011/05/11/what-is-the-war-of-gog-and-magog-part-two-as-we-remember-israels-63rd-day-of-independence-is-this-prophetic-war-close-at-hand/; Walvoord, *Every Prophecy*, chapter 6.

8. Many aspects of the Rapture are strongly debated by believers, and it would not serve our purposes in this book to attempt to resolve them.

Chapter 14: Altar of Sacrifice

1. See Richard Wurmbrand, *Tortured for Christ* (Bartlesville, Okla.: Living Sacrifice Book Co., 1967); Wurmbrand, *Christ on the Jewish Road* (Bartlesville, Okla.: Living Sacrifice Book Co., 1970). Wurmbrand founded the ministry The Voice of the Martyrs.

2. Nanos, *Romans*, 274.

3. Wistrich, *A Lethal Obsession*, 927.

4. Basilea Schlink in Evangelical Sisterhood of Mary, *Changing the Future*, 207.

5. Schlink, *Israel: My Chosen People*, 85–86.

6. Dan Gillerman, in a speech to the UN Security Council, October 5, 2003.

7. Corrie ten Boom, *The Hiding Place* (Grand Rapids: Chosen Books, 1996), 77.

8. Ibid., 95.

9. Marshall Roth, "The Rescue of Bulgarian Jewry," Aish.com, October 23, 2011, http://www.aish.com/ho/i/The_Rescue_of_Bulgarian_Jewry.html.

10. Freda Mary Oben, *Edith Stein: Scholar, Feminist, Saint* (New York: Alba House, 1988), 36–37.

11. Dietrich Bonhoeffer, *Dietrich Bonhoeffer Works*, ed. Clifford Green, trans. Douglas Scott, Reinhard Krauss, and Charles West, vol 6., *Ethics* (Minneapolis: Augsburg Fortress, 2005), 117.

12. Christian Quotes, http://christian-quotes.ochristian.com/Jim-Elliot-Quotes/.

Index

Sandra Teplinsky has been in Messianic Jewish ministry since 1979. She is president of Light of Zion, an outreach to Israel and the Church based in Southern California and Jerusalem. From an Orthodox Jewish background, Sandra obtained a J.D. from Indiana University School of Law, B.A. in political science from the University of Illinois and Bible training from Talbot Seminary in Los Angeles.

Sandra is an ordained minister and prophetic conference speaker. She has taught seminars about Israel and mobilized prayer in many nations, including the Muslim Middle East. Together with her husband, she developed intercessory prayer groups and humanitarian aid projects in Jewish evangelistic outreach in the former Soviet Union.

A former attorney, Sandra has authored several books and articles about Israel and the Church, including *Why Care about Israel?* (Chosen Books, 2004) and *Israel's Anointing* (Chosen Books, 2008). She has been a frequent guest speaker on international television and radio. Sandra and her family maintain their primary residence in the Jerusalem area. You may contact Sandra at www.whystillcareaboutisrael.com or:

Light of Zion
www.lightofzion.org
PO Box 27575
Anaheim Hills, CA 92809
USA

As the biblical clock counts down, the destinies of Israel and the Church are converging.

✔Chosen

Stay up-to-date on your favorite books and authors with our *free* e-newsletters. Sign up today at chosenbooks.com.

Find us on Facebook. facebook.com/chosenbooks

Follow us on Twitter. @chosenbooks